If you want to profit from the Internet Boom you must act now!
-Ted Ciuba

If we could be alive at any ONE time to get rich,
it would be here and now, because of the Internet!
- Forbes

There is no faster way to get rich than on the Internet!
-Robert Allen

It really doesn't matter what business you're in,
where you're located, or what your
product or service is. You need *the Internet*
-Ted Ciuba

How to get Rich on the Internet

Internet Marketing Millionaires Reveal...

America's 21 Top-Gun Internet Marketers Reveal Their Insider Secrets To Outrageous Internet Marketing Success!

by

America's Foremost Internet Marketing Consultant

Ted Ciuba

How To Get Rich On The Internet™
by Ted Ciuba

ISBN: 0-9672414-1-3

Published by:

Parthenon Marketing, Inc.
2400 Crestmoor Rd #36
Nashville, Tennessee 37215   USA

1-877- 4 RICHES
615-662-3169
fax: 615-662-3108

www.GetRichOnTheInternet.com
tedc@realprofit.com

Ted Ciuba, America's Foremost Internet Marketing Consultant
Book Ted Ciuba at your event! Speeches, workshops, copywriting, consulting. Contact publisher.

Book Production by DS Lisi Inc. • 315-865-5845

Printed in U.S.A.

Dedico este libro, y todo lo que hago, a tí, mi amada Ana
¡Te amaré para siempre!
¡Gracias a Dios por el Internet!

Para obsequiar a la gente de mi sangre

A portion of the proceeds from the sale of this book
go directly to select child development agencies active in
Latin America. For an up-to-date list of these charities
send an e-mail to sangre@realprofit.com

Acknowledgements

The problem with making acknowledgements is that you leave out more than you include. I think of my parents first, Ted and Shirley Ciuba, who I remember and honor with profound love. My children, Alysha and Ted Jr., and my wife Ana. Family, friends, business associates, teachers, influences... That being said...

I hereby express my genuine love and gratitude to all influences, family members, peoples, sexes, governments, ideas, philosophies, and religions. I see God's world is a place a-riot with diversity.

I'd like to acknowledge the tremendous influence certain people have had on me personally and professionally – people like Napoleon Hill and Tony Robbins, Tolly Burkan and Peggy Dylan.

A handful of super rare marketers like Ted Nicholas, Ron LeGrand, and T.J. Rohleder. Jay Abraham, Robert Allen, and Dan Kennedy. Michael Enlow, Joe Cossman, Joe Karbo, and Mark Haroldsen. Melvin Powers, whose landmark *How To Get Rich in Mail Order,* has been a driving inspiration in this project. Thank you for your tremendous influence.

My mentors and MasterMind partners in the creation of this book, top-gun Internet Marketers all, including Terry Dean, Jay Conrad Levinson, T.J. Rohleder, Clay Cotton, Mike Jay, George Tran, Mike Lauria, Armand Morin, Ron LeGrand, Carl Galletti, Michael Penland, Marlon Sanders, Don Bice, Jeff Gardner, Russ von Hoelscher, Chris Lakey, Kirt Christensen, Jonathan Mizel, Joel Christopher, Mike Litman, Robert Allen, Phil Huff, and Ken Kinnett. I couldn't have done it without you.

Well-chosen friends help you achieve your goals.

My competitors in this rough-and-tumble, fast-moving Internet world. My greatest wish is that we can help one another profit! Competitors no more – co-operators.

And especially to my students and special clients who have taught me more than anyone else. Yes, you CAN get RICH on the Internet!

Table of Contents

Table of Contents

EXTRA! 2 Free Special Reports

Special Bonus Chapters

The Internet, The Richest Land In All The Earth

Ted Ciuba *America's Foremost Internet Marketing Consultant*

Introduction

Are you ready to get your share? Here's how!

6:49 a.m. Saturday - Overlooking The Misty Tennessee Hollows

Friend:

I am not Charles Dickens, this ain't revolutionary France, and there is no contrary statement.

When we're talking *Internet* -

"These Are The BEST Of Times!"

Congratulations! You've jumped into the middle of the biggest revolution in history – the Internet.

This is the best time ever to be alive! Our children, grandchildren, and grandchildrens' children will look back on us and wish they could have had these opportunities. Industry people will remember the good old days of easy and outrageous Internet profits when anybody with a dream and a little action could get rich overnight! All available to you today!

Right now the incredible window of opportunity on the Internet when the little, educated, nimble guy can compete with major corporations in a world market is wide open.

Opportunity on the Internet is not tapping at your window like a lover who doesn't want to be discovered by your parents - it's POUNDING ON YOUR DOOR LIKE A HUNGRY GRIZZLY BEAR!

Congratulations for having the insight, resolve, and daring to get your share!

The advantages you have on the Internet are nothing short of stupendous! I could write a whole book about it, or we could just cut to the chase right now...

> *What you do on the Internet costs practically nothing, goes out to an infinitely large global audience, makes money in seconds or minutes, not in weeks, months, or years, costs nothing to deliver, and stays put and keeps making you money forever!*
>
> *-Ted Ciuba*

What you do on the Internet costs practically nothing, goes out to an infinitely large global audience, makes money in seconds or minutes, not in weeks, months, or years, costs nothing to deliver, and stays put and keeps making you money forever!

With the proviso that you're getting targeted traffic to your web page, the power you possess to compel others to send you their hard-earned money in ridiculous amounts is staggering!

How To Get RICH On The Internet

We don't have to beat around the bush on this one...

We have ONE PURPOSE in this book.

If this one purpose doesn't sit well with you, you'll never enjoy this book. Honestly, you ought to tiptoe back and return the book now.

On the other hand... If you *share* this one purpose, if you want to get *rich* on the Internet, charge forward! Today you encounter destiny!

THE ONE PURPOSE OF THIS BOOK IS

TO GET YOU RICH

ON THE INTERNET

... And if you're already doing well, to get you *RICHER*!

In a way, I feel like Napoleon Hill asserting the tremendous power rendered in *Think and Grow Rich*. It's not an arrogant contest of trying to control the future. It's an authorial respect for the awesome power of what's in the book.

You really do find everything you need in this book to get rich, or if you're already getting rich, to get a lot richer on the Internet.

You can do it in record time at costs approaching the disappearing point. On the Internet.

This Has To Be The Easiest Business On Earth...
Success On The Net Lets You Do What You Want With Your Life

Prefer an office? Have one. Like to travel? Take the wife and kids to an exotic location. Work from there. You might even write your trip off your taxes! Like to visit the school or little league in the middle of the day? Or maybe scoot out to the golf course or lake? Do it, nobody's stopping you or thinking bad things about you!

Want a new house? A nicer car? Investments for the future?

Things you've dreamed of for years, now that you don't have a crummy job holding you back, appear overnight!

If others insist on suffering the mediocrity of the job-bound, let them. You don't have to participate in what's going around no more.

Startup And Promote Virtually Any Business, Product, Or Service On The Internet

You can start and promote virtually any business, product, or service on the Internet! It literally doesn't matter what business you're in, where you're located, or what your product or service is.

Aside from making the obvious positive legal, ethical, and moral choices, the skills you learn in this book apply 100% to every type of product, service, industry, personality, or cause.

We're talking about doing it low-cost/no-cost... We're talking about how to do it entrepreneurial-style, right from the convenience of your home...

There is no legitimate business reason under the sun to not get on the Internet, no matter what your product, service, personality, or cause!

$100,000 Startup Pay

We're talking from home Internet marketing, where you can make an easy $100,000 this year.

In fact, I've got special high-priced BootCamps where I offer a 90-day, $25,000 earnings guarantee. Do the math - that's $100,000 per year.

Speaking of which... A cop from Cleveland approached me about a year ago... Working blue. Brave. A family man. In harm's way. Barely above survival.

> *In a way I feel like Napoleon Hill asserting the tremendous power rendered in* Think and Grow Rich. *It's not an arrogant contest of trying to control the future. It's an authorial respect for the awesome power of what's in the book.*
>
> *-Ted Ciuba*

I told him what to do and how to do it. I gave him the insider tools to make it happen. Still, when I spoke of $100,000, he had some doubts.

Me? I was worried if what I said didn't work he might arrest me. (Smile).

He's now an *ex*-cop. Here's what he confided to me just yesterday...
 "You told me anybody could earn $100,000 on the Internet. You were right. I've done that easy!" - Chuck Smith

It's all there for you, too!

ANYONE Can Make Money On The Internet!

Anyone can make money on the Internet today! It doesn't matter what your field or area of interest, and you don't have to work hard.

You only have to work smart.

Success on the Internet is a science with proven formulas that have been tested. The only reason people fail is because of lack of information or, more commonly, because of *mis*-information from listening to unsuccessful marketers claiming they are successful.

There are reasons why web sites succeed. There are reasons why web sites fail.

Once you get it, you can repeat the process repeatedly. Earning more and more money.

When You Want To Know The Truth About Internet Success Go To Someone Who IS Successful!

It should be obvious that when you want the real lowdown to Internet marketing success, you should go to someone who is successful.

For my part, I have brought you the best of the best of Internet Marketers... The guests in this book are top-gun marketers, every one of them. They are all making good, solid six- and seven-figure incomes. From home.

They are respected names on the Internet.

Learn from studying these proven top-gun masters. They are super-successful themselves. And they're great teachers... Got the grit of a drill sergeant and the patience of a nun.

> *The skills you learn apply 100% to every type of product, service, industry, personality, or cause.*
> *-Ted Ciuba*

They have the secrets, and they reveal them to you here!

Apply The Cutting-Edge Strategies And Secrets

Everyone wants these secrets. As an investigative reporter, uncovering the deepest Internet profit secrets of these high-profile marketers, I conducted these interviews for two simple reasons. Guess which one was the most important...

One: To root out, gather, classify, and share the secret powerful strategies, techniques, tips, resources, mindsets and breakthroughs of these top-gun Internet marketers with all the world .

Two: To discover and apply the cutting-edge strategies and secrets these masters reveal to my own business, products, clients, and efforts.

The secrets these marketers share hurl you light-years beyond your earth-bound competitors and companions.

"Brought To You LIVE!"

Though you find them in print now, these "interviews" were originally radio broadcasts. They were recorded live on the air, broadcast out of KFNX, Phoenix, Arizona. They were simulcast on the Internet at *www.InternetMarketingInterviews.com*

Why did I want these shows live? On the air? I mean, we could have gone into a studio. For that matter we could have just recorded a telephone conversation. That's how most programs are captured.

I can tell you this… As an investigative reporter with my own radio show, *How To Get Rich On The Internet*™, I'm very familiar with both live and "canned" events…

Accordingly, I *had* to have this *live* because there's a *juice* you never otherwise get…

With the adrenaline boost of a live event, the guest, trying to "show out," is boosted to even higher levels – all to *your* benefit! Flying in show form!

In the enthusiasm of a live event, these experts reveal far more than you'd ever otherwise get from them in a reasoned midnight hour with their own word-processor.

They just can't resist spilling the beans on their latest successful Internet marketing strategies and tactics!

MasterMind Sessions

I'm a famous author, sought-after public speaker, frequent guest in newspaper articles, ezines, web sites, interviews, radio, and T.V. But it wasn't always so good.

As low as they go, I was there… Living at the end of a long country dirt road in a 12' camper trailer in Tennessee where detectives and bill collectors fear to tread. Like I said in an earlier book, *Mail Order in the Internet Age*, "Them rednecks there pay taxes on their wages, pack an array of guns, and still fly rebel flags from their trailers. And they mean it."

But I even had to run from that outlaw lair… They were closing in on me. All they found was an empty trailer with the door swinging on the hinges in the wind… I outran them! They didn't repossess my dinky Renault because I disappeared overnight for the Promised Land, California.

It was there one day that I met a very special man who shared some stuff with me. Now this was not an ordinary man. Nor did he show me ordinary things. This was not a teacher, a friend, or family member. This was someone who was doing the direct response marketing business. He took me under his wing and shared a few things over a 3-day weekend we spent together.

I went out and applied what Ted Nicholas showed me. Direct response marketing. Copywriting. Backend. Adapting it the best I could to the Internet. Miraculously it worked. I am grateful to him.

That's what first got me starting to believe, "Huh, maybe there's something in this Napoleon Hill talk about the *MasterMind principle*."

And then I noticed, as I spiraled rapidly up in the world of success, that my noticeable boosts and jumps in income, significant products, significant contacts, significant opportunities always came in association with the word, the teachings, or the meeting of another person.

As Mark Victor Hansen says... 1 + 1 doesn't equal 2, it equals 11!

That recognition was the genesis of the radio show. It evolved into the purpose and the format of the show - where we have different marketing guests, all biggies in Internet marketing, coming together to share and stir up profitable new ideas with you. MasterMind sessions giving you the best advice, insight, and instruction available on the planet!

Now, even though you couldn't be there, it's yours in print.

Meet Your Top-Gun Faculty

Every guest and speaker you meet in this book is remarkable. Each has their own area of specialty, their own insights or techniques that can contribute to *you* getting rich on the Internet.

Each of them is imminently qualified to show you how to get rich on the Internet. Each of them has done it.

I present to you my mentors and MasterMind partners in the creation of this book!...

In the order they appear...

- Terry Dean
- Jay Conrad Levinson
- T.J. Rohleder
- Clay Cotton
- Mike Jay
- George Tran
- Mike Lauria
- Armand Morin
- Ron LeGrand
- Carl Galletti
- Michael Penland
- Marlon Sanders
- Don Bice
- Jeff Gardner
- Russ von Hoelscher
- Chris Lakey
- Kirt Christensen
- Jonathan Mizel
- Joel Christopher
- Mike Litman
- Robert Allen
- Phil Huff
- Ken Kinnett

Most people would consider these individuals competitors of mine.

Success Clues

But, as America's Foremost Internet Marketing Consultant, that's not the case... Truth is, I couldn't have done it without them. We are *co-operators*.

We are colleagues, resources for one another, mentors, teammates, joint venture partners, and okay, "competitors" at the same time. That's co-opetition.

You'll hear more about co-opetition shortly...

But here's the bottom line - we each make each other better marketers, and - working TOGETHER - we present you a far better, more accurate and more powerful rendition of how easily *you* can get rich on the Internet.

And every word, every insight, every trick they tell of is important...

But there's another message in this *How To Get Rich On The Internet* saga.

There are certain things you'll discover the speakers reinforcing each other on... Such as...

- ◆ The importance of building your own list
- ◆ Using e-mail rather than your web site as your Internet marketing workhorse
- ◆ Writing an article to establish yourself as an expert and gain credibility, click-throughs, and e-mails to market to
- ◆ Cooperation rather then competition in the Internet world
- ◆ Focusing on no-cost and low-cost marketing methods

When you find something repeated repeatedly it's got to be important. *Pay attention*!

Like top-gun Internet Marketer Randy Charach says about the importance of building your own list...

> *"Every super successful marketer has one...*
> *Does that mean you need to have one?*
> *YES! It does!"*

Jump, Jump, Jump On This In The Living Present!

Act on the sound Internet marketing advice you receive from Ted Ciuba and the Top-Gun Internet Marketers he's assembled for you here and you almost can't help but get *RICH on the Internet today*!

It could happen with your very first web page.
These are the BEST of times!
Your BEST is yet to come!

[signature: Ted Ciuba]

Ted Ciuba, President Parthenon Marketing Inc.
Author, America's Foremost Internet Marketing Consultant

P.S. The Internet really is a field of dreams! Do you think it's any coincidence that the Internet masters in this book identify the elements of Internet marketing as *skills* that you can learn and improve at?

Marketing on the Internet is a learnable, improvable skill. Duplicable, repeatable, dependable.

P.P.S. It's something you can do! Like playing the guitar or learning to swim, anyone with desire can learn the rudiments of putting up a good web site.

Anyone willing to invest a little more *extremely pleasurable time* can become a master on the guitar, in swimming, or in Internet marketing in short order.

Take your pick…

> The guitar will make you popular
> Swimming will make you healthy
> The Internet will make you rich

How to Earn $33,245 Next Weekend On The Internet

Chapter 1

Ted Ciuba *Interviews* Terry Dean

Terry, welcome to *InternetMarketingInterviews.com*'s *How To Get Rich On The Internet* show.

Terry Dean (TD): Thank you for having me here, Ted. I'm glad to have the opportunity to help others create their own online success stories.

Ted Ciuba (TC): Terry, you're one of the Net's most famous personalities. How did you get started?

From Zero To Hero In 6 Month's Time

TD: My start wasn't quite as quick as your three week start-up time, Ted, but I started from a similar position. I was a pizza delivery driver, basically going nowhere. I found the Internet and started a successful online business. It was that direct... That quick. I was able to get my business up and running and producing a full-time income in about six months.

TC: Most listeners would think generating a full-time income in six months is pretty good, Terry!

TD: I don't think it's bad at all!

Super Hero Overnight – Earn More Money In A Single Weekend Than Most People Earn All Year Long!

TC: I recently saw you take on an amazing challenge. I watched you earn more money online at *www.TheInternetBootCamp.com* in a single weekend – on stage before the world - than most people earn in a whole year of slavery for a wage. Can you give us a little insight on that?

Pick Up A Quick $33,000 In A 3-Day Weekend

TD: That demonstration began as a challenge. A marketing guru asked if I could make $10,000 online in ten days. That's where I got the idea to launch an online offer during a three-day conference and see how much money I could generate. People could see the action live and learn how they could produce a good online income. That one little promotion produced exactly $33,245 of income.

TC: Terry, that is truly amazing!

The Rest Of The Story... I Earned $55,000 In Three Days...

TD: It gets better... When we talk about those three magic days, I sometimes say I made $33,000 in three days... Other times I say I made over $55,000 in three days. That's because I had other business offers going on during that same three day period that generated an additional $22,000 in income. Either way you look at it, we actually made $55,000 in three days.

I'd like to refer back for the one promotion that generated $33,000 in three days. Because I was offering an online informational product, 95% of that income was net profit. My total staff consists of my wife and myself, so that $33,000 three-day income is wonderful. That's as much as I'd earn in three years back when I delivered pizzas.

> **$55,000 In 3 Days**
>
> *We made $33,000 from a single promotion I did on stage. The other $22,000 was made from other offers going on, and other things that were going on in my business. But either way you go, we still made $55,000 in three days.*
>
> *-Terry Dean*

Rake In Obscene Profits With Internet Orders

TC: You said 95% of that is net profit. Are you delivering your products over the web also?

TD: I do both physical and online digital delivery. That specific product was delivered on CD Rom which costs approximately a dollar plus some shipping costs. On that specific offer, customers got three CD's.

TC: Tell us a little about digital delivery...

Digital Delivery EQUALS 100% Profit!

TD: Sure! How about a for instance? I sell a product for $97 at *PaperlessNewsletter.com* For $97, once they pay their money, purchasers are sent immediately to download the product, which is a set of e-books teaching you how to have your own membership site.

When they download it, they have the product with no delivery cost. The money that comes in is 100% profit after processing fees.

TC: Wow! So either way you cut it, when you're marketing on the Internet, and when you're marketing information products, you're marketing products with an insanely low cost of goods sold!

It *really* is possible to earn 95% - 100% profits!

You don't have a *conventional business* do you?

> *$33,000 in 3 days is wonderful.*
>
> *Back when I was a pizza delivery driver that was as much as I'd earn in 3 years!*
> - Terry Dean

TD: No, definitely not. The main reason is because costs go down to virtually zero. Part of the reason I can say I earned 95% profit was, with that promotion, *I simply went to my existing online e-mail list and made an offer!*

Sending out an e-mail to my list costs me nothing.

It's not like sending out a direct mail piece, where you have to spend thousands and thousands of dollars in print and mailing costs. I sent out 35,000 e-mails (that's how large my list was at the time) to the 35,000 subscribers who were subscribing to my free publication. I sent them an e-mail - and it cost me nothing. Think about trying to contact 35,000 people for free in any place other than the Internet.

These Kinds Of Results Were Impossible Before The Internet

TC: Those kind of numbers are phenomenal! You earned $33,000 because you sent out an e-mail that was *free* to you, and you had 95% profit in it. I mean, this couldn't have been done before the Internet, could it?

> ### 100% Profit$
> *It really IS possible to earn 95% - 100% profits!*
> *-Ted Ciuba*

TD: There's no way you could have done it before!

TC: What about the risks? Aren't the risks you take to earn that much money that fast reckless?

Riskless Profit$

TD: Okay, let's talk *risk*. When I sent out that offer, how much was I risking? Nothing. If the offers wouldn't have worked, all that would have happened is I might have looked bad.

If I would have made the web site link something stupid and given the wrong order form - which people have done in direct mail sales letters - or if I had done something bad and not gotten any orders, how much would I have lost? Nothing. I could just have made the offer again with the correct link, or I could make a different offer tomorrow or next week.

Use Your Greatest Asset To Produce Endless Money On Demand

I can continue to produce money from the same thing over and over again. A lot of people don't understand how I made $33,000 in one weekend but that's not anywhere near the overall profits of my list! About every two weeks we send another offer and continually generate income from it.

TC: So you just keep repeating this whole process... And that's how you're living the "Internet lifestyle." Is that right?

Formula To Outrageous Internet Success: Build List, Send Offers, Bank Money, Repeat

> ### No Place But The Internet!
> *I sent out 35,000 e-mails... I sent them an e-mail – it cost me nothing. Now think about that trying to be able to contact 35,000 people for free, in any other place, besides the Internet.*
> *-Terry Dean*

TD: That's exactly right. That's what I teach everyone who comes to me now, how to do the same thing I have, which is build a large, opt-in e-mail list, send out offers to it, and continue to make profits over and over again.

I don't want just a one-time sale. I want to develop a relationship with customers and generate sales from now until the day I retire. My income is constantly increasing along with my subscriber list.

TC: That's fantastic, your list is your greatest asset!

Let The Facts Speak For Themselves:

"$55,000 In A Single Weekend, IS 'Get Rich Quick'!"

You talk distinctly about a *relationship*, not a one-time shot.

TD: Exactly. A lot of people mistakenly think of the Internet and immediately think "Let's go online and make a bunch of money, real quick."

TC: Be that as it may, the facts speak for themselves: $55,000 income in a single weekend is kind of "Get Rich Quick."

TD: Yes, the Internet can get you rich quick, but that's not the *mentality* of success. If I would have had the mentality, "I'm going to go on the Internet, make a quick offer, and make a lot of money," I wouldn't have gotten that response.

The reason I was able to generate that response from my list is those subscribers have gotten to know me. They know what I offer; they know how valuable the products I offer are.

The Lazy Man's Way To Riches

TC: Terry, that's all well and good for you to say – you already have 35,000 subscribers to your list, and you've already built the all-important relationship with your fans... But what about Joe or Jean Average riding around in their car right now?

TD: Someone could come online, and do exactly what I did – tomorrow - simply by going out and finding someone who has a large list already, someone who already has that *relationship* built up with their subscribers.

They could tap into it, partner with them, maybe divide the profits 50/50, and do exactly what I did, *this* weekend, just like I did. They don't have to take the whole time I did, to build up my subscriber base, because there are people who are already doing it.

You just need to go to them, and make them an offer they can't refuse, so that you can benefit together... The Internet is based on that relationship.

It's simple... If you don't have the list, then you need to find somebody who already has a list and has built a relationship with their subscribers.

You can tap into it because that's where everyone's online profits come from. Profits come from the credibility and trust that has been produced between a publisher and their subscribers, between a list owner and the list subscribers.

Secrets So Simple Even A Beginner Can Do It

TC: So you've then identified the secrets for your success - and you're identifying anyone's big success keys as 1) develop that relationship, 2) service your customers and clients, treat them with respect, and 3) bring them other products that are similar.

But you also said that a beginner could go out and put a deal together with an already existing marketer, and replicate your accomplishment this weekend!?

TD: They could. The only difference between what *they* could do, and what *I* did, is I got 95% of the money; they would have to settle for 50% of the money, since they'd have to split it with the publisher. But I don't think that 50% of $33,000 would be too bad for a beginner.

TC: I think it'd be pretty good! In fact, very often we talk about how our goals and objectives are to help anybody who wants to get on the Internet *earn $100,000 their first year*.

But you just dropped a third of that in their first weekend!

Success Is Duplicatable

I've seen you enjoy a lot of other successes online, Terry. You had an e-book campaign that ruled the web for a couple of years. I see you running an e-zine, that has a tremendous subscription base that's very loyal, and I know you've got an Internet membership site that's doing real well.

Fill us in a little bit, how can we replicate and duplicate your success?

FREE E-zine Forms Foundation Of Millionaire's Empire!

TD: Most of my business relies back on the free "Web Gold" e-zine, which we've already mentioned. Those wishing to subscribe can log on to *www.BizPromo.com* They can subscribe for free on the main page and sign up to receive extra bonus e-books.

The Internet Success Formula Restated

I use this free e-mail publication to give people good content and start building relationships with prospects. I then use that relationship to sell additional products and services subscribers want or need.

I produce intense, informative e-books for download and purchase and offer them to my subscriber list. They buy in droves. They've found so much good information inside the free publications I've given them, they immediately think, "The information he's selling must be even better" and purchase the e-books.

Reprint Rights Are A Good Strategy

Not only do I sell my own products to my list, I also regularly buy reprint rights to other people's products. Basically I buy reprint rights then sell the product to my list.

For example, I bought reprint rights to Monique Harris' *Paperless Newsletter*. I paid something like $1,600 for the reprint rights, took her sales letter (I didn't even have to write my own) and sent it to my list.

At that point in time my list was a lot smaller than it is now, - around 17,000 subscribers. I sent it to my list and made over $10,000 - all within 24 hours from buying the reprint rights.

TC: Wow!

TD: That's a pretty good profit. I've continued to sell the e-book on my web site... Generating somewhere between $4,000 and $5,000 a month since that launch.

TC: $4,000 and $5,000 a month... If it averages $5,000 a month, that's $60,000 from a product that you didn't even create! And that's just one more additional stream of Internet income for you!

TD: That's right, a product I didn't create. People don't have to create everything themselves.

TC: There's really no limit to the number of different products you can repeat this strategy with, is there?

TD: No limit... And it's usually a lot faster than creating your own product. Let me explain. Of course I have good success from my own products but I get much quicker success when I buy reprint rights or do a joint venture with somebody else's product. I don't have to spend all this creation time, and as you know, creating or writing a book takes a lot of work and time.

TC: Amen!

TD: You know buying reprint rights to somebody else's product is quick.

TC: Only takes $1,600 and less than 14 minutes, right?

TD: I've definitely got the money back, and that's just one aspect of what I do in

> ### Reprint Rights A Good Deal!
> *I bought reprint rights... Took her sales letter... Sent it to my list, and made over $10,000. All within 24 hours from buying the reprint rights.*
> *-Terry Dean*

my business. You're right. It's all about multiple streams of Internet income. I sell my e-books, buy reprint rights, and sell those e-books. I have joint ventures with other companies, such as selling web hosting to my list.

Offer Related Services To Your Market

When I talk of selling web hosting, don't think for one second that I'm running a whole different business. I don't do the hosting myself. That would be too much work, too much technical detail... So I found a host who has a good service and I offer it to my list for a split of the profits. I simply joined their *affiliate program*.

I've done that a few times and now I get a check every month, from a number of different companies. Those checks come in every month - month after month!

Earn 50% Off Others' Products

TC: Terry, you mentioned an affiliate program. Can you explain what that is?

TD: Online we have what we call free *affiliate programs*, a lot of people offer them on their web site for their own products. You sign up for free to promote their products - usually getting somewhere between 20-50% commission - and promote their products to your list.

2 Dozen Checks A Month

I get over two dozen checks a month, from different companies who pay me for promoting their products. I get enough checks from free affiliate programs that I could actually stop everything else I was doing and live on those checks with a full-time income.

Affiliate Programs For Any Subject On The Planet!

TC: That's phenomenal! There are affiliate programs that relate to whatever interest a person has, aren't there?

TD: You can actually find affiliate programs for just about any subject on the planet. Since I own a subscriber list that has to do with marketing tips, most of the programs I join have to do with marketing or provide tools that marketers need online.

If a web-site owner had a passion for golf, they could find multiple sites with affiliate programs offering golf clubs, golf travel packages... Anything golf related... And promote these products at their own site.

TC: So if I'm reading you right, the other companies have to keep the inventory of golf shoes, golf clubs, golf packs, and golf vacations.

They're the ones who have to be the experts, have the connections, and actually deliver the product - and you simply promote it and get a piece of the action?

TD: That's exactly right. If you own a small or home business and are just starting out, you're going to find that kind of business is a whole lot easier. If I wanted to start a big company and inventory a lot of different products I could... But that's too much work! I want to stay where it's just the two of us working and hire freelancers to do the work. Let's let them do some work.

I want to earn a really nice lovely income but I don't want to have a big company. Right now with just two of us working at home part-time and keeping business simple, my monthly income usually reaches what a lot of people get for working full-time in a year.

> **It Could Be You!**
>
> *I get enough checks from free affiliate programs that I could actually stop everything else I was doing, and live on those checks, with a full-time income.*
>
> *- Terry Dean*

TC: That sounds pretty simple! Most people think it's complicated to make money and double-complicated to make money on the Internet. But you're saying that you actually keep it simple by building your list, joint venturing, and letting other people do all the hard work?

TD: That's exactly right. One of the most stressful components of running a business is staff and employees. I don't want to have to deal with all those kind of problems. That's a real pain.

One Marketing System Makes Money Repeatedly In All Markets, In All Political Climates

It's much easier to just learn a *system of marketing*.

I use the same system of marketing no matter what I'm selling. I just apply that one system of marketing to different products and services and generate multiple income streams... All from the same system.

TC: The Internet has come a long way! You were still delivering pizzas when you first started doing business on the Internet, weren't you?

TD: I was, for a short period of time. But I've never held a job for more than thirty days - including delivering pizza.

TC: Is there any hope for the working stiff who has held a steady job for the last thirty years?

TD: I'm sure they actually have a better chance at succeeding on the Internet than I did. I was wishy-washy... Back and forth. That's probably part of the reason it took me a whole six months to actually get up and running online.

People who have been working for someone else for a long time might actually be able to learn quicker than I did because they're probably more disciplined. All they need to do is sit down, make a strong commitment and decide, "This is what I'm going to do *no matter what...*"

TC: The formulas and strategies you're talking about will work for anyone, regardless of their product or area of interest... Is that right? They don't have to be Terry Dean to get rich on the Internet?

TD: They'll work for anyone, in any market. I don't recommend that everyone model themselves after me in every detail... I'm one of the laziest marketers I know.

The Freedom, The Independence, The Money

TC: And one of the richest too, I might add! Is it true that the *Internet lifestyle* idea you promote attracts people who want freedom, independence, money, and those kinds of things?

TD: That's true. When I talk about the Internet lifestyle I'm not just talking about money. A lot of people have a goal to become a millionaire. That's not really a goal you should be looking for.

The Quality Issues Make For True Wealth

What's really going to help you be successful is determining what you want to do with your life, where you want to live, how you want to live... Then setting a goal to build a business that will help you accomplish that.

Some people like to live in big cities... They like the hustle and bustle of a big city and the noise and confusion. I like to live off in the country. I own eighteen-and-a-half acres with a lot of it woods and live in the middle of nowhere. That's the lifestyle I choose and this business enables me to live it.

TC: Very good advice, Terry. Everyone should think about how they want to live in order to maximally enjoy their lives while making enormous contributions.

The Most Important Thing You Can Do Is Build A List

We have a caller joining us from central Indiana.

Caller: I'm a subscriber to Ted's e-zine and a member of a number of different affiliate programs, basically marketing-type things. I've been jumping from one thing to another... Mail order, Multi-Level marketing, and Internet marketing. What do you suggest I do as far as zeroing in on specific Internet and affiliate programs?

TD: The first thing we need to determine is if you're building a list. Have you started an opt-in list of any type?

Caller: I'm in the initial stages of that... But from what I read on your site, instead of just advertising the web address of my affiliate link on my site, I should send visitors to an autoresponder in order to build my list automatically. Is that correct?

TD: That's exactly what you need to be doing. The big mistake most people make when linking with an affiliate program is to promote only the affiliate link. You can be in my affiliate program, but if you're promoting *my* product and sending visitors directly to *my* site, you'll make some money in sales, but whose name are you building? You're building my name - not your own.

To be successful you need to brand yourself. Specifically, you need to *brand* yourself as something or someone people think of when they think of *you*. That's the key to being successful with affiliate programs.

What you need to do is decide what personality trait you have that can be marketed as an advantage. For example, my personal advantageous branding trait is the fact that I am very direct, specific, and a little bit laid back.

If you read my *Web Gold* e-zine, you'll see that I consistently come through this way. I let people see who I am. You need to let yourself show through in some type of e-zine. It's not that difficult either because there's so much free content on the Internet. Grab one of these free articles, write a paragraph or two introducing yourself, add it to the top of the article, and you're off!

Some people say, "Maybe no one will like me... There's nothing special about me." A lot of people think that but the truth is, people want reality, they want credibility, they want to know you are a real person.

TC: Alright, Caller. You got some million dollar advice there!

Caller: Thanks a lot, Ted and Terry.

TC: You've got it!

Be Yourself – You Are Promotable!

Terry, are you saying people like to do business with someone that comes across as *real*?

TD: Yes, many people are so afraid of rejection that they refuse to be themselves and try to be someone else instead.

TC: So are you saying that if they would be themselves, they could actually promote being themselves and enjoy life more?

TD: That's right. The truth is, some people aren't going to like you. I get hate e-mail every time a newsletter goes out because somebody doesn't like it. Somebody gets mad about it... But guess what? I get a lot more *sales* from my newsletters than I do hate mail.

TC: And you can handle a few pieces of hate mail with all those sales, right?

Where Is All The FREE Advertising Online These Days?

TC: Speaking of e-mail, a listener just sent an e-mail question to us at *tedc@realprofit.com* She heard us talking about your $33,000 weekend and the fact that you sent your message out for free. Her statement is, "I thought that all free marketing on the Internet was gone."

TD: No, free marketing on the Internet is definitely not gone. When one of my NetBreakthroughs subscribers recently asked about free marketing, I told him what a lot of people previously looked at as free marketing is gone. They think about free Internet marketing as no-charge classified ads or free link pages. Those free offers are pretty much a thing of the past. Even most search engines are not free anymore.

But what still *is* free is building relationships and making deals. *Example*: If I created an offer that I knew was going to generate good profit, Ted, and I came to you and asked if you'd like to offer this to your subscriber list and split the profits, I'm pretty sure I could convince you we should agree to this deal.

TC: You've got it! It would be easy to get me to do a deal like that.

TD: It would be easy... And how much would it cost me?

TC: It wouldn't cost you anything, would it?

TD: No, and it wouldn't cost you anything either. See, there is still *free* advertising. The free advertising that really works is relationship advertising.

TC: Boy, that's a very big distinction on what's free... But, once a person has their basic access set up, sending an e-mail is totally free. It didn't cost you a penny to send that famous e-mail, did it?

A joint venture, such as you just proposed to me, is free. Definitely, free advertising is working.

www.InternetMembershipSites.com

TC: Terry, you, Kirt Christensen, and myself created the killer program, *www.InternetMembershipsites.com* During the filming of this project you featured *www.NetBreakthroughs.com* And you've made some references to it today.

Can you fill in the cracks on this site? What is it, what do you do, how can our listeners benefit?

TD: *NetBreakthroughs.com* is my monthly membership site which produces a good income every single month. I feel it's a good model for anybody to look at who's considering - and everyone should - their own membership or subscription site.

What I do at the site is actually review what type of advertising is working, what type of advertising is not working, and where you should be spending your money when marketing online.

TC: First, anyone who is advertising ought to go to your site. Your condensed information, I'm testifying, will pay them back multiples of the monthly toll.

Second, if they want the lowdown on starting their own membership site, they should check out *www.InternetMembershipSites.com*

Follow The Steps Of The Master

But the bigger issue, in our immediate discussion is... When visitors go to your site, they get into your marketing funnel because, as you said, you start the relationship with free info.

TD: Exactly.

TC: Then they'll be able to learn what you're doing.

TD: For example, when someone goes to my site at *BizPromo.com* they can download a free e-book called, "*How To Start Your Own Traffic Virus*," which explains all about viral marketing and how they can use viral marketing to build free traffic to their site.

TC: You've said e-books as a form of viral marketing is working.

TD: Exactly, they're generating traffic to web sites, they generate a lot of traffic from my web site.

Do you want to know the number one traffic generator for *BizPromo.com*?

TC: Yes, please!

Turbo-Charge Your Internet Marketing

TD: The number one traffic generator is viral marketing in two forms.

Form number one is free e-books.

Form number two is free articles.

These two tools, which are both viral marketing tools, are the number one traffic generators for *BizPromo.com*

TC: They are also free marketing techniques, is that correct?

TD: That's exactly right. They're free marketing techniques, and with all the paid advertising I do, those free techniques still out perform paid advertising.

TC: Wow that is phenomenal! Terry Dean, I'm glad I tuned in and caught you today!

How To Get Rich On The Internet

We have just had the phenomenal Terry Dean with us and some of the things that he shared with us was how he made $33,245 in three days off a single, *free* e-mail. I mean is that impressive or what? And if you count the other things he had going on, he really earned $55,213. Not too shabby for three days work.

He revealed the real secrets he's using to build his business and talked about forming a relationship with customers. Starting off, he gives away a free e-zine.

He talked about, and this is an important secret for all of us to learn, making your own personality visible. *Be yourself*, he says.

He revealed how we can start and make $33,000 ourselves this weekend with a joint venture. Bring a product to someone who has a list, who's got that relationship with their customers, while, of course, you are building your own.

Terry talked about free marketing and dispelled a myth that there is no more free advertising on the Internet. Most of all, he really did convince us that yes, you can do it, and no, you do not have to be exceptional. You do not have to be a major company and well-funded.

Yes! You really did discover how to scoop-in $33,245 this weekend on the Internet! Now go do it.

News Flash! Urgent Update!

At the last minute, after this interview, as this book was going to press, Terry Dean shattered his own Internet income record. I just had time to skate down here and get this news in here for you before the presses rolled!

On the stage of *TheInternetBootCamp.com* Terry Dean proved again that the ordinary guy or gal can get *rich* on the Internet. This former pizza delivery driver sent out a single e-mail and within 24 hours pulled in $72,930! With the cameras running.

Only on the Internet.

Congratulations, Terry Dean!

Reader, YOU can do it, too!

Special thanks to the contributors to this show...

*Terry Dean * www.BizPromo.com*
*Ted Ciuba * www.InstantInternetMarketing.com*

If you enjoyed this interview, there's more just like this! Tune into *www.InternetMarketingInterviews.com*

Other resources to supercharge your progress!
   www.GetRichOnTheInternet.com
   www.GetRichOnTheInternet.com/seminars
   www.AutoPilotRiches.com
   www.KillerWebCopy.com
   www.ProtegeProgram.com
   www.MailOrderInTheInternetAge.com
   www.LowCostInternetAdvertising.com
   www.PrePaidLegal.com/go/parthenon

The Ultimate Internet Guerrilla Marketing Attack

Chapter 2

Ted Ciuba *Interviews Jay Conrad Levinson*

Jay Levinson, as he likes to be called, is the author of the famous Guerrilla Marketing Series, which I'm sure, if you have any interest at all in business, you've heard of. You've seen his Guerrilla Marketing flooding the bookstores. As a matter of fact, Guerrilla Marketing books are the best selling marketing books in history. Translated into thirty-seven different languages, they are required reading in many MBA programs.

You normally wouldn't think of Guerrilla Marketing as going along with MBA programs and Fortune 500s. This is another area where Jay has absolutely distinguished himself. He is the ultimate marketer for everybody from home-based entrepreneurs and Fortune 500s to the university. What he's pulled off is almost impossible. He's also one of the most respected marketers in the circle of marketers, his peers.

So, marketing consultant, author, university professor, executive in several businesses, extremely successful entrepreneurial marketer, and Internet marketer, Jay Conrad Levinson... Welcome to *How To Get Rich On The Internet*!

Jay Levinson (JL): Thank you, Ted, it's great to be here and to share some of my powerful marketing concepts with your Internet marketing audience.

Guerrilla Marketing Is...

Ted Ciuba (TC): Jay you are famous for the *guerrilla marketing* concept. Could you give us a good idea of what guerrilla marketing is, and especially how it applies to the Internet?

JL: I'd be happy to do that. The bottom line is that guerrilla marketing is going after conventional goals using unconventional means. One of those unconventional means is the Internet, which didn't exist in its present form when I wrote the first *Guerrilla Marketing* book.

Discover Your Greatness

I wrote that first *Guerrilla Marketing* book, while I was teaching at the University of California at Berkeley.

I was teaching a course on succeeding as an entrepreneur. The name of my course was, *The Alternative For The Nine-to-Five Job*.

One day my students asked me if I could recommend a book that would tell them how to market aggressively without having to spend a lot of money. I said I would be happy to find a book like that for them.

I scoured the library at Berkeley, went to Stanford, the public library in San Francisco, then Sacramento, but came up empty handed. There were no books on the topic of marketing for people with limited budgets then.

> *You never know where something will lead! Follow your heart! "And that book seemed to take on a life of its own."*
> *– Jay Levinson*

So, as a service to my students, I wrote *Guerrilla Marketing*. The reason I had to write that book was to give my students exactly what they were asking for... That book seemed to take on a life on it's own, and it now sells in thirty-seven languages! (Of course, that's a polite way of saying I don't understand thirty-six editions of the book...)

The Internet Is The Strongest Guerrilla Weapon!

JL: Nonetheless, it shows that the whole world seems to be embracing the ideas of guerrilla marketing, which are quite different from traditional marketing.

TC: And though the Internet didn't exist at the time you wrote that first book, everything you wrote and espoused *does* apply to the Internet, doesn't it?

JL: Oh, the Internet is the best marketing weapon ever developed of any one out of a hundred marketing weapons. There are ninety-nine others, and it's the strongest of all, and we're just beginning to scratch the surface of what it can do for a business. Essentially, a business can make unlimited income with minimal advertising and operational costs!

TC: Jay, for a man with your experience and your track record to be saying that the Internet is the strongest marketing tool the guerrilla marketer has is incredible!

I believe that, of course, because I'm always saying to people, "You must get on the Internet... Your only choices are whether you want to have a 100% Internet business, or whether you want to integrate the Internet as a component in your overall success..."

The Value Of A Marketer's Work

Jay, before we get into some of your teachings, why do you continue to write? You don't *need* to.

JL: It's a great delight to me that my work has touched so many people. When people say, "I like your book," or "I like the talk you gave," it doesn't mean nearly as much as somebody who says, "I read your book and now my business is three times the size it used to be."

That's why I write - to have something like that said to me... And, I'm hoping that the results will be the same from the time that we are spending together today.

TC: Absolutely. I can guarantee that everybody I know, including myself, is surrounded with your materials because it is very easy to pick up one thing after another and amplify the ways we market our businesses... That's why I invited you into the studio today, to share your teachings to a broader market.

JL: It's crucial for people to pick up one thing after another and to understand marketing, because it's the key to success for everything. If you know what you're doing, why, and how, there are many ways to market on the Internet for practically nothing!

Guerrilla Marketing vs. Traditional Marketing

The first thing people should know are the differences between guerrilla marketing and *traditional* marketing. I used to compare guerrilla marketing with textbook marketing but now that *Guerrilla Marketing* is a textbook of the University, I compare it to traditional marketing.

When you hear these differences you'll understand which of these apply to the Internet.

The first difference is that traditional marketing has always said "In order to market, you have to invest money." Guerrilla marketing says, "If you want to invest money you can, but you don't really have to."

Your primary investment should be time, energy, and imagination. If you're willing to invest those things, you don't have to invest much money. Of course it takes time, energy, and imagination to market *with* money, too.

A second difference is that traditional marketing intimidates most people so they're scared to even try it. They're not sure if marketing is advertising or sales, or if it's being on the Internet. Guerrilla marketing completely removes the mystique from marketing. Anyone who understands guerrilla marketing skills knows *they're* in control of marketing, rather than the other way around.

The third difference is that traditional marketing has always been aimed at big businesses with unlimited budgets. Guerrilla marketing is geared to small businesses with tiny budgets. And, although it's true that Fortune 500 companies buy up several thousand copies of *Guerrilla Marketing* books to distribute to their sales and marketing people, the reality is that every word, on every page of every *Guerrilla Marketing* book is geared strictly for small businesses.

I've been working from my home three days a week since 1971 and all these things I talk about are things that I have been doing myself. My books offer freedom in your life and balance in your life. One of the ways to do that is to be a good marketer.

The fourth difference is that traditional marketing is always measured in performance by sales or responses to an offer. Guerrilla marketing says it's okay to get high sales and responses to an offer, but that the only number that you should be looking at are *profits*. If your profits are increasing on a regular basis, you are going about things right. It has nothing to do with your sales or responses to your offer.

The fifth difference is traditional marketing has always been based on experience and judgment. It's a fancy way of saying guesswork, but guerrilla marketers can't afford to make wrong guesses, so guerrilla marketing is based, as much as possible, on psychology - laws of human behavior.

> *If you know what you're doing, why, and how, there are many ways to market on the Internet for practically nothing!*
> *– Jay Levinson*

For example, we know that, *a)* ninety percent of all purchase decisions are made from the unconscious mind and, *b)* the way to access the unconscious mind is through repetition. When you put these two ideas together, you begin to have an idea of how the process of guerrilla marketing works.

The sixth difference is traditional marketing says - know your business *then* diversify. Guerrilla marketing says - know your business, maintain your focus, and keep your mind off of diversity. Did you hear that Gerber once thought their name meant *baby*? They introduced a line of baby furniture, lost twenty-nine million dollars, then decided perhaps their name meant *baby food*.

Coke thought, "our name means *beverages*, so let's buy a winery." After they lost $89 million they thought, "maybe our name doesn't mean *beverages*, it just means *soft drinks*."

Somebody lost their focus. Guerrilla marketers maintain their focus.

Seventh. One of the biggest differences is that traditional marketing says the way to grow your business is linearly, adding one new customer at a time. Guerrilla marketers say that's an expensive way to grow.

The best way to grow is geometrically. Which means, *a)* enlarge the size of each transaction, *b)* go for more transactions per customer per year, and *c)* harness the enormous referral power of your existing customers to add new customers on a regular basis. If you're growing in four directions at once through largest transactions, more transactions, the referral power of your customers, and adding new customers through regular marketing, you are growing geometrically. It's almost impossible to go out of business if you grow like that.

Eighth. Traditional marketing does everything it can to get a new customer, then loses that customer sixty-eight percent of the time because that person is ignored after the sale has been made. Guerrilla marketing never lets that happen because guerrilla marketing is all about follow-up. E-mail is such a wonderful follow-up device. Guerrilla marketers never lose their customers because they stand up for them and never ignore them.

The ninth difference - traditional marketing says, "Scan the horizon for your competitors so you know whom to obliterate." Guerrilla marketing says, "Forget the competitors for a minute, scan the horizon for those businesses that have the same kind of prospects you do, and cooperate with them." No market medium in history is as good a medium for cooperating as the Internet, because you can offer your competitors a piece of the action simply for putting a link on their web pages or sending out a free e-mail.

TC: That's what an affiliate program is all about, isn't it?

JL: Yes.

The tenth difference is that traditional marketing is *me* marketing. *Let me tell you about MY company!... Let me tell you what makes ME great!* Guerrilla marketing isn't me marketing at all, it's *you* marketing. Everything a guerrilla marketer says in their marketing is about the customer, about the tours of their web site, about the visitors to their web sites, it's about the *customer*.

The eleventh difference is that traditional marketing has always been about *getting* while guerrilla marketing is all about *giving*. The Internet is the greatest guerrilla marketing weapon because it allows us to give information away for *free*. The information is free to the prospect or customer, and it's also delivered free. A fancy brochure is *not* free to the marketer. The Internet lets the guerrilla marketer give away valuable information to help their prospects succeed, at no cost.

The twelfth difference is that traditional marketing would have you believe that advertising works, or having a web site works, or doing direct mail works. Guerrilla marketing says that's nonsense, nonsense, and nonsense. Advertising doesn't work, having a web site doesn't work, and direct mail doesn't work. The only thing that works in the twenty-first century are *marketing combinations*. If you do advertising, and have a web site, and do direct mail, all three will work. All three will help the others work.

The thirteenth difference is that traditional marketers look at the bank statement at the end of the month and count up how much money they brought in. At the end of the month guerrilla marketers count up how many new relationships they've made. Again, the

Internet is the best thing known to humankind to establish relationships with people.

The fourteenth difference is that traditional marketing doesn't make much of an allowance for technology, because technology of the past was so expensive. Mainly it was too complicated. They don't know there's been a technological revolution. Guerrilla marketing requires you to be very techno-cozy. If you are techno-phobic, make an immediate appointment with your techno-shrink because techno-phobia these days is fatal.

There are nineteen differences in all and we've covered fourteen. Traditional marketing aims at large groups, the larger the better. The fifteenth difference is guerrilla marketing is aimed at individuals or smaller groups. The smaller the group the better. These are called "niches."

Sixteen. Traditional marketing identifies only a few ways to market and overlooks important details such as how your telephone is answered (which is an important way to market) or how fast you get back to someone after they've said via your web site that they're interested in something. Guerrilla marketing is always intentional, and it includes all the details.

The seventeenth difference between traditional and guerrilla marketing is that traditional marketing attempts to make a sale with marketing while guerrilla marketing only intends to gain consent from people to receive more marketing materials from you.

> *Guerrilla marketing isn't* me *marketing at all, it's* you *marketing. Everything a guerrilla marketer says in their marketing is about the customer.*
> – Jay Levinson

Number eighteen in our list of differences is that traditional marketing has always been a monologue, one person does all the talking. Guerrilla marketing is a dialogue, back and forth between the marketer and the prospect or the customer. The Internet encourages dialogue... Magazine ads don't, radio commercials don't. Aside from the Internet, few kinds of marketing allow for a dialogue - but Guerrilla marketing is all about a dialogue, back and forth.

The nineteenth and final difference is that traditional marketing identifies just a handful of marketing weapons - radio, television, magazines, newspapers, direct mail, telemarketing, and the Internet - that's about it. Guerrilla marketing identifies a hundred different weapons you can market with and sixty-two of them are free.

Having A Web Site Alone Won't Do It

TC: Excellent. Jay, the nineteenth point that you ended up with, a hundred different weapons... Are you suggesting that just putting up a web site alone is not enough to get rich?

JL: If you just put up a web site all by itself, no matter how good it is, you're invisible. No one knows that you're there.

They're going to find out about you once you start connecting with other people who are online, once you start advertising your site, once you start speaking to people by postcards and letters and letting them know that you are there. It's crucial to realize that having a web site alone won't do it.

You've got to mix it with other marketing weapons. There's lots of ways to do that. You can, for instance, write an article for a local newspaper, establishing yourself as the expert, and use reprints of that story to get people to your web site.

TC: It works the same way online, doesn't it – providing content to other web site owners that refer back to you.

JL: Yes it does!

The bottom line is, having a web site is very important, because that is where everything comes together, you've got to let people know that you are there, and the only way that you can do that is by cooperating with other people who have a web site or by driving off-line people online.

One Thing That's For Sure About The Internet Is That Nothing Is For Sure About The Internet

TC: Jay, you were marketing before the Internet came along, and you embraced it immediately. What can you say about the changes you've seen during its short life-span?

JL: Here's something I can say specifically about the Internet. First of all, and I guess everybody knows this, nothing about the Internet is for sure except that it's going to change. Everything that people thought about the Internet last year has changed. And what people are learning about it this year is also in the process of changing.

One thing that's for sure about the Internet is that *nothing* is for sure about the Internet.

You've Got To Know "Marketing" To Market Online

Secondly, the important point that I make when I talk to my clients is - you want to market ON the Internet. I tell them you've got to know *marketing* in order to market online successfully. I just mentioned that there are a hundred different weapons of marketing. Being on the Internet and having a web site is only one of those weapons, there's ninety-nine others, and you've got to know the whole spectrum of marketing in order to see how you can have a web site and how to market online, and how to make everything work together to empower everything else.

When people think about marketing online the first thing that comes to their mind is having a web site, but the reality is that the best way to market online is by e-mail.

TC: Most people do not understand that, Jay, and they say, "But I don't have any names to market to." How could this person get started?

JL: One way is to first join forums and see the groups and look for people that are talking about your field of expertise. Go into the chat rooms and talk about your particular industry or the topic of your expertise. Participate in those forums and chat a little with those groups. You will get access to a lot of e-mail names and these are people that have demonstrated that they're interested in the topic that you have to talk about.

You're going to get a lot of people that way. You'll find that loads of sites would love the content you provide. You could write an article for their web site, charge them nothing, just ask for a paragraph at the end of the article letter linking to your site and talking about you. It costs you nothing to do these things.

> *The best way to market online is by e-mail.*
> *– Jay Levinson*

Join the forums, go to the chat rooms, post articles at other peoples' web sites - those are three ways of marketing.

These are the things that you have to think of first, how you're going to *market* your site. Then think of having a web site.

The 8 Elements To Success On Your Web Site

TC: Okay, Jay, so we've figured out how we're going to market our site when we get it up. What do we need to think about when we're building the actual site?

JL: When you think of having a web site, there are eight elements you need to emphasize, and if you only emphasize seven of these elements, you are just not going make it. Most people only emphasize five or six elements then wonder why success is eluding them.

Here are the eight elements. Implement them and I don't think there's any way to fail... No way that you cannot make a lot of money online.

The first element is the most important – you have to do it first to get the other seven elements in line, to ever make any serious money from your web site.

The first element to emphasize is *planning*. Why do you want a web site? What do you hope to accomplish with a web site?

I'll tell you a little story about this. I have a client in Berkeley, California who sells mattresses. He manufactures and sells mattresses and has a lot of young bright people working for him who told him, "You should have a web site. You ought to have a web site." He said, "No, no, no, I don't like technology, I don't want a web site, and I don't want to sell mattresses online."

Eventually he found that these bright employees were possibly going to leave unless they could get him involved with a web site. To appease them he said, "Okay, you can create a web site, but I don't want to sell beds on the Internet. I don't want to sell mattresses online. If you want me to have a web site to help me in other ways, then I'm willing to go along."

He put up a web site which does not attempt to sell his beds or his mattresses - all it does is to get people to his store. That's all his web site does... And his advertising, radio, and newspapers direct them to his web site.

> *The most important thing you are going to get from your web site is the list of people who care about you.*
> *– Jay Levinson*

He told me a few months ago that he's been doing marketing for thirty years and no marketing weapon has ever been as good as his web site. "I never sold one mattress that way, I haven't sold one bed online, and I've never had more traffic in my store! The people who come in know what they want to buy! How dare I resist having a web site!"

The point is *plan*. Why do you want a web site? Do you want to make sales? Do you want to get people to call a phone number, and do you want to engage in a dialogue with them on the telephone? Whatever it is, plan why you want a web site.

The second element is *content*. What content should be included on your site? How will you get reoccurring, fresh, updated content - something that will make Internet users want to return to your site?

I have a total of eight elements. We've only talked about two of them. The first was planning, the second was content.

The third is *design*. In the online world now there's something called the stay or bail moment. Within three seconds, visitors to your web site decide whether they are going to stay there or whether they are going to bail (to click over to some other site). The thing that's going to keep them there is design of your web site. You've got to limit the number of ideas you present at once. You've got to make your ideas very clear.

The fourth after planning, content, and design is *involvement*. Involvement is realizing that the Internet is an interactive marketing medium. It's not just you; it's you plus the people who are visitors to your web site. You've got to involve them.

You can involve them by asking them to click to sign up for your free newsletter, enter your sweepstakes, or to get a free report on something. The point is, involve visitors to your site and get their name and e-mail address. These names are going to be worth more to you than anything else. The most important thing you are going to get from your web site is the list of people who care about you.

We have covered planning, content, design, and involvement. The fifth is *production*. How do you produce a web site? It's not too hard these days. There's simple-to-use software that lets you produce and design your web site.

The sixth of the eight areas is *follow-up*. It's crucial, if a person gets in touch with you, that you get right back in touch with them. If you're a real true guerrilla, you will get back to them in two hours, and if you're somewhat of a guerrilla, you're going to get back to them that day. If you're almost a guerrilla, you'll get back to them the next day. But if you get back to them after twenty-four hours, you're not really a guerrilla. People use the Internet because they're in a hurry and appreciate the convenience. If you don't get right back to them with follow-up, you're blowing the genuine opportunity laid in your lap.

Those are the first six of eight web site success elements. I mentioned earlier that many people have all six of these: planning, content, design, involvement, production, and even follow-up.

Basically they fall on their face with the seventh area, which is *promotion*. When you go online and do a web site, you become invisible and nobody knows you're there. That's why promotion is what it's all about. There is something we call the "rule of thirds." The rule of thirds says "Once you determine what your budget is going to be for marketing online, put one third of it to developing your web site, one third of it to promoting your web site, and one third of it to maintaining your site."

Most people put all three thirds into developing their web site then don't promote it. Don't overlook promoting your web site off-line - that's a crucial element. The moment you think of marketing online, start thinking, "How am I going to promote my site off-line?"

The eighth element is *maintenance*. A web site is a lot like a daily newspaper ad. It's an organic medium and needs to be fresh to be interesting. A web site is like a brand new baby; it needs constant attention, constant changing, and constant nurturing. If you keep your web site fresh and new like a baby every day, you will be implementing all eight of the elements.

Planning, content, design, involvement, production, follow-up, promotion, and maintenance. If you do those eight things, you're going to find you can make a lot of money on your web site.

Make It Simple To Sell – Or You Won't Sell

TC: Jay, you were speaking earlier of design as one of the eight elements of success. Can you elaborate a little on that?

JL: Here's the story. You've got to make it as simple as possible for people to buy what it is you're selling. Kinko's, for example, offers a good case study of this principle. In one of their offers, they described an eight-step order process. Sales weren't good at all. When they rewrote their copy with a three-step process, sales shot up thirty-five percent. You've got to make things as simple as possible.

Most people listening to this show know more about the Internet than people who will visit their site. They may be technologically adept, but the people who visit their sites might not be.

You don't have to have a lot of bells and whistles or flash, dazzle, and special effects on your web site if you offer something of value. In fact, it will probably be counter-productive.

You and I both know that the Internet isn't about technology, it's about people. The Internet is a wonderful way for people to develop relationships and stay in touch with each other.

TC: That's what it's about; it's not about technology. Marketing on the Internet, like all marketing, is about people.

Even Your Local Business Needs To Be On The Internet

Jay, here's another point I've heard you speak on before... Someone might say, "Why would I want to be on the Internet because I have a local business?" Could you explain your take on that? Maybe give us a real-life example from one of your clients.

JL: Exactly! I talked to a couple of hot tub manufacturers last year and that's what they said to me. "We have a local business. We sell hot tubs and can't sell them online. Why do we need a web site?"

I told them a local business really ought to have a web site because people are learning to buy things in a new way, and the way they are learning to buy things is to go online first.

The people that had the hot tub company set up a web site. They called me within thirty days and said, "We sold several hot tubs as a result of our web site, and we didn't even think we needed one!" A web site is very important, even to a local business. Even locally, people don't go to the yellow pages anymore, they go online.

> *Marketing on the Internet, like all marketing, isn't about technology, it's about people.*
> *– Jay Levinson*

That's why a show like yours is so darned valuable for our economy and your listeners.

TC: Going online first really is the way it's happening. It's reflecting societal trends and evolutions in the world that we get to be part of. I like that, Jay!

Guerrilla Marketing Strategies To Make You Rich
On The Internet

Okay Jay Levinson, with your experience and with the breakthroughs that you've seen, give us a couple more down-and-dirty Internet marketing guerrilla strategies that any good entrepreneur could employ to really make big money, quickly on the Internet.

The Best Product Is "Free"

JL: One of the most important things people can do on the Internet is to offer something free or at a very low cost. The reason you do that is because you get names for your mailing list.

For example we have a web site at *GMarketing.com* We spelled it that way because a lot of people don't know how to spell guerrilla, so we called it *gmarketing.com* The site's been up since 1995 and when people go there, they find they can sign up for a tip every day. The cost of getting a marketing tip every day online is $3.00 a year. Now that's almost free, but what really happens is when people sign up to get the guerrilla communiqué, we get their name, and we know they are interested in marketing!

As a result, the site compiles a very large list of people we can mail to, and it costs us next to nothing to do that. I highly recommend that you offer something free or low cost at your site so you can get peoples' names and e-mail addresses, then start sending to them. Send them good information, stay in touch with them, and you're going to make money on the Internet.

Become An Industry Expert By Writing One-Page Articles

Another thing to do is to offer a newsletter to your online list. It's not too difficult, because these days, the most popular kind of newsletter is just one page long.

It's another way of getting your name in front of people. They'll see you as an expert and everything you say and do will have more impact - including the offers you make to your list.

The Secret To Earning $625,000 On The Internet In 4 Months With Zero Advertising Costs!

TC: Jay, how could someone write an article and turn it into a lot of money?

JL: Most newsletter owners would be happy to publish an article by you. It's very easy to find out what newsletters are out there then start sending them articles. I did a BootCamp in Las Vegas three months ago. We charged $2,500 a person for one day. To publicize the event and get people to the BootCamp, I wrote articles

> *The amazing thing is, we didn't spend one penny in marketing, and we didn't do anything but market online.*
> *– Jay Levinson*

for a whole lot of newsletters. No one paid me for those articles, we distributed them free.

TC: But on the other hand, you didn't have to pay anyone for advertising!

JL: And we got a whole lot of coverage. As a result of that, over 250 people showed up at my $2,500-a-person BootCamp. The amazing thing is, we didn't spend one penny in marketing, and we didn't do anything but market online.

That is *FREE* marketing!

People have got to realize that there are opportunities out there... Lots of free ways to market. This technique, public relations, is very powerful!

TC: So you just go to work and get press and list coverage for your site that drives traffic and subscribers to your e-zine, which means purchasers for your offers. It couldn't be simpler... Or more guerrilla.

JL: That's the beauty of these newsletters; it doesn't cost you anything but time, energy, and imagination.

TC: That's pretty doggone good! You just illustrated what you were talking about: You had names in your database and made joint ventures or deals with others who had names in their databases. You wrote a free article, published it, and if I did the math right, Jay, without any cost in advertising you pulled in $625,000 - more or less?

JL: That's about right. Actually, it was a little bit more than that.

TC: Outrageous!

It Didn't Cost Us Anything

JL: But the point really is - and it blows me away - it didn't cost us anything!

TC: That's a mighty big point.

JL: Only on the Internet.

Special thanks to the contributors to this show...

*Jay Levinson * www.JayConradLevinson.com*
*Ted Ciuba * www.InstantInternetMarketing.com*

If you enjoyed this interview, there's more just like this!
Tune into *www.InternetMarketingInterviews.com*

Other resources to supercharge your progress!
www.GetRichOnTheInternet.com
www.GetRichOnTheInternet.com/seminars
www.AutoPilotRiches.com
www.KillerWebCopy.com
www.ProtegeProgram.com
www.MailOrderInTheInternetAge.com
www.LowCostInternetAdvertising.com
www.PrePaidLegal.com/go/parthenon

Confessions Of A Mail Order Millionaire Gone Internet

Chapter 3

Ted Ciuba *Interviews T.J. Rohleder*

Our featured guest today is T.J. Rohleder, a tremendously successful mail order and Internet marketer. In fact, the truth is, he was the very first person I heard about Internet marketing from. In fact, like 1992 or 1993, and he was talking about *bulletin board systems*.

If you don't know what a Bulletin Board System (BBS) is, don't worry about it. It faded away. The important thing is that it was a precursor to the commercial Internet.

Even at that time, I knew T.J. Rohleder was a man to be listening to, because he had already made over $10,000,000 in mail order the old way. He pulled that in during his first four years in the business.

I looked at him and said, "Man! There is so much going on, let me jump in!"

What T.J. has done can be replicated. He is, in every sense of the word, an "ordinary" person like you and I. In fact, he comes from Goessel, Kansas. How much more heartland America can you get than rural Kansas? He has done some extraordinary things in mail order and on the Internet... And his customers love him.

T.J. Rohleder, welcome to *How To Get Rich On The Internet*.

T.J. Rohleder (TR): Hey Ted, I am so excited that I just can't wait to get started.

Ted Ciuba (TC): I'll tell you what, I know our listeners can't wait to get the insight and advice you'll give them. Tell me, how did it start for you?

I Was Sending Away For Every Single Program You Can Imagine On Getting Rich

TR: About twenty years ago I was sending away for every single program you could possibly imagine on getting rich. And, as some of our listeners might know, once you start sending away for these programs on how to make money, you end up getting on mailing lists and companies that sell money making plans and programs start sending you a ton of different offers.

I was buying every single program that I could possibly get my hands on. Back then we were pretty broke, but we really believed in the American dream and believed it was possible to get rich. That's how I found out about the mail order business... Simply by buying a series of programs on how to get rich in mail order.

Start Your Business With $300

My wife, Eileen, and I started our first business in 1988, a small mail order business in Goessel, Kansas. Goessel is a very small rural town about an hour north of Wichita. We started the business with $300. We ran a small display ad in a national magazine for $300. We were broke and that was about all the money we could scrounge up at the time. We had to sell one of our old, beat up vans just to come up with the $300. But like you said, Ted...

$10 Million In First 4 Years

...Within our first four years we brought in over $10,000,000. No one was more shocked and amazed and stunned than we were! None of our family members could believe it, and we couldn't believe it ourselves!

That's the power of this kind of business.

Pyramid Your Profits

TC: Indeed. You must have done something right... Because I occasionally hear someone say, "I tried mail order once, and it doesn't work."

TR: I'll admit we got lucky to begin with. My wife actually talked me out of one of the first ideas I wanted to try to sell by mail. Thank God she did, because now, years later, I realize she was right and I was wrong.

We found the right product at the right time, rolled it out and brought in $10,000,000 with no outside additional financing whatsoever. We just let the profits roll back into more profits.

There was an element of luck there, of course, but as you know...

People get lucky when they go out there and think big and try to accomplish big things and when they're not afraid to take a chance, a calculated risk.

TC: Did a $300 risk seem like a pretty big one to you at that time?

Last Way The Little Guy Can Get Rich

TR: You bet it was. I mean, at the time $300 was a lot of money. But we knew that mail order marketing was one of the last ways the average person could really have a chance at getting rich. We had read enough books about it and, actually, I was kind of a mail order junkie. I already knew quite a bit about the business because we had been sending away for all kinds of plans and programs and so forth. So, any way, we already knew quite a bit of stuff that needed to be done and that helped fuel it all.

Scientific Marketing

TC: It's even easier today with the Internet. It's faster and you don't need to even spend $300.

I know a little bit, because I've seen some of your promotions in action. I know that you are what I would term a "scientific mailer." That is, out of all your customers who ever bought anything from you, you have the clear intention that you want to serve them some more and in doing so, you can make more money. You also segment your list. Can you speak a little on those ideas?

Most of all it's having the desire to do it and the willingness to put it into action.
- T.J. Rohleder

TR: Well, it's vital. The longer people study these kinds of things and the more programs they invest in, the more they'll find out about the eighty-twenty rule. It's a simple concept stating that eighty percent of your profit comes from twenty percent of your customers. So, what you have to do early on, and this can be simple or advanced, is separate the "better" customers from your "other" customers. Simply do more with your better customers, the ones that are representing eighty percent of your profits. Those are the people you need to focus on and do more business with... The people who will get you more money.

"If I Can Do It, You Can Do It"

TC: It does sound very simple when you say it like that.

TR: Ted, if it wasn't simple, I couldn't do it. Believe me, the one thing we try to tell people is that if *we* can make millions of dollars, *they* can make millions of dollars. We're in the business of helping people make money in mail order and Internet marketing... That's part of our business, part of what we do. Customers come to our seminars, spend a few days with us, and at the end of the seminar when they're shaking our hand, they're saying, "You are right. I do believe now that if you can do it, I can do it." There's absolutely nothing special about us.

> ## BFO: Blinding Flash of the Obvious!
> *This is the future right now, it's still unfolding, it's still brand new, and we're getting involved in it, taking a big position in the market right now...*
> *- T.J. Rohleder*

BFO: Blinding Flash of the Obvious!

Most important to our success, as you well know, is having the desire to do it and the willingness to put it into action.

TC: Now you've really brought it down to a very simple level. But most people hate their jobs. Everywhere we go we hear people crying and moaning about their jobs. I heard two people today complaining about their jobs... One laughed the laugh of resignation and said, "There's never a good day on the job!"

$50 Million In Sales From Nowhereville

TR: I'll tell you, there's nothing like this business as far as getting excited in the morning.

Having people from all over the nation, all over the world, send you money is about the most exciting thing I've ever experienced. Year after year after year I only get more excited about it, as you do, Ted.

It's so exciting to think that, from where I'm standing right now, in the middle of nowhere, a small little tiny rural area in the middle of Kansas, we've done over $50,000,000 in sales.

TC: You mean you don't have to be in New York, Miami, or L.A.?

The Average Guy Can Get Rich On The Internet

TR: Absolutely not. That's part of the thrill of it... You can move anywhere you want. You can live anywhere in the country, or for that matter you can live anywhere in the world, thanks to the Internet. It's so thrilling! It's an exciting time to be alive because what this does, Ted, is give the average person more power then they've ever had in the recorded history of the world! I know that might sound like hype to some people, but it's the absolute truth.

TC: It surely is and that's why we're on this radio show. Since you have become so embracing of the Internet, give us some of your ideas on exactly what the average ordinary person can do to get rich on the Internet.

Invest In Yourself

TR: What you have to do first is invest in yourself and your future by purchasing books and tapes. You have to become familiar with some things. When I'm talking about becoming familiar with some things, I'm not talking about a bunch of computer technology crap, because that's the wrong thing to become good at or become an expert on.

You have to learn the marketing side of the business - the Internet. Too many people get caught up in the technical side, and I realize that to some degree knowledge there is helpful, but what is more helpful than anything is using those old-fashioned mail order techniques. (*Direct response marketing* is a more politically correct term these days.)

Learn how to use direct response marketing techniques on the Internet, like techniques for attracting new customers, then reselling to those customers again and again. You're probably better off letting some low-cost high school age computer person handle a lot of that part of your business. That's just my opinion, Ted, and I know a lot of people will disagree with me. I barely know how to turn a computer on. I don't want to learn all that crap.

TC: That's the curious thing... A lot of people think you need to be an expert on technology to market on the Internet, but that's not the case. That's excellent.

Embracing The Internet

TC: T.J., you started in mail order eighteen years ago, before the Internet came along. Now I've seen you move and embrace the Internet. As I said earlier, you were one of the very first to give instruction in Internet marketing, you're a massive marketer on the Internet, and a massive marketer for programs that help people make money on the Internet.

Give us a little background about how you made that change.

We Didn't Know What A Computer Bulletin Board Was

TR: We started back in '93 with computer bulletin boards. We heard about a small handful of people across the country who were using computer bulletin boards to sell all kinds of different things... Everything from office supplies and software programs to publications, books, etc. It was exciting!

> ### Very Important Lesson
> *We didn't know what a computer bulletin board was, but we weren't going to let anything like that stop us.*
> *- T.J. Rohleder*

Very Important Lesson

We didn't know what a computer bulletin board was, but we weren't going to let anything like that stop us. So, we went out and found some people in the Wichita, Kansas area who were running a very successful computer bulletin board system.

A lot of people these days don't even know what a computer bulletin board is.

TC: It's become antiquated, hasn't it?

TR: You bet, and it's amazing how all of this has changed so fast since we began in '93. A computer bulletin board was a closed computer network of people who were connected together. Sometimes, especially towards the end, they all had Internet access. It was kind of like America OnLine is now.

TC: Good description, kind of a closed club?

Market For Zero Cost, Make A Killing!

TR: Yes, but the idea about being able to market stuff without the high costs traditionally associated with printing, postage, and advertising was the thing that got us so excited.

You know, Ted, that's the thing that gets us excited to this very day... For instance, we have thousands of customers. We've got their e-mail addresses and we're constantly staying in touch with them, selling them, offering them a variety of products and services that our company provides... And it's *free* to us!

We can send them as many messages as we want, it's absolutely free to us. There's no cost of printing or postage and all of the stuff that goes along with that... You know, the graphic art work. So, when you're able to spend no money whatsoever on any of your marketing, every penny you make is pure profit!

> *When you're able to spend no money whatsoever on any of your marketing, then every penny you make is pure profit.*
> *- T.J. Rohleder*

That is, besides the hard costs of your product or whatever.

TC: And that could be *zero!*

TR: That's exciting to us! Mail order is a fascinating business. Once you get involved with it and start getting checks, money orders, credit cards, and orders from around the world, you just get hooked! But, mail order in the Internet Age can even be more exciting, because your marketing costs go away! There's *no* cost now!!

Exaggerated Profit$: Viral Marketing & Digital Delivery

TC: T.J., I know that for some of your programs, not only are you marketing to your e-mail database customers at zero cost, you've also done some viral marketing in which one person refers another. That's also at zero cost, isn't it.

I know you actually deliver products and e-books that don't cost you anything, also.

Step Into The Future Today

TR: We're doing a lot of electronic books now... We're publishing a lot of what are called *e-books*. These e-books are so exciting, this is the future right now, it's still unfolding. It's still brand new and we're getting involved in it, taking a big position in the market right now because it's still brand new.

I think that any of your listeners who are really excited about making a lot of money on the Internet should definitely look into e-books. With e-books - it's a book that's sold *and* delivered electronically so you don't have any of the printing or have to worry about the weight of the book. Our company has shipped hundreds and thousands of regular books over the years, and those things are heavy and postage fees cost a fortune. With electronic books, it's all done digitally, so one hundred percent of the profit goes straight into your bank account. That's the most incredible feeling in the world, Ted.

> *Making $100,000 a year in mail order or on the Internet is nothing.*
> *- T.J. Rohleder*

TC: Yes!!

TR: You know... To be able to make sales but not have all of the costs associated with traditional sales and services...

TC: Right, T.J., and that's one of the reasons that I wanted our listeners to hear you. I know with your massive success in mail order you've also encountered massive expenses, as you referred to... Printing, typesetting, graphic work, handling, postage. Today, of course, I see you running for the Internet, and reduced expense is the reason, isn't it?

The Difference Between Revenues And Profits

TR: Yeah, it's exciting to bring in millions of dollars every year. And we recently topped a million dollar month! That's exciting, but when you can only keep ten cents on the dollar, that's not exciting. It's one thing to bring in millions of dollars, but with traditional mail order you have quite a bit of costs involved, and those costs can eat away at your profits. Don't get me wrong, the profits can still be phenomenal. Some of the richest people in the world are in the direct response marketing business - and the profits can be *phenomenal*!

This Thrilling Internet

With the Internet you have a chance to get out from under some of the onerous costs and procedures associated with mail order, as profitable as it is! That's the kind of thing that keeps me awake at night. It keeps me awake at night because I'm excited. Some people are kept awake at night cause they're worried, but some of us can't get to sleep because it's just too darn exciting.

TC: That's a better reason not to be able to sleep at night!

TR: This is a thrilling business, Ted. I know you've dedicated your life to helping people get started and make money on the Internet, and our company does the same thing. We truly get so much pleasure out of helping people get into this fascinating business, because it's really one of the last opportunities for the average person - the person that doesn't have a great education, a lot of skill, or a super high IQ.

This is one of the few remaining ways to get rich. That's exciting because *I'm* an average person. In the past, our opportunities would have been so closed. I mean, a hundred or two hundred years ago average people stood no real chance of making it big. It was always the people who were born with the silver spoon in their mouth, or who had some special abilities or talents.

With the Internet and mail order, ordinary, average people, which most of us are, have the opportunity to make as much money as the richest people in our area make... Lawyers and doctors. That's very exciting to me.

Earn $100,000 Your First Year In Internet Marketing

TC: So I'm absolutely certain you'd have no problem with me telling people that it's pretty easy for them to earn $100,000 their first year in Internet marketing?

TR: Well, you know, this is the funny thing, Ted. For those people who have never made $100,000 in one year... It seems impossible.

TC: T.J., if you've never made a $100,000 a year... Where would you go with that one?

TR: Well, Ted, if you've never made $100,000 a year, it's going to be very hard to believe that you can actually do it - and I'm speaking from experience here. Before Eileen and I got started in the mail order business, we had never made more than $26,000 a year in our entire life - and that was with both of us working. That shows you how poverty poor we were, with both of us working full time, we never made more than twenty-six grand a year.

Back then, $100,000 a year was an awful amount of money and it was kind of out of reach for us, as it is for most people that have never made that kind of money.

But once you hit that mark... I'm not sure how to explain it, Ted.

To the guy that makes $100,000 a year, it might seem impossible to make $500,000 a year. To the guy that makes $500,000 a year it might seem impossible to make $1,000,000 a year.

Believe me, there are plenty of people out there making $500,000, $1,000,000, or $10,000,000 a year. It's a matter of perception.

Making $100,000 a year in mail order or on the Internet is nothing. It's just that if you would have told me that when we first got started, I would never have believed it.

I'm sure a lot of your listeners are having a hard time believing it.

Selling In The Global Marketplace

TC: A lot of people have been pleasantly surprised. I mean, you talked about the web page. Put up a web page and instantly you've got a global market, not a neighborhood market. $100,000 in that market is just not that big, is it?

TR: No, not when the world, or even just the country, is your market place. Some people get hung up on the fact that they don't want to take orders from, say, Indonesia, and deal with money transfers and all those things. They may want to do business in the continental United States, but still market on the Internet. That's fine! How many millions of people are there in this country, 600,000,000 or something like that.?...

A Small Group of Repeat Customers

The point is, and this is how we made our fortune, Ted, and this is how you are making all *your* money... You only need a small group of customers with whom you do business again, and again, and again. Over a period of months and years you can make millions and millions of dollars. There's no guarantee that you will, no promises or guarantees. Nobody can guarantee that you're going to make millions of dollars, it's up to you.

All you need is a relatively small group of customers to bring in millions of dollars in sales every year.

TC: I know exactly what you're saying, but I want to ask this question because I'm not sure all our listeners understand. You said all you need is a small group of customers to do business with over and over again. I thought when you got a customer – if you've got a book for sale, for instance, you sell them, and they're gone.

What can you do? How do you sell to customers again?

How do you apply what you hear? How bad do you want it? And what are you willing to do to get it?

TR: It's a funny thing about human nature, but the person who buys one type of product or service is never fully content. Some markets are different - some are even more *insatiable*. That's what I call it - an insatiable market. Human nature being what it is, people who buy once from you will buy again and again if you just sell them products and services similar to the kind they bought from you the first time. It sounds simple, and really it is simple, although like everything it can be advanced, and there are certain techniques…

I don't mean to be too simplistic about it, but the concept is pretty basic.

How To Crank Out 2 Books Every Month

TC: I think we're all happy to hear that, but you touched on a point that I hear listeners asking about, and since you touched on it, it's fair game. You said all you have to do is give customers more products similar to what they first wanted. Now T.J., I think you are a veritable *product machine*. I've never seen anybody who can turn out books and products like you. The normal author takes two years to write a book and I've seen you turn out two or more in a month. You must have some secrets and simple techniques that you can share.

TR: We crank a lot of stuff out here because it's our passion. This is what we love to do, and it's taken a number of years to get as good at it as we've gotten.

We have a staff of very talented people here that we've developed over a period of time, so I don't want to take undue credit. My wife, who ran the company for the last fourteen years before I took it over, built a very good staff of people. Now that I've taken over, those people are still here and they're very talented, very good at what they do, and we all work together as a team.

> *It's the* content, *it's the* material, *it's the* message, *it's the* how to, *it's whatever the information you're selling is. It's not if all the commas are in place or if you have a dangling participle, whatever that is… In other words, it's not literary print, it's the* information.
>
> -Ted Ciuba

People spend an awful lot of time doing unnecessary work. Publishers are a perfect example. People who write and publish information products spend way too much time trying to make everything perfect. We try not to fall into that trap. We've got an obligation to sell good stuff because if we don't, customers are not going to come back and buy again and again. You have to achieve a level of quality or customers will be so upset they're never going to buy from you again.

We strive to make it good, but just good enough… That's it… Just good enough. We don't get caught up in the perfection game of having to make everything perfect. We make it good enough so the customer will be happy and come back and buy again and again, year after year.

Good Content Is The Important Thing

TC: I want to clarify a point. What I hear you saying, and correct me if I'm wrong, but what I hear you saying is you've got the *content* and the *material*, it's the *message*, it's the *how to*, it's whatever the information you're selling is. It's not important that all the commas are in place or if you have a dangling participle, whatever that is... In other words, it's not literary print, it's the *information*. Is that correct?

TR: That's exactly right!

Recycle Products For Rapid Production

All of our products are pretty much the same. We tend to recycle a lot of our products... I'll give you an example, Ted. Right now we're creating one hundred different e-books. A lot of the content we're using to create those one hundred e-books is used in more than one e-book. As long as the customer is getting good value, it works.

Most customers are never going to order all one hundred anyway. They'll order a few here and there, but in most cases they're not going to order the whole batch. In creating one hundred e-books, we're able to use the same material, weave it through various publications, and mix it up a little bit. As long as the customer gets good value in each one of those e-books, they're happy and we're happy, and in a very short period of time we can crank out one hundred different products.

TC: Believe me, when you say *one hundred e-books*, that makes the average person think W-O-R-K. I would say that you revealed a major, major secret there. You're talking about what I recently heard called *repurposing*. To put it in other forms to use parts and pieces that apply in other works. T.J., thanks for that one, and for the way you stress you've got to deliver value, but you don't have to have every "*t*" crossed in the grammar part of it.

On behalf of all our listeners, thank you so much. You have really revealed some deep and tremendous secrets.

TR: Well, Ted, this has been real exciting!

Multi-Millionaire Internet Marketer T.J. Rohleder
Reveals Greatest Secrets

TC: We're nearing the end of our magic hour on radio. I don't want you to get away without giving us your greatest secrets that you think that we might need to know. I'll just throw it open to you. What is it our listeners need to know to get rich on the Internet?

TR: Okay, well this is about getting rich in mail order or the

Internet, period. The one thing we see a lot of people getting hung up on is wasting an enormous amount of time, in some cases *years*, trying to come up with a product to sell. I think that is the *biggest* mistake someone can possibly make. Forget about what kind of product you're going to sell. Don't get caught up in that! Most people just sit around and all they can do is think about products they're going to sell to millions of people.   What a bunch of crap!

Market First, The Product Will Follow

This is the kind of marketplace where you get rich selling to very small groups of people. I'm talking about narrow target markets - and that's been the secret to our success. We started with $300. We're very average people who have now made over $50,000,000 in sales... But who's counting?

I'm not saying that to brag, believe me, I hate people who brag. There are people making a lot more money than we're making, but they're all doing it in a *target market.*

Forget about the product, forget about what you're going to try to sell. Instead, put some of your time and attention on the *market* you want to sell to.

Get Rich In A Niche

Now what is a market? A market is a group of people that have something in common - it could be many things. Our company sells to the opportunity market. We sell to people who are looking for business opportunities... Particularly opportunities to make money in mail order and on the Internet. That is our niche market.

Your niche market might be people who want to lose ten pounds in one week.

Once you decide the marketplace, it's a matter of figuring out who the competitors are in that marketplace and who you want to model after. What are they selling? What is your market clamoring for? Then you develop some type of product or service that is right along the lines of the top competitors of that marketplace.

TC: So you're saying, find the market you know is spending money *first*, one which you know is providing riches for others, *then* find out what to provide to those customers?

Get On Your Competitor's Mailing Lists

TR: Right. Look around and find the people who are making the most money in those markets. Get on their customer mailing list, buy the stuff they're selling, and experience their customer follow-up and attempts at upsell. Get to understand the market that you want to reach and how it works... How it's currently being serviced.

All of a sudden, the ideas of what you're going to sell become very easy. You're not trying to sell to a nameless, faceless audience of millions of people. Let the large corporations with the deep pockets worry about those markets. You're trying to sell to very small markets that don't cost a lot of money to reach, but who have a very specialized interest.

That is the key to how the average man or woman can get very rich in mail order or on the Internet.

TC: Sounds good to me because I certainly don't want to spend millions trying to reach the public, and I know that's what you're saying... Find a niche.

Model Your Successful Competitors

TR: Right, that's better for large corporations that have deep, deep pockets. The average man or woman needs to find small markets of people who have something in common, then find out which companies in those markets are doing the very best. Those are the ones you want to model after as closely as you can. Especially in the beginning, without copying exactly what they're doing, try to find a way to do something similar or better. That was how we got started and that's been the whole key to our fortune.

TC: Therefore, that is a major secret to success.

Work With Real People Really Doing It

TR: Another one, Ted, is that you've got to work with people who know what they're doing. Eileen and I have had a lot of help over the years from people who have helped us along the road.

These are people out there who are actually doing it, not some retired consultants who were doing it twenty or thirty years ago, and now spend all their time talking about the past. We're talking about people out there doing it right now. *Those* are the people you need to get as close to as possible, the ones you need to follow. You need to work with people that are out there doing it right now so you can use the best ideas in today's world.

TC: Absolutely, T.J. Rohleder! Thank you for everything. You've been a tremendous guest and you've shared so many good secrets for our listeners to grab hold of.

How To Get Rich On The Internet

Okay listeners, we've had a fantastic guest with us. T.J. Rohleder from More Inc. out of Goessel, Kansas has shared so many great things with us. He started with a humorous story about how twenty years ago he sent for everything he could that related to making money at home. Sure enough, he read it all, started putting something in motion, and took that courageous step. He even had to sell a van to put $300 down to pay for an advertisement - you could do that - and the rest, they say, is history. He's made a fortune in mail order and

> *Forget about the product, forget about what you're going to try to sell, and instead put some of your time and attention on the market you want to sell to.*
> *- T.J. Rohleder*

in recent years has shifted into Internet marketing where he's making more, more easily, at a lower cost and with less hassle than ever before!

He gave us a lot of different insights as to why we're all involved in Internet marketing.

We love it. It gives the average person who has no money, no real contacts, and no extraordinary quality traits, an information goldmine. It gives them the ability to enter a worldwide market and compete. There's just a mouse click between Microsoft and you. T.J. also revealed, and this is very important, that he has taken a lot of his direct response marketing (his politically correct term for mail order) techniques and used them on the Internet to attract new customers and re-sell them again. That's important!

Attract new customers and re-sell them... He emphasized that. Of course, re-selling on the Internet with no cost gives you a tremendous marketing advantage! T.J. gave us the example of sending out thousands of e-mails at no cost, then said he's into e-books, which he recommends you jump on to, too. Electronic books have zero production or delivery costs.

Yikes, this Internet has some real advantages!

When I asked for some of his really great secrets, he said: find a market with insatiable customers, then, since people in any market *do* buy again and again, simply provide what they want. One of the easiest ways to get started is by zeroing in on the competition – what are they succeeding with? Can you go one better?

T.J. told how you can provide a series of products by repurposing, dividing and conquering, and sending out different things that you have. Recreate one product, maybe a book, and make it into several reports, which you can then put into an audio tape. Share parts of your work and research with other products...

What a lot of secrets he's shared with us! Thank you for that, T.J.

TR: Thank you, Ted. I really enjoyed talking with your listeners.

TC: Thanks. Listeners, what you are getting here is MasterMind insight. Real, genuine. *Helpful!*

T.J. was one exceptionally good example of that type of help. The best marketers in the nation are here freely sharing their thoughts, successes, and maybe some of their failures, so that you learn easily.

It just don't get any better than that. Coincidently, that's what T.J. closed with, saying, "*Go to the people who are really doing it.*"

And yes, just like T.J., *you* can get *rich* on the Internet!

Special thanks to the contributors to this show...

*T.J. Rohleder * www.TheWorldsGreatestInternetBusiness.com*
*Ted Ciuba * www.InstantInternetMarketing.com*

If you enjoyed this interview, there's more just like this! Tune into *www.InternetMarketingInterviews.com*

Other resources to supercharge your progress!
www.GetRichOnTheInternet.com
www.GetRichOnTheInternet.com/seminars
www.AutoPilotRiches.com
www.KillerWebCopy.com
www.ProtegeProgram.com
www.MailOrderInTheInternetAge.com
www.LowCostInternetAdvertising.com
www.PrePaidLegal.com/go/parthenon

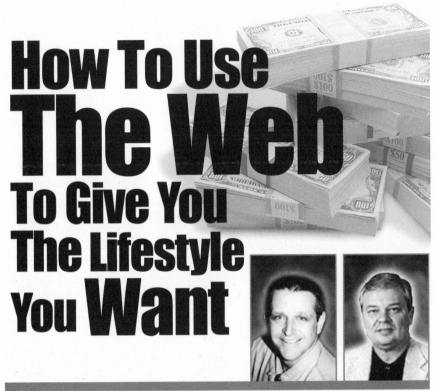

How To Use The Web To Give You The Lifestyle You Want

Chapter 4

Ted Ciuba *Interviews* Clay Cotton *&* Mike Jay

Let's jump right into the purpose and whole position of our show. We bring this show to you introducing some of today's greatest marketing experts, exhibiting many aspects of Internet marketing, as a live MasterMind session. You meet, one by one, people from that select group of rich people on the Internet - someone who's a mentor, someone who knows what's going on on the Internet, someone who's *doing* it.

The title of our segment today is "How To Use The Web To Give You The Lifestyle You Want." These two guys are experts on that.

Lifestyle Driven

Allow me to introduce Clay Cotton. He's a man who has a real interesting history. Back in the days of real rock-and-roll he was playing with Janis Joplin, Jimmy Hendrix, and the Rolling Stones. Even today, I'd say he's got a little bit of that in him because he's really the *doctor of love* in marketing and, though I'm not free to share all the names, he's doing some real high profile work on *love-based marketing*.

He's the big chief behind the Marketer's Hall of Fame, with which he's really making some great contributions to this industry. He's doing a regular six-figure gig, working from home, part time, making the Internet serve his lifestyle.

> *I'm just sitting out on my porch and listening to the brook here in Santa Barbara. I got up this morning, whenever I felt like it, and I took a little drive and then came back to the house for the phone call. My time is really my own.*
> *- Clay Cotton*

Ted Ciuba (TC): Clay Cotton, good day! How are you?

Clay Cotton (CC): I'm doing fine, Ted. Thank you so much for the wonderful introduction.

TC: Hey, Clay, you're a tremendous guy and we're glad to have you with us.

Our second guest is Michael Jay, who is also a fascinating entrepreneur on the web. In fact, he's the one who corrected me one time. He said, "Ted, you've got the whole title wrong. It's not '*How To Get Rich On The Internet*,' but more correctly, '*How To Use The Internet To Get Rich*.'" I certainly don't disagree with him there.

Michael and his lovely wife are enjoying life, traveling around the country in their Winnebago, living the Internet lifestyle in total freedom. And brother, you know that if you can do that... It ain't cheap to be on the road all the time. It's a specific lifestyle.

So Michael Jay, welcome aboard!

MJ: Thanks for inviting me. Hi, Clay! How are you doing? I love you, man.

CC: Thank you, Mike. Bless your heart.

TC: Hmm... That's love-based marketing at work!

Santa Barbara, Paradise

I'll tell you what, just to get things started, Clay, why don't you tell the listeners what you're doing and why they might want to be sure to keep their ears tuned closely to this show?

CC: Well, right now I'm sitting out on my porch and listening to the brook here in Santa Barbara. My wife and I are living in Santa Barbara now, where we just came from Santa Fe, New Mexico. Those are not bad places to live.

I got up this morning, whenever I felt like it, took a little drive, then came back to the house for this phone call. My time really is my own, and I think that's what a lot of people would like.

I'm a hard-core unemployable person. I was a musician for twenty years, would not take a regular job, and still won't, so I've always looked for a lifestyle that would adapt to me and to my needs. Direct response marketing met that need in the early 90s.

It wasn't until seven years later that I was able to utilize the Internet as a tool of automation and of delivering messages and collecting interest. I've been able to mold the direct response marketing principle into a system that produces, as you say, a six-figure income. It's pretty nifty.

Run Your Internet Business From The Caribbean

TC: I'd say so, especially since it sounds like you're just going from one beautiful location to another, and enjoying your days as you wish!

CC: We may even head out to Costa Rica or down to the Caribbean and live there. With the Internet, it doesn't really matter. You could live in the south of France or Hawaii, or wherever, once you have developed something that's working.

It may not happen overnight. As in any craft, you have to practice the basics and study the craft. In this case, it's technology, psychology, and direct response marketing. Most of all, study your target market - study the mindset and needs of your market, then serve those needs efficiently.

TC: There seems to be a real attraction to doing it on the Internet, because, as you said, you could live in the south of France or anywhere you wanted. Which brings us to...

"I Couldn't Have The Lifestyle I Have Without The Internet"

Michael Jay! Since you're living on the road, tell us what the Internet does for you, and how fascinating it really is in your life.

MJ: I couldn't have the lifestyle I have without the Internet. Five or six years ago, I decided I wanted the freedom to do business wherever I wanted to. Of course, in order to do that, you've got to have connectivity, and the Internet becomes the medium that enables all of us to connect, share, and do all the things we do.

That's primarily what I chose and why I offer it to you. Rather than getting rich on the Internet, we use the Internet to get rich. Of course, richness comes in many ways for many different people in terms of whether they want freedom, as I do, and a lifestyle that affords me the opportunity to hang my flag wherever I'd like to, or whether or not they want to make a lot of money, or serve a lot of people, or make contributions all over the world. Those kind of things are available to us all.

I think many people who have started experiencing the Internet realize that connectivity is going to lead us to wherever it is we're headed in terms of a global world.

I think the Internet is a very powerful place, and when you add marketing to it and begin to understand that you can set up very simple and easy-to-use systems that will, in effect, leverage your ideas...

Why Sell To 1,000 When You Can Sell To A Billion?

TC: The scope of it is awesome!

MJ: About five years ago I had someone say, "Why sell to 1,000 when you can sell to a billion?" It's *that* type of mindset that we need to begin to develop - that the Internet allows us to do.

We work with people in our business. We're not in the "Internet marketing" business, but we do Internet marketing. We work with clients all over the world, on six continents, and we're able to do that and still have the freedom we want in terms of our lifestyle.

Bill Gates calls it the "web work-style" in his book, *Business At The Speed Of Thought*. It's a profound read for anyone.

You Have Ultimate Freedom

The point is, once you develop this work-style, you have ultimate freedom. You are doing business 24 hours a day and you're still able to enjoy other things while it's working for you. It's really nice to get up in the morning, look at your in-box, and find not only wonderful words from friends, but also transactions that have taken place while you were sleeping because others were buying your products or enrolling in your services.

It's kind of hard to believe that.

"I Know It Will Work For Everyone Else..."

TC: We run across people all the time who say, "You can't make money while you're sleeping!" or "It's impossible to earn $100,000!" But guys, is that true? What would you say? What do you say to help someone who simply has a few doubts?

Clay, let's start with you. What would you say to someone who doubts, not that it can be done, but whether *they* can do it?

CC: Well, if a person has doubts, then that deals with psychology, and I would say, "Speak with a therapist or a psychologist, or read some books on self-esteem."

People who have been entrepreneurial, independent, or free-thinkers for any length of time, have had to overcome their doubts.

The Law Of Large Numbers

If you're going to be a marketer or in business promoting anything, or if you are a non-profit organization or charity promoting a message or a spiritual message, *whatever* you're going to do, you're going to find many people who are not receptive to your message. There are going to be rejections... And that's fine. If 99% of the people reject me, that's perfectly okay. I have to be able to look to the 1% that say yes. That's another reason why the Internet is so awesome - it's called "the law of large numbers."

The insurance actuarial industry makes their statistical analysis based on the law of large numbers. If you're going to send a message or query to a million or one-hundred million people and try to get them to respond, you can get a low percentage of positive responses and still do very well. That's another awesome thing about the Internet.

When marketing to millions, you only need a very small percentage of positive responses in order to generate the revenue that we all need to get by.

TC: On the Internet the world really is your market. That's fascinating!

CC: It really is. Compare Internet marketing with conventional selling. If I were to go out on the street corner or into the local town and try to get somebody to respond positively to me or to my message, I'd be beating my head against the wall. The same one out of 10,000 would be interested, but the time and personal rejection would be debilitating!

There's lots of reasons why most people don't do things like this. They don't have the self-esteem. They've got an ego problem or some success problem, some psychological problem, or they don't want to face the rejection because they're going to take it personally for some reason. That's often because they were just knocking on the wrong doors, the wrong way, and they weren't thinking in terms of the law of large numbers and statistics.

The Internet allows us to do that, without spending an arm and a leg to do initial testing. These are topics that anyone who has been a student of marketing would understand.

"But Will It Work For Me?"

TC: Michael, because it's such a prevalent question, what do you say to people who say, "I know there's fortunes being made on the Internet, but will it work for me?"

MJ: I wouldn't encourage anyone to drop what they're doing and run onto the Internet unless they're totally committed and don't have any doubts about making it work. It will work eventually, *if* you continue to persist. That's part of the issue.

Start Out With A Pilot Project

The second thing I'd say is, continue doing what you're doing and try a pilot project. Try something small, try something that keeps your interest so that you can have some motivation around. At the same time, you're going to have to try and find what people want.

A lot of people develop a product then try to sell it. That's backwards. What we've learned in Internet marketing is to go find a market, then find out what the market wants, and then use your particular plan and the way you do things to provide a product that the market already wants. That's really a shortcut in my view. It took me about twenty years to learn that, and that's probably one of the reasons I wasn't successful for a long period of time. I kept thinking that I had this mouse trap and if I just kept making it better, people would come.

One secret I say people should use is to try a pilot project and, in that project, find a market that exists then determine what that market wants. Try a couple of products or services or things you think you'd like to be involved with in that market place. Test it. It's really easy to test on the Internet.

You don't have to spend a lot of money to test something on the Internet. Of course, you'll know right away whether or not you've got something that will sell.

We've got all kinds of things, like search engines, that can be used to drive Internet traffic. Get other people to help you drive traffic to a little pilot project. If people actually buy what it is that you have to offer, then, of course, you roll it out.

That would be my advice to people who are just getting started. Start small. Carve out a little bit of your income and sort of invest in

Internet marketing. Make a few investments up front... Allow your-self to lose a little bit of money while you try to figure out some of this stuff.

While everyone wants to get lucky, luck won't carry you through the long term. You've got to learn what you're doing to create rev-enues.

Use a good plan and a good system, like all of *us* have.

I know Clay has a great system, and I have one, and you have one too, Ted.

There are a lot of systems out there that set up really good Internet marketing opportunities. They use a good system patterned after some-one else's success, and I would say that's really going to help you avert a lot of failure.

Find A Proven System Someone Else Is Already Using

I know you're probably like me... We fail our way to success, and just keep trying things until something works. But I wouldn't say go that route. I'd say go find the proven system that someone else is using, then use it on your own e-book or a small product or whatever your service is. Try that out in a target market... Use that test as your sample and survey, and when you know there's some interest in it, roll it out.

TC: Michael, if I'm hearing you right, you seem to be advocating something that might begin to sound like *scientific marketing*?

MJ: Well, of course! You know I wrote an e-book called *Creating Scientific Marketing Systems*. That's exactly what I learned over the last fifteen years of making mistakes - use something that has been around a long, long time. This stuff has been around since the turn of the cen-tury. There's a tremendous amount of material out there that teaches how you should approach selling, marketing, and advertising things. None of the basic rules have changed. They've just been adapted for the Internet Age.

TC: Just as in flight, the same principles that lifted the Wright broth-er's first bi-wing, cloth plane also lift supersonic military test planes? Big difference in application - same principles.

MJ: If people are not already in marketing, advertising, or promo-tion, I think it's silly for them to think they have enough expertise to go right on the Internet and start marketing their mousetrap. They're going to get real disappointed. There are a lot of disappointed people on the Internet.

Done Right, It's Hard To Fail

However, if you follow the process I'm talking about; go out, find an established market, test that market to see what they're interested in, then use whatever it is you have to help that market get what they want - *then* it's going to be really hard for you to fail.

Too many of us have tried to take the short way. We keep thinking that we've got these great ideas then we throw the ideas out there without finding a market and testing. We end up in trouble then can't figure out why our idea's not selling.

The Internet Is Only A New Tool Of Communication

TC: Both of you have made some interesting comments. Mike, you said that these principles have been around since the turn of the century... And, Clay, you talked about direct response marketing.

Now, how do we apply the information you're sharing to the Internet, which has only been here as a commercial thing since 1994-95? Clay, what's your opinion on that?

CC: Well, the Internet is only a tool. Before the Internet there were fax machines, and before that, the telephone, television, and radio. These are all just tools and mediums which communication can go through. Marketing is basically communication, and communication depends on messages, psychology, listening, cognitive science, and what not. The actual tools are the channels you use to send and receive messages, to get communication, transactions, or whatever. Technology is always bringing us newer, greater, faster tools, but communication - that doesn't change a great deal.

The Marketer's Hall Of Fame

The fundamental principles of direct response marketing were originated around the turn of the century by great ones like P.T. Barnum, Al Lasser, John E. Kennedy, Claude Hopkins, and many of the people I feature in the Marketer's Hall of Fame.

I hope people will come to *www.ClayCotton.com* and sign up for the autoresponder that will give directions on how you can get to the Hall of Fame and study some of these people. I have biographies and reviews of their best work and what they contributed to the industry. I know Ted Ciuba is featured there, and I'm getting some information from Mike Jay to put in his exhibit.

I have a lot of exhibits there. I'm not selling anything. I just want to help people learn the things I've learned. I think people need to study psychology and communications and, as Mike said, it's not about the product. That was my original thought of marketing.

It's better to fall in love with your market, not your product. That's the first step I have in my little five-step marketing mini-course. Just take out your gun and shoot your product, forget it, then break the mirror. It's not about you, it's not about your product. It's about the market.

TC: That's absolutely right, because if you get your market first - a market that's hungry, has money, and is large enough - you simply provide what they want for guaranteed sales. Then, as your market progresses, you can furnish other products for additional income.

> *It's really nice to get up in the morning, look at your in-box, and find not only wonderful words from friends, but also transactions that have taken place while you were sleeping because others were buying your products or enrolling in your services.*
> *- Michael Jay*

Generating Traffic To Your Web Site

Michael, you were talking about what most people think is the all-important *traffic*. You said you can do a test quite affordably using prepaid search engines and getting others' traffic. Can you elaborate a little on that?

Prepaid Search Engines

MJ: Sure. It's easy for me to slip into jargon, like talking prepaid search engines, so I appreciate you saying something about it. An example of a prepaid search engine is *Overture.com* How you get into that search engine is that you literally go in and bid on keywords. For instance, let's say you were selling a new iron to iron clothes with. Under the keyword "iron" or keyword phrase "ironing board," if you bid a certain amount of money, you're listed, and your web listing comes up whenever someone searches on those words.

If you have the highest bid on the keywords, whenever someone enters "iron" or "ironing board," your listing would come up *first*. Of course, you know that when a listing comes to peoples' attention, if it matches their desire, they are more likely to go ahead and select it. The idea is that you could drive traffic, in other words, send people to a test site that you put up.

Successful Internet marketing is as simple as being on track with your keywords and your idea, then selling something to a target market that wants it.

Instant Mailing Lists

The other thing is, you can get market to people who know you. Clay, you, Ted, and I - and a lot of people I know - have a list of people that are on our *opt-in list*. An *opt-in* is someone who has come and said, "I would like to receive some information from you."

You don't want to spam and you want to stay as far away from spam (unsolicited e-mail) as you possibly can, because that will cause you problems.

What you *want* to do is offer people the opportunity to come and say "I would like to see some information." You've no doubt seen these invitations on many sites. When they no longer want to receive it, you give them the option to unsubscribe.

Use these opt-in e-mail lists and draw traffic to a particular test site or a product. For a really powerful boost, have someone well-known in your market endorse your offering. That will really boost your traffic meter because the people on a marketer's list know and respect them.

Start With Small Investments

Those are some cool secrets in terms of starting out with a small, well-targeted investment and getting someone to endorse you or spending a little money at *Overture.com* to drive some traffic to your test.

Of course, this assumes your sales letter or product is aligned with the target market - the people coming into those keywords.

TC: That's fascinating, because I know a lot of people think that all search engines are free. You're saying that today you can actually get yourself an edge just by paying a moderate amount of money for a click through?

MJ: Yes, probably less than you would by taking the time to learn how to rank your site in a search engine and going to all the trouble of doing all that stuff that everybody teaches, like sending your links to a thousand search engines. You're competing with millions and millions of other people who have similar sites.

When you want to do a short, quick test, drive some traffic from a pay-per-click search engine. It doesn't have to be expensive because you can set a budget. For instance, if you only want to spend a hundred dollars, track the number of people who come through on those clicks. What was your conversion rate? How many sales did you get?

You can drive quite a few people to your offer if you're creative about your keywords and know what your target market thinks is important. You'll find out quickly if people want what you're selling. If you have any kind of conversion rate with your test, then you know it's now just a matter of getting more traffic.

You Can Buy Traffic

Now you can go out and buy traffic. Wait until you've tested your conversion rate, because you'll have to pay whoever gives you traffic. *They* don't care what the traffic does, because they charge a fee, but *you* want a profitable venture.

Once you know it works, it's just a matter of driving traffic to your offer and making money. That's part of why the Internet can make you rich. All you have to understand are these simple processes. Don't try to make things complicated by studying search engine rankings and everything. You don't even know if your offer works yet. Pay for a little traffic, direct it to your offer, look at

> ### Internet Profit Alert!
>
> *TC: You can actually get yourself an edge just by paying a moderate amount of money for a click through?*
>
> *Mike Jay: Yes, probably less than you would by taking the time to learn how to rank your site in a search engine and going to all the trouble of doing all that stuff that everybody teaches, like sending your links to a thousand search engines. You're competing with millions and millions of other people who have similar sites.*

your conversion ratio, do some tweaking, maybe pay a little bit more, test it again, then once you've got something that will convert, start diving traffic to it.

Target Your Market For Guaranteed Success

TC: And I think Mr. Clay Cotton has an idea about how to help that conversion rate with his love-based marketing.

CC: Thank you, and Michael, good thinking! Most people are product-centric. They've built a better mousetrap and they think tradition. That's the way they are going to enter the world of business... Build a better mousetrap and go out and promote it. We've discovered that's futile in many cases, and really uncomfortable and rather insufficient.

It's far better to go and target people in groups that have similar wants and desires. Then you can test and measure whether this group wants what you're selling. You can quiz them and get market research. It's work. It's about study and measurements, statistics and behavior. You have to determine the psychology of a particular market and the mindset of that market. If you can target them halfway, you can come into harmony with that market, and honor and serve them in some way.

Following this pattern, you can't help to be successful eventually. On the Internet, you can get money for selling somebody else's product. You can make money for generating a sale the original owner may not have otherwise had. That's the basis of an *affiliate* program. You get a piece of the action, sort of like a sales commission. It doesn't matter if it was your product or somebody else's product, as long as you're serving the market.

Fall In Love With Your Market

I like to call that good-hearted marketing, warm-hearted marketing, and a market-centric approach. I say fall in love with your market, start your product, work with value and devotion for the highest good of all concerned for that market.

If you do this, no one's going to resist you. You are giving value worthy of devotion, and you're going to feel real good when you go to sleep at night. You're going to deliver the highest value to a group of happy people, your preferred market. Everyone's going to be happy to the highest good of all concerned.

That's what I talk about: love thy product, become a servant of a group of people... It's going to embrace you and pull you in. You'll have their loyalty and trust, you'll earn it everyday or anytime you interact with them.

TC: That's really a fascinating idea, and you're one of the best people I've heard articulate it. That immediately attracted me to you, but it's also common sense. Unless you're delivering value, people in this free economy will not give you their money. You can screw a few people sometimes, but you can't have a long-time career that way.

Clay and Michael, I wish we could spend the whole day with you, and even then I know we wouldn't get everything. You've got to have some special secrets that you cherish, ideas that have been particularly successful for you or others.

Mike, let's go with you first. What secrets do you have that can really benefit our listeners and help them get rich on the Internet?

Find A Team

MJ: I think the thing that helped me most was getting over my fear of rejection, or my fear of not doing the right thing, or of not putting an offer out there because I didn't think it was any good. I think that's really important.

Author Robert Kiosaki said his rich dad told him, "A third of the people like you, a third of the people hate you, and a third of the people don't care. You can't worry about pleasing everyone when you do marketing."

It's a good idea to have a strong purpose behind what you are doing and to understand your market, then get after it. Don't mortgage your farm - do a pilot project and see how the pilot project goes. Learn how to do a few things on your own with your web so you don't have to hire expensive webmasters anytime you want to make a little change. Go find someone to work with - in other words, find a team. You don't have to do it all yourself.

One of the things we've done is look for other people who want to do certain aspects of this business and are good at it, then we all get together as a team and share the profits. That's an easy way of helping with risks and, it's a good way to help if you don't have a lot of capital to get started.

Learn marketing the way it should be done, the way people have been telling us to do it. It's not falling in love with your product. Like Clay said, it's *"Love your market."*

TC: Fabulous. Thank you Michael and Clay. I knew that you would have interesting input on this.

Crank The Knob Up To Number 10 And Go For It

CC: I learned from being in music that you've got to be willing to step out and start blowing. It's your turn, get out there and blow. Crank the knob up to number ten and go for it.

Another thing I learned from music is that the first ten thousand hours don't count. If you're going to be a professional musician, you've really got to practice, practice, and practice. I think that is what Michael is saying, you have to make small experiments over and over again.

Don't risk the farm, don't risk everything, but you've got to make these experiments and be willing to fail forward, to fail 10,000 times in order to learn, learn, learn. The thing is to not cripple yourself by one failure, just do it small and test it.

Study Psychology, Influence, Persuasion

I tell people, "Study psychology, study neuro-linguistic programming, study the history of psychology, influence, persuasion, study the hypnotic conversational hypnosis..."

I think people have to learn how to be flexible, they have to learn how to immerse themselves in whatever they're doing, especially in this day and age. As long as we are talking about the Internet, you're going to have to immerse yourself in how the Internet works, the culture of the Internet, and the technology of the Internet. You have to do things according to the protocol and politeness of the Internet. You can't spam, you can't be rude, you have to be respectful.

A Little Technical Know-How Goes A Long Way

You have to learn how to build your own web pages, otherwise you're going to have to pay somebody else. Most likely, they'll overcharge you and you'll be dependent upon them forever.

At some point you're going to have to learn how to design HTML web pages using some sort of an editor/visual editor. Learn how to FTP (transfer) the files from your machine to the server machine. You have to learn how to do that stuff. It's like learning a new language... You go to a foreign country and if you don't learn the language, you're isolated unless you hire an interpreter. You can't hire an interpreter to constantly walk and ride around with you unless you're super wealthy. Most of us aren't super wealthy enough to hire our own personal interpreter.

TC: It goes back to the old adage that knowledge is power... And now you're saying we can get that power through education.

How To Get Rich On The Internet

Indeed. I'll tell you what, we've picked up so many good things from our guests. I'll review a few...

Clay Cotton talked about direct response marketing, and Mike Jay reminded us that this information has been available since the beginning of the century.

Basically, as Clay mentioned, the Internet is a medium of communication, but we're still dealing with humans. The universe is so much larger using the Internet, but we've still got to use psychology to appeal to them.

Then we've got numbers - we approach them, tweak them, and make our offers better - which these men communicated very well today. Many other valuable things were mentioned today, including the importance of self-esteem and getting over doubts.

Discover prepaid search engines, they give you instant results. And make sure you deal with *opt-in* lists. An easy way to launch a product or test a product is to offer it to your opt-in list or to an opt-in list of another marketer, but do *not* spam.

It's the culture of the Internet.

The Internet CAN give you whatever lifestyle you want. Study the basics of the game, learn from others, pace yourself... And have fun!

Jump up, crank it to ten, and share the action with others on the Internet stage!

Special thanks to the contributors to this show...

*Clay Cotton * www.ClayCotton.com*
*Mike Jay * www.b-coach.com*
*Ted Ciuba * www.InstantInternetMarketing.com*

If you enjoyed this interview, there's more just like this! Tune into *www.InternetMarketingInterviews.com*

Other resources to supercharge your progress!
www.GetRichOnTheInternet.com
www.GetRichOnTheInternet.com/seminars
www.AutoPilotRiches.com
www.KillerWebCopy.com
www.ProtegeProgram.com
www.MailOrderInTheInternetAge.com
www.LowCostInternetAdvertising.com
www.PrePaidLegal.com/go/parthenon

Maximum Automation To Make
Maximum Money with
Minimum Effort

Chapter 5

Ted Ciuba *Interviews George Tran, Armand Morin & Mike Lauria*

We've got three special guests with us today. First is marketing genius, George Tran, a true trans-national. Born in Viet Nam, he escaped to Australia and was raised there before coming to Eugene, Oregon to make his fortune. His web site, one of many, is *www.AutoPilotRiches.com* George is highly educated in business, having earned an MBA as well as a MS in Computer Programming.

What a combo to put together! It's really no exaggeration to say that George is the first one to ever bring together such an automated sequence - one that all the major marketers are using – the ultimate, integrated e-commerce solution.

We also have with us Mike Lauria from e-Commerce Exchange. Mike offers *merchant accounts*. You know, the Visa/MasterCard thing? When you combine the automation of *AutoPilotRiches.com* with merchant account processing, you can have money roaring into your account all hours of the day and night, whether you're on the golf course, sleeping, or relaxing with the spouse and kids.

I've also invited my good friend and marketing wonder Armand Morin to share the greatest single secret to his success – which hasn't been too shabby. Armand made $4.2 million his first year on the Internet, and he's going to share exactly how he did it so that you can do the same thing!

It's an enchanting idea, and it works just fine on the Internet... *Hallelujah! Your income is independent of your "work."* What you do you do once – and that's get your systems up and running - but *you get paid forever*!

Money comes in on autopilot. You don't have to do anything to earn it. You can live, vacation, work, travel, buy a new home or car... Only on the Internet!

Ted Ciuba (TC): Guys, welcome to Ted Ciuba's Famous *How to Get Rich on the Internet* Show!

Mike Lauria (ML): Thanks Ted.

George Tran (GT): Thanks for inviting us, Ted.

Armand Morin (AM): Good day, Ted, and good day, listeners!

TC: Let's rock!

Automation Puts Money In Your Pocket While You Sleep

George, I'd like to start by asking you a question, because you're the king of this. In fact, I frequently refer you to as "Genius George Tran," because you have designed and maintained a suite of incredible web site automation tools, and you've done it in such a way that you've created a virtual monopoly.

Because of my position, I know hundreds of super-successful Internet marketers and it seems every single one of them is using your product - Terry Dean, Ron LeGrand, Carl Galletti, Randy Charach, Marlon Sanders, Joel Christopher, Kirt Christensen, Phil Huff, and even myself, Ted Ciuba... Just to name a few.

You seem to be really deep into maximum money with minimum effort and maximum automation. Is that a fair statement?

GT: Yes, Ted, that's an *exact* statement. I like the fact that every morning when I wake up there's more money in the bank than when I went to bed the previous night. And that happens automatically.

TC: Tell us a little bit about what you do.

GT: Well, I've created a program with *AutoPilotRiches.com* which enables merchants - people who want to sell products and services online - to get a shopping cart and process credit cards. But it goes way beyond that to doing marketing things like creating a contact database, data mining, maintaining relationships with customers, and automating the whole process in a holistic and integrated manner.

And I do my entire business right on the Internet.

Helping Others Repeatedly Can Make You Rich!

TC: Of course listeners sitting there listening to George Tran are going to say, "That's great for George Tran, but how does that apply to me?"

You used a lot of jargon; could you simplify it a little for some people who don't have the MBA and computer programming degrees that you've got?

GT: Let's take it a step further by defining more about building *wealth* and what that really means, because the medium and the technology is, for all technical reasons, irrelevant.

There are several basic principles that are relevant, whatever the medium. One of those, as you mention frequently, is the *MasterMind*. You don't know, you *can't* know everything... It's who you surround yourself with that matters! It's your winning team that gets you to your goal - and the medium is irrelevant.

TC: Of course the Internet makes wealth acquisition cheaper, quicker, outrageously fun, and splendidly more profitable!

But the principles you're outlining now, such as the principle Napoleon Hill in his landmark *Think and Grow Rich* identified as the MasterMind principle... These apply generally in the life and affairs of anyone who acquires great wealth, don't they?

GT: Yes. And another basic principle of wealth is, taking a line from Kennedy, "Ask not what people can do for you... But what you can do for people." The function of how wealthy you become is really *how many people you can help*.

The more people you can help, the more money in turn you'll make. It's applying your skills, creatively and strategically, in giving to the world.

TC: This is easy, common sense math...The more people you help, the more money you make.

People will only buy a product they need or desire; and they're always going to be looking for a good relative value. If your product fulfills a need or desire in the marketplace...

The more you sell the more you make.

Manifest Residual Income

GT: Using that principle, marrying it with another principle, creates *residual income*. Meaning, you need to look at a sale more as a series of transactions, of how you can make money from people on a regular, residual basis.

For example, if people pay rent to you every month, that's residual income. If you sell vitamins on a monthly drop-ship program, or sell a subscription to your newsletter every month, that's residual income. But if somebody buys a lamp from you and never comes back, well that's just a one-time sale, and the amount of money you make from that person is limited. You've really got to combine these two principles together, to maximize your worth - helping the maximum amount of people and helping them on a continuous return basis.

TC: How sweet it is! Ongoing residual income! By the way, George, doesn't *AutoPilotRiches.com* offer an *affiliate program* so that anyone can resell it and make good residual income?

GT: It sure does, Ted! Not only does it incorporate an affiliate program so that any Internet marketer can offer one for *their own products*, but we offer an affiliate program, which we call a *referral* program to distinguish it from the tools in *AutoPilotRiches.com*, so anyone can sell the *AutoPilotRiches.com* system to their friends and customers and get paid lifetime, residual income.

> *I like the fact that every morning when I wake up there's more money in the bank than when I went to bed the previous night. And that's automatically.*
> *- George Tran*

TC: That, I might suggest, would be a good product for anyone to sell – for the same reason it is for you: ongoing, residual income.

I've invited Armand Morin to join us because he's really got the inside scoop on why everyone needs to run an affiliate program for their site, for their own products. Armand, what's your scoop on affiliate programs?

AM: It's just been the biggest secret of my success. And that is... *Start your own affiliate program.* If you don't have one, you need to do it immediately.

Think about it like this: if you owned a Coke machine and had it sitting in the hall, you could only sell to as many people as would come to your Coke machine. That's your own web site.

But if you had ten Coke machines placed all over, you would sell to as many people as come to ten different places, twenty-four hours a day, seven days a week. Those are the ten affiliates you have selling your products for you.

Imagine having one, two, or three *thousand* Coke machines all working for you twenty-four hours a day, seven days a week!!! That's exactly what's happening when you have your own affiliate program.

If you don't have an affiliate program, get one immediately. You could have thousands of people selling your products and services almost overnight.

TC: Thank you, Armand Morin! These are millionaire secrets!! True secrets! Genuine.

Looks like we all agree; residual income, recurring sales, keeping the relationship, an affiliate program... These are major aspects of how to get rich on the Internet.

An Easy-To-Use Shopping Cart

George, *AutoPilotRiches.com* seems to be something of a phenomenon. What is everyone so excited about? What do they see? What does *AutoPilotRiches.com* do?

GT: Ted, just so people understand what exactly I offer, I want to spend some time explaining the simple automation process we have and what I've done to the system. Then we'll talk more specifically about how to make money on the Internet.

Typically, when you want to make money on the Internet, you need to sell some kind of product or service. Most people either know how to make a web site, or they can get somebody to make a web site for them pretty easily. But, getting a shopping cart so you can actually *do business* on the Internet costs a lot of money, a lot of time, and a lot of pain.

Our shopping cart gives anyone who wants to sell a product or service on the Internet the ability to set up shop within five minutes or less. What I did was discover a way to make a shopping cart that is very, very easy to use, you can virtually set up a shopping cart in minutes.

For those who don't know what a *shopping cart* is, when you go to a web site and want to buy something, you see a button that says "Add to shopping cart" at the top. That's a shopping cart and that's the technology that we provide at *AutoPilotRiches.com*

Five minutes or less! That's an amazing amount of time, because until my program, it normally took a number of weeks and thousands of dollars in setting up some custom software.

TC: And what about setting up an *affiliate program*?

GT: We make it very easy. Point and click.

Regular Communication Leads To Recurring Sales

Not only that, *AutoPilotRiches.com* lets you capitalize on the principles we're speaking about - residual income and managing customers and turning them into customers for life.

There's awesome sales power in getting into a system in which you effortlessly communicate with your customers on a regular basis. Our system sends automated e-mails to your customers every week, every month, every two weeks, or whatever time periods between e-mails you choose, for as long as you want, with as many messages as you want.

Let's say you want to sell nutritional products. You can have the system send out automated follow-ups to your customers reminding them to come back to your web site to buy refills.

Oh, by the way, the same system works if you're running 1, 2, 3, or 125 web sites... This one system can handle them *all*.

TC: Incredible! What's the name of that technology? They have a name for that, don't they?

GT: *Autoresponder marketing.* Instead of writing out e-mails to your customers individually, over and over again, the system does it for you. Once you have more than fifty customers, the manual method becomes a very tedious task. We've automated it, so it's much easier to use.

For example, I send at least one hundred e-mails off of my automated system every day - and I'm sitting in bed doing nothing. The software does it automatically, and it's done in such a

> *Our shopping cart gives anybody who wants to sell a product or service on the Internet the ability to set up shop within five minutes or less.*
> *- George Tran*

way that people think it comes from me. That's how I'm able to deal directly with my customers and have them buy and return and make more purchases on a regular basis.

TC: Listeners, what George is saying is that, instead of making a one-time sale, there's an automated sequence of letters every two weeks or thirty days that goes out, reminds the customer, and keeps that healthy relationship alive. It keeps the money flowing in. That is great.

Recurring Billing

George, I would assume with a product like vitamins, which people want and need regular delivery of, *AutoPilotRiches.com* is smart enough to automatically bill their credit cards on a regular basis. Am I correct?

GT: Yes, Ted, one of the things it allows is *recurring billing*. So, if you're a merchant selling something on a web site that needs to be filled every month - let's say a vitamin product, or a newsletter, or anything that people would want month after month - our system allows you to take their credit card and charge them a certain amount on a certain day of every month, automatically.

So once you get a customer, you've captured that customer and they become part of your regular income stream, your cash flow, and that automatically builds up a residual for you. As I said, it's exciting to wake up and have more money in your account than when you went to bed the night before.

Residual income, recurring billing, and recurring sales.

TC: How sweet it is!

A License To Print Money

George, you are just loaded with different techniques for making massive money online. I'd like you to reveal some more of your secrets, some of the things that our listeners can really use and apply.

GT: One of the things that I really like to joke about is that I have the ability to *print money*. No, seriously - *print money*.

When I say that people just look at me and say, "Isn't that illegal?"

No, on the Internet it's never illegal to print money. The secret to being able to print money is in your database and the products and services you can bring to your customers. The more people in your database, the more products you have, the more money that you can print.

Joint Venture Deals Make The Pie Sweeter and Larger

Not only that, but you can get additional products to offer to your list and profit from very easily.

I'll give you an example, and my marketing and the same profits could be replicated by *any* marketer in *any* market. I currently have approximately 20,000 people in my database whom I can send e-mails to and talk to about marketing principles. I could send them a solicitation that says, "If you currently have a shopping cart, but you don't have the ability to take credit card orders, I know how - and I have a great deal for you. If you're interested, come to this web site and sign up."

What people don't understand is, in the background, I may have made a deal with Mike so that every time somebody signs up for a merchant account, I get a certain percentage of that sale. That's another way you make money.

The more people I have on my list who need the products or services I have to offer, the more I can let them know. I can capitalize on that, help them along the way, and, in the meantime, make some money for myself. And I continue to do that with new deals as I go along.

If, for example, I know someone who has a very good product that can help in the business, for example, being able to drive traffic from the Internet to their site, and I bring that deal to them, I can make money by offering that *needed* service!

So one of the ways you make money is your influence to your database.

TC: If you want to make *real money* on the Internet, build your database and communicate with them regularly.

There's another distinguishing feature in the scenario you just described.

> ### A License To Print Money
> *This certificate hereby grants you, the owner of this book, How To Get Rich On The Internet, an unobstructed, unrestricted license to print money on the Internet, 24 hours per day, 7 days per week, from all countries of the world! The only thing you must do to cash in on this bonanza is build and nourish your own list.*

Even if your product isn't by nature a recurring billing product, such as vitamins or a newsletter, by offering other related products, you can make your list an asset that produces residual income.

Marketing like that truly gives you a *license to print money*!

Provide The Leads And Fill Their Needs

I want to make one other point clear. As a merchant, you're making available something the people on your list need - something that's high quality, and something they are going to buy and pay for anyway.

Consequently, because *you* offer it to them, when they buy, which they were going to do anyway, you get a piece of the action. Is that what you're saying?

GT: Absolutely, and I'm not talking about spamming. I'm so annoyed by that. I'm talking about building a relationship and bringing to their attention some products and services that my customers need and will have to pay for anyway.

Alchemy From The Information Age

TC: George, earlier in the studio you were talking about one of your friends who has capitalized on the Information Age in an interesting way. Can you share that story with us now?

GT: People say that we are in the *Information Age*, but not many people understand what that means. I want to spend some time explaining what it means.

It means that we value information more than we do other things. What that means to you is that you can sell *nothing* - empty air - and make more money than you would selling a good physical product!

Information is something in terms of leads and know-how. Because the costs are so low, you can make riotous profits very easily. Everyone should investigate information. *Information* could be your *key* to success.

My friend makes a quarter of a million dollars selling *leads*. He works about two hours a month, and all that involves is sending out invoices. His business is in selling leads, and it's all automated!

TC: $250,000 is a pretty good business, too!

GT: He jokes that I'm in the wrong business. He says I work for my money, but he just *collects* money every month.

Actually, that's a business for your listeners to consider, *brokering leads*. And how do you sell leads?

Let's use the insurance business as an example. Getting leads for people needing insurance is very difficult because people don't want to talk to insurance salespeople. Most agents can sell to an interested prospect, but they get beat up and lose their enthusiasm trying to *find* that interested prospect. As a result they get fatigued, and often don't present a good case even when they encounter a good prospect.

So, as an agent or a firm, if you could provide a name of someone interested in buying insurance, I would be willing to pay a lot of money for that lead.

> *If you want to make real money on the Internet, you'll build your database and communicate with them regularly.*
> *- Ted Ciuba*

That's just an example of what you could do on the Internet by selling information.

TC: That's right. Wrapping up this particular thought about information marketing, of course we always think about books, manuals, videos, audios, and software. They're easy to create. They're cheap. The handling costs and hassles are cheap or, on the Internet, non-existent.

These types of products have a high perceived value. You can make outrageous money selling information products. Literally thousands of people have become millionaires in short order by selling information products.

People readily understand the benefits of selling *information* in these forms, but your example puts a spin to that. I like it. Selling and brokering leads is truly *information*, and that's a market that's not going to go away!

Automated Credit Card Processing On The Internet

Now, Mike Lauria, you're a merchant account vendor for E-Commerce Exchange. You help everyone get the ability to accept MasterCard, Visa, American Express, and Discover. It used to be a real battle to get credit card processing, but today it's pretty simple, isn't it?

ML: Yes, getting a merchant account today is simple, Ted. It's just the ability to accept all major business cards, and we've all used those. You go into a store, they swipe your card, and you make your purchase.

On the Internet though, it's a whole different ballgame... There's no swiping and no signatures. It's a whole different system, but it's not difficult to get a merchant account, there's just no swiping.

The system works like magic. Someone goes to your site, enters their credit card information, fills in the amount and the expiration date, and within three seconds our system tells them if the credit card is good or not. If they're over the limit for Visa, a message appears saying, "Why don't you try a MasterCard or Discover, American Express or Diners Club, because you are over your limit." Our system verifies that the billing address matches our records. It will verify the name, match the account, do the transaction, print a receipt - and within forty-eight hours put the money in your business or personal checking account.

Basically, twenty-four hours a day you've got your web site proactively working, verifying credit cards, accepting orders, printing receipts, and sending out products, doing everything you need to run your web site.

> *Twenty-four hours a day you've got your website proactively working, verifying credit cards, accepting orders, printing receipts, and sending out products, doing everything you need to run your website.*
>
> *- Mike Lauria*

It Takes Two To Tango...

AutoPilotRiches.com And A Merchant Account Are Complementary

TC: Mike, I frequently hear the question... "I'm convinced I need *AutoPilotRiches.com* – but do I need a merchant account?"

ML: There's a difference between the shopping cart function of *AutoPilotRiches.com* and the merchant account I offer.

Think of the supermarket for a minute. That's where the *shopping cart* metaphor came from, you know. There's the shopping cart going up and down the aisles holding all the food and products you select. When it comes time to purchase your items, your shopping cart doesn't buy the product for you; you have to go through the checkout and pay your money.

It's the same with us. You use George's product, surf all over a web site, pick out the products that you want, put them aside, and keep a running tally on how much you're spending. Then, when it comes time to pay for the whole thing, the message reads, "To pay by credit card click here." People click. Now my product jumps to the fore and they make the *purchase*.

Do You Have To Have A Merchant Account To Sell Goods And Services On The Internet?

TC: That brings up another question. Does someone who's just starting out absolutely need to have a merchant account?

ML: No. You can get to the point of George's product where it adds up everything you want to buy, and you could write a check and mail it to the person who owns the web site to buy the products. You're not going to get many sales doing that, but theoretically you could do that.

There are a lot of impulse buyers. Eighty percent of all Internet sales are done between eight o'clock at night and eight o'clock in the morning. That tells you something about after hours. People are quiet, they're at home, the kids are asleep, they're on the Internet, and they're buying. It's a low-stress environment for them and an impulse buying environment. All they have to do is click right here; they have a credit card, and two days later FedEx pulls up with the product. That's a great impulse buy. So, you really have to have a merchant account to accept credit cards.

> *Eighty percent of all Internet sales are done between eight o'clock at night and eight o'clock in the morning. That tells you something about after hours. People are quiet, they're at home, the kids are asleep, they're on the Internet, and they're buying. It's a low-stress environment for them and an impulse buying environment.*
>
> *- Mike Lauria*

TC: Indeed you do.

Current "Hot" Internet Businesses

Now, Mike, I want to make sure we hear more inside secrets. Since you see the inner workings of thousands of businesses, which businesses are hot right now? Which ones are raking in the dough?

ML: Information businesses are booming. Any sort of insider newsletters for various clubs and organizations are really hot. Auction sites are extremely hot right now, as are newsletters and certain techniques for auction sites. Vitamins, personal nutrition, and personal care products always do well. Diet products are always good. Products on how to make money or stay out of debt or clean up debt are always popular as well.

Retire Early When You Cultivate Residual Income

TC: Okay, George Tran, you've got to explain something to our listeners. You are thirty-one years old, so why are you talking about retiring in a few months? Going back to Australia... What's up?

GT: Well, because of the business that I set up and the fact that people will be paying for the shopping cart service as long as they're in business, they will continue to feed me for the rest of my life. I decided to retire and set up home for my family.

TC: You're going to live off the residual income you created in just a few years on the Internet?

GT: Two years, to be exact.

TC: Two years! Can our listeners do that?

GT: Sure they can!

Get Rich On The Internet Today!

TC: You heard it! You too can get rich on the Internet, and even retire within two years!

We've had an exciting, fast-paced show with George Tran, Mike Lauria, and our special guest, Armand Morin! These ace marketers fit in completely with the theme we are always talking about - bringing the greatest marketers, the people who have the most to offer to you, to help and teach you, to give you resources and tools like you received today, so that you can get rich on the Internet.

> *You too can get rich on the Internet, and even retire within two years!*
> *- Ted Ciuba*

Just a quick run-by of some of the MasterMind ideas that we talked about: we talked about shopping carts, e-mail broadcasts, and managing relationships, and we brought in merchant processing, which Mike Lauria helped us understand.

Early on we identified the real key to building wealth, which is creating something with residual income - a system where you can bill again and again.

Armand Morin reminded us that if you want to get *rich* on the Internet, you must have an *affiliate* program.

George Tran talked about *printing money* with your database. We all talked about information marketing and how, in today's Internet age, it's really the easiest no-cost/low-cost way to make money on the Internet.

Information Marketing

In today's Internet Age, it's the easiest, no-cost /low-cost way to make money on the Internet.
- Ted Ciuba

There are so many ways to make money on the net, but whatever you do, you've got to have the two e-commerce tools our esteemed guests are talking about: *AutoPilotRiches.com* and a merchant account.

Special thanks to the contributors to this show...

*George Tran * www.AutoPilotRiches.com*
*Mike Lauria * www.eccx.com*
*Armand Morin * www.eBookGenerator.com*
*Ted Ciuba * www.InstantInternetMarketing.com*

If you enjoyed this interview, there's more just like this! Tune into *www.InternetMarketingInterviews.com*

Other resources to supercharge your progress!
 www.GetRichOnTheInternet.com
 www.GetRichOnTheInternet.com/seminars
 www.AutoPilotRiches.com
 www.KillerWebCopy.com
 www.ProtegeProgram.com
 www.MailOrderInTheInternetAge.com
 www.LowCostInternetAdvertising.com
 www.PrePaidLegal.com/go/parthenon

The P.T. Barnum's of Internet Marketing

Chapter 6

Ted Ciuba *Interviews* Ron LeGrand, Carl Galletti & Michael Penland

Today we have a very special group of guests with us. I call them "The Men Who Make Internet Marketing Success Stories." I also refer to them as "The P.T. Barnum's of Internet Marketing."

These are the guys who are putting on Internet Marketing Conferences, Super Conferences, and BootCamps. I believe their workshops, along with the one I myself sponsor, are the very best in America.

Truth be known, each of our guests deserve their own separate show, but they've agreed to come together and give – in one concentrated presentation – the best of their insight as large scale trainers of Internet marketing success stories.

Coming From Nowhere But Desire

These guys have come from nowhere with nothing but a desire and have learned a few secrets which can give you a giant leg up in your own pursuits on the Internet.

What I'd like to do now is introduce these guys, because if you want to get rich on the Internet, it's their business to show you how.

Ted Ciuba (TC): Carl Galletti, how are you doing?

Carl Galletti (CG): Good, Ted, how are you?

TC: Excellent, thanks so much. We're so happy you could be here. Carl, what is the name of your Internet marketing conference?

CG: It's called the Internet Marketing Super Conference and it's based out of the website *www.InternetMarketingSuperConference.com* We stage the event in Las Vegas.

TC: That sounds cool. I'd like to go to Las Vegas!

CG: It's a good place to have the conference because it's an exciting town with a lot of new things going on, innovative things... Lots of action going on there.

> *Can people still get rich on the Internet?*
>
> *Most definitely, they're doing it now!*
> *- Carl Galletti*

TC: I think it ties in real well with your showmanship.

And Michael Penland, we're happy you could join us today.

Michael Penland (MP): Hi, Ted. It's great to be on your show.

TC: Thanks, Michael, and what is the name of your show?

MP: It's the Internet Marketing and Mail Order SuperConference. Our last event was in Atlanta, Georgia. We packed it out and people loved it.

TC: Fabulous, so you're teaching to full crowds, too.

And Ron LeGrand, good day. How are you doing?

Ron LeGrand (RL): I'm outstanding!

TC: As always, Mr. LeGrand. And what is the name of your BootCamp?

RL: It's called the Internet Marketing BootCamp. The next one will be held for three days in Orlando.

"Can People Still Get Rich On The Internet?"

TC: Well, guys, this is going to be real interesting. Carl, let's start with you. I get this question from our listeners all the time. Can people still get rich on the Internet?

"Most Definitely, They're Doing It Right Now!"

CG: Most definitely, they're doing it right now. I've known several people, especially in the early days but some still today, who claim that people really don't make money on the Internet. Of course, when you see news stories about one dotcom after another going under, you may think, "Gee, you really can't make money on the Internet."

That's far from the truth. The truth of it is, dotcoms go under because they don't know the formula. They're not really doing it properly. The people who are doing it properly are the small entrepreneurs who have been innovative in applying standard marketing principles to the technology of the Internet.

> *The people who are doing it properly are the small entrepreneurs who have been innovative in applying standard marketing principles to the technology of the Internet.*
> *- Carl Galletti*

They are producing phenomenal results with very few people. Most of the people I know are running one-man businesses, working a few hours a day to maintain something. Once they get it established, the thing practically runs itself.

TC: That certainly sounds good. Michael Penland, what's your experience? Can people still get rich on the Internet?

"Do Something, The Money's Waiting For You!"

MP: Absolutely, Ted! Remember that there are a lot of misconceptions about the Internet. The Internet is like any other business. It is a business and it's a people business. It's more about people-to-people relationships, and, if you do that right, certainly the money is waiting there.

I really appreciate an expression I recently read; "More money will be made through movement than will ever be made through meditation." I think everyone should post that saying on their refrigerator or mirror. You can think about making money or you can do something about it. That's really the bottom line. If you're willing to get out there and do something, the money's waiting for you.

TC: Thanks for that insight. Ron LeGrand, what is your opinion? Can people still get rich on the Internet?

RL: Heck no! You, Carl, and Michael have made it all!

TC: {laughter}

RL: There's none left.

CG: It's all over now, right?

"It's A Cash Cow On-Going Money Machine"

RL: We all know better than that. Truthfully, there's plenty of money to be made on the Internet but it really comes down to learning more about marketing. The Internet is just a tool.

Some people think that box is the magic pill. It's not, it's just a delivery mechanism. You learn a few basics that apply to marketing on or off the web, then learn how to apply those online. It's a cash cow ongoing money machine that literally produces revenue while you're sitting around in your shorts. That sounds kind of trite, but it's absolutely true. You and I both know a whole bunch of people who are sitting around in their pajamas making money on the Internet.

TC: We sure do. I know a bunch of them that the first thing they do when they wake up in the morning, still in their pajamas, is go down and check their e-mail and see how much income came in.

RL: Correct.

"What Are The Secrets To Internet Marketing Success?"

TC: Your unique position as promoters of Internet marketing events gives you a very special insight into the people who succeed – and even those who fail – on the Internet.

So, what are the secrets that help a person succeed in Internet marketing?

Powered By Testosterone

RL: Well, that's easy. The problem with us males is testosterone. We have way too much of it and the last thing we want to do is read directions. We want to go out pillaging on our own and go to the school of hard knocks. This really applies to any kind of a business we go into and most everything else we do. Males would rather just go do it, and not take time to learn it.

Making money on the Internet is very simple. Actually, everyone on this call can

> *Making money on the Internet is very simple. It's about a fraction as hard as people think it is, but it does have some basics that apply. If you don't first learn and apply those basics, you're going to be chasing your tail, never getting anywhere.*
>
> *- Ron LeGrand*

attest to that. It's about a fraction as hard as people think it is, but it does have some basics that apply. If you don't first learn and apply those basics, you're going to be chasing your tail, never getting anywhere.

> If I were starting over, I would simply find out who is making money on the Internet, not who's talking about making money, but who's *making* money on the Internet, and do exactly what they tell me to do.

TC: That, of course, is the business you're in... Bringing people who are making money together so they can tell others what to do.

RL: That's called *Information Marketing*, and that's the business I'm in. I have a rather large company which sells information products to people who want to learn how to buy and sell houses. You can do that both on and off the web.

My other company, Global Publishing, which I founded with my daughter Vicki Sessions, teaches people how to make money online and how to sell information products like I do. After about twenty years of doing this and making a few million dollars in the school of hard knocks, the best advice that I can give someone is to follow those who follow their dreams and quit trying to recreate the wheel. There's so much information available today, Ted, and it's so cheap!

It took me twenty years to learn what I know, but today, someone who follows these instructions - which are based on proven practices and principles that have worked for thousands and thousands of students - can get it all in a long weekend.

I can't imagine why anyone would want to do it the hard way – but some will. It's testosterone.

> *Follow those who follow their dreams.*
> *- Ron LeGrand*

TC: A lot of people want to make it more complicated than it really is.

RL: That's a lesson.

A Cut Above Thinking That Buying A $29.95 Manual Will Turn It All Around

TC: Carl Galletti, how about sharing your view on those special secrets, insights, and actions that predispose someone to Internet marketing success?

CG: I concur with what Ron said. By holding these seminars, we're in the unique position of attracting the type of people who are a cut above those looking to get rich by buying a $29.95 manual and expect to learn everything they need to know in a short little book.

> *They come from a lot of different areas, they're tuned in, study hard, and are not afraid to invest their money. They're not skittish and are more positive than the average person.*
> *- Carl Galletti*

The people who attend our seminars are more educated in the means of how to make a business out of something, business principles, marketing principles... They come from a lot of different areas, they're tuned in, study hard, and are not afraid to invest their money. They're not skittish and are more positive than the average person.

The greatest enemy anyone has in *any* business is themselves. It's very easy to talk yourself out of doing something you've never done before. There are a lot of excuses you can make, and it's easy to rationalize in fear, "That will work for that person, but it won't work for me."

It pays to have a positive attitude, and I believe people who come to seminars are much more serious about making a go of it and being successful. As a result, they *are* more successful.

RL: I agree with that a hundred percent. I think the reason they are ready to make a go of it is because they've already jumped through hurdles and have been sifting and sorting.

TC: You've got it. I always encourage people to attend seminars because good conferences are MasterMind events. It's an opportunity to meet and put your palm with the people who are successful and who came with the express intent of showing *you* how to be successful, too. It's an incredible opportunity!

Michael, we're not going to let you off the hook. You've got to tell us - based on your experience as a promoter and a person who sees so many people - what are the special insights or actions that help a person become really successful and rich on the Internet?

To Know The Game

MP: That's a great question. Just this morning I received an e-mail from an individual who is $50,000 in the hole because his pet project had gone south on him. I contrast that with other clients who have earned $100,000-$200,000 in a day. The difference is the latter group understands they can no longer have a *consumer mentality*.

Consumers are people looking for no risk, no effort - do it my way or no way.

What we do as promoters is teach people to play baseball. Let me explain what I mean by that. Really, we teach people how to make hits, consistent hits. In baseball, the guy who continues to get hits day after day after day is an important person. It's not the guy who blasts away trying to hit the home run, but striking out.

Learning to hit singles, doubles, even occasional triples, keeps money coming across home plate. Really, *that's* what separates the winners from the losers. It's developing the attitude and mind set that says, "I'm going to follow what is tested and proven. I'm going to apply it in my situation."

I find that the people who are consistently doing something are the ones making money - not the people who are just meditating, wishing or wanting. It's the people who are actually *doing something*.

That's really the key to success on the Internet - learning to be a good hitter and learning how to play the game successfully. That's what we give to people.

TC: It's kind of funny, and then, of course, it's really the epitome of what a person might expect... Every single one of you have identified similar traits that involve *doing something*... Getting the education, getting the instruction, then going out and doing it intelligently.

How To Get Started On The Internet

I'd like to throw this out to any of our guests today. Every day someone asks, "How does a person get started? How do I start?"

This Stuff Really Works!

CG: You know, Ted, there are many ways to start, but I think the most important thing is to quickly get some kind of positive feedback that what you are doing is working. You don't want to risk a lot of money testing your ideas - the implementation of the things that you've learned. Even the most astute marketers don't hit every time they get up to bat, and you don't want to pour your life savings into testing out some new concept you have.

You want to test something cheaply and inexpensively and see if it works first before rolling it out - which means to put it on a grander scale.

There's nothing like going to your mailbox or your e-mail box and finding a ton of orders. I know in the mail order business it wasn't until I found a five thousand dollar check in my mailbox that I said, "Wow, this stuff really works!" There's nothing like getting cash in the bank to convince you, "Yes, this stuff really works!" Getting to that point as fast as possible is real important.

TC: Anyone else want to comment on that one?

Give Your Market What They Want

MP: Ted, once you understand who your target market is going to be, the safest and quickest way to success is to deliver what it is that people want. Sometimes as marketers we fall in love with our own ideas about what people need instead of what they r-e-a-l-l-y *want*.

If you can help people solve a problem or situation they're facing, or make their life easier, better, richer, and more exciting, that really helps to accelerate your potential for success.

You have to remember that the Internet is still relatively in its infancy. We're at a turning point where the Internet is going to become so acceptable it will be like the cellular phone or microwave oven... I believe that can only be a few years down the road.

We talk about targeting the needs of people so let's not forget that this isn't about technology - it's about people and their needs. Online marketing isn't any different than offline marketing in that regard. Focus on your market *first*, then the product will be easy. Find out what your market wants then deliver that. In my opinion, that does more to guarantee success than simply using technology.

TC: It's a people business as we've all heard before. Ron, I know that you've got a lot of good insight. Where do you start?

RL: Truthfully, I can tell you from my experience that most people don't have a clue of where to start. The first thing everyone should do is decide how they want to go about making money on the Internet. There's really an endless list. Obviously, the best way to decide is to put yourself in front of people who are doing it..

If I were starting any business, I'd find someone who was doing what I want to do and I'd listen to them because they've already paid the price. Making money on the Internet seems like a giant problem because most people don't have a clue where to begin. Most people believe they have to have a product to make money on the Internet and that's not true.

The Smartest Thing For You To Do Is Build A List

The people I know who are making the most money on the Internet have come to the conclusion that the smartest thing you can do is build a list. Build a list of e-zine subscribers - people who want you to send them information on a regular basis. If that information contains an offer giving them a special bargain on a product or service they're interested in, that's great. There's only two ways to market to a targeted list: build your own list or tap into somebody who's already built one.

To get started, you simply have to decide what direction you want to take first. I've found that most people are afraid of the technology side of an Internet business. They're so concerned about how to move around and how to set up web sites that they don't do anything.

> *The smartest thing you can do is build a list. Build a list of e-zine subscribers - people who want you to send them information on a regular basis. If that information contains an offer giving them a special bargain on a product or service they're interested in, that's great.*

One thing I've learned from the school of hard knocks is that I don't want to get involved in technology. I have no desire to do that, in fact, I don't spend my days sitting in front of the computer. I spend my days managing my business which means I can get other people to do all that technical stuff for practically nothing. In fact, there's a web site you can go to called *www.Elance.com* where you can get copywriting and just about any service you might need for practically nothing.

The idea is to figure out how you want to generate revenue and how you want to go about doing that, then let the other people do the stuff you don't need to be doing.

TC: Fantastic, Ron.

"I've Only Got Limited Funds, How Do I Get Started?"

Okay, here comes the hard question - "I've only got limited funds but I really want to get on the Internet. I've been hearing a lot about Internet businesses but I don't know what to do or where to turn, I don't have a product. How do I get started?"

The Three Steps To Internet Profits Plan

MP: My answer is, break it down into three steps.

Step one, I would find a market. Surfing the Internet, get familiar with the Internet and look at discussion groups that deal with the specific market you feel might relate to a product you now have or want to develop. Determining what that market wants is your first goal, then create a product around the needs of that market. The Internet is an excellent tool for doing this. It allows you to find "experts" who are willing to contribute to the development of your product by searching through discussion groups and forums, and finding the information relative to the market and what that market wants. You've really got to live with people, talk with them, laugh and cry with them, just to learn what they really need. That's the first step, I think, to target a market.

The second step is to create or license a product to your target group. Create a scenario or build a story around a product so that it relates to the needs of the individuals in the market. This is when you write advertising copy and put up a simple web site with a single web-page and e-commerce processing.

The third step, of course, is to solicit those customers. I recommend that you build your list of potential prospects by e-mail, e-zines, and site sign ups. Send your offer to those e-mail addresses or do a joint venture and blast to the list of an individual who is already in that market.

Basically, that's the three steps - find a market, create a product and write the copy, then market.

TC: It sounds like a pretty good deal to me. Any other comments on that?

Direct Hit: Joint Venture With List Owners

RL: What I would probably do if I were starting over with limited funds would be to license products I knew already had a market, which - as you know - are all over the Internet. In fact, at our BootCamp we always have tons of products you can license for pennies, and have total rights to sell. Then, I think I'd probably go on the web site *www.Listz.com*

That's the site with all the joint venture partners on it, isn't it Ted?

TC: Well, that's a site with a lot of Internet marketing resources - people who have e-zines.

RL: That's what I'm looking for, a list of e-zine owners... In other words, this is a list of list owners.

I would simply go to a list owner, work out an affiliate agreement, and let them use the copy that comes along with any product you've licensed. (I wouldn't suggest that any one license products that don't already come with marketing materials that have been tested.) Simply contact those list owners, have them do an e-mail flash to their e-zine list, and split the proceeds.

TC: You know Ron, there's got to be something to that because I saw a guy named Terry Dean demonstrate this at one of your shows. He used his own list and sent something out on Friday morning. Before Sunday evening, he'd made something in the neighborhood of $33,245.

RL: He made $33,245 on the single promotion he blasted during the BootCamp, and then, counting a few other things he had going on, his income totaled over $55,000 for those three days!

During the BootCamp, while we were sitting there watching it happen, he earned $33,245 live, online. That happened simply by releasing a little low-end product using his own e-zine list.

In that case, it wouldn't have much mattered if the blast had been to his e-zine list, your e-zine list, or my e-zine list, because the list owner - as a list owner - would have endorsed the product when it was sent to their list, and they would have bought the same amount.

In Terry's case, he kept all the money because he used his own list. Let's assume Terry was using your list - you guys would split the money. Terry's cost would be absolutely nothing except for the cost of delivering his product, and if I'm not mistaken, his product was delivered online, so he had zero cost. What did his product sell for? I think it was $495, wasn't it?

TC: I believe it was.

RL: Terry could have said, "Here, Ted. Put this message out to your e-zine list, give them a deal and we'll split the gross." He could be sitting back doing nothing but collecting checks for $247.50 while you're doing the work blasting to your list.

TC: Ron, I want to make sure I'm understanding this correctly. If I developed a product doing what Michael Penland suggested – finding a market, finding what they needed, licensing or creating a product, going to Elance to get copy written – if the product fit into Terry Dean's market, I could go to him and say, "Send this to your list and we'll split the proceeds," and I would possibly make half of $33,000?

RL: Correct. Let's say your hobby was... What's your hobby, Ted?

TC: Let's say I like mountain climbing.

RL: Let's say you have a mountain climbing hobby and you licensed a product to teach people to climb Mt. Everest or whatever. You simply tap into lists of folks that are catering to that kind of market, just like Michael said.

You can offer them this product to show them how to climb Mt. Everest without getting killed. The list owner usually takes the orders and processes all the money and sends you your check. It's an auto-pilot way to create tons of revenue without doing anything except licensing a product, contacting list owners, and letting them do the work.

Look at it from a list owner's point of view. All they have to do is take all written copy, throw a little endorsement on it, and send it out to their list. Remember now, this is an opt-in list. People have asked the list owner to send them an e-zine every week, every month, or whatever period of time it is. The list owner sends out their normal e-zines and adds a little blurb at the end about this product.

Just go to *www.listz.com* where you'll find thousands and thousands of list owners. The subject is already right there so you can identify who you want to target and who you want to joint venture. If I'm not mistaken, list owners aren't even on the site if they don't want to do joint ventures.

TC: It gets amazingly simple when you get the real inside secrets, doesn't it?

RL: Herein lies the problem, most people try to make Internet marketing a whole lot more complicated than it really is.

But, the magic key that unlocks the vault is building your own list. When you control the list, you control the money. Until you get a list, just tap into somebody else's.

> *It gets amazingly simple when you get the real inside secrets.*
> *- Ted Ciuba*

TC: We're really getting some good information here. Carl, I'm sure you have insight on this.

CG: Of course! We've known this from non-Internet marketing - before there was an Internet. The most valuable thing you own is your customer list. Building a customer list is *the* most valuable thing you can do in your business. Of course, if you're just starting out you don't have a list, so doing what Ron suggests is an excellent idea - joint venturing with other list owners.

Establish Yourself As The Expert

Having something to sell is the next situation. Of course you can get things from other people to sell but I think it's better to establish yourself as the expert. If you're selling information on, say, mountain climbing... If you're the person who created the product, you're the expert. That doesn't mean you have to write the whole thing yourself or even get all the words right yourself, have someone pretty up the words for you once you put the concept down - but put your expertise down. I think a good place to start is with something you have interest, passion, and expertise in.

RL: Carl, what if we split the difference? What if we let people license the products and start marketing them while they're developing their own product, to get the cash flow coming in?

CG: Right!

RL: Regarding your point, I would absolutely agree, and I know Michael will too, that you're always going to feel better marketing your own product. But I'd venture to say most people don't have a product or a clue where they're going to get one, and don't know how to write the marketing copy if they found one.

MP: Exactly, but if you at least identify your market, you can get someone else's product and begin with that.

CG: Then you're making money as you're working on your own product. When you have your own product, you really have total control. You can spread it around like Terry Dean. One of the reasons Terry is so successful is because he's a good writer. He writes his own products, he writes other peoples' products, and he also knows how to write copy.

TC: If you happen to enjoy writing, maybe that's an angle.

The Top E-Commerce System

So much as been said about the importance of a list that I'm going to give you a good resource to build your list - *www.AutoPilotRiches.com*

It's a web-based e-commerce system that takes visitors' names and e-mail addresses - and there you have your list. Check it out for yourself at *www.AutoPilotRiches.com*

Where Does A Beginner Begin?

Ron, here's my question: How does a beginner get in?

Get Your Education In A Focused Manner

RL: One way is to attend Global Publishing's Internet BootCamp. It's an absolute killer phenomenal three-day event!

TC: Indeed!

RL: Incidentally, the BootCamp is for beginners who want to start from scratch and build a step-by-step income producer system.

I think anyone who doesn't get their education from someone providing it in a focused manner in a two- or three-day event is kind of foolish - especially when our sessions are so inexpensive. All three of today's guests, and you yourself, Ted, have killer training events. Truthfully, people should go to all four of them.

> *I think anyone who doesn't get their education from someone providing it in a focused manner in a two or three-day event is kind of foolish.*
> *- Ron LeGrand*

TC: I would recommend that, too.

RL: It's impossible to go to all four of our Internet marketing training events without picking up a wealth of information. But again, the idea is to figure out what you want to do. When you get that in mind, the rest is just a systematic approach - like eating the elephant one bite at a time - to getting revenue coming in as quickly as possible.

I don't know where better to get an Internet marketing plan in place than at an event where they teach that plan. Speaking for my event, we've got tons of products that people can license for pennies. It's literally like handing people a business in a box. As soon as participants register for our BootCamp, and for everyone here, they have the rights to resell the BootCamp and keep half the money. They also get the tools to do it with.

TC: So they've got an *instant product*. That's excellent!

Start With The Direct Response Marketing Classics

RL: Carl Galletti, do you still have that huge library of marketing books?

CG: Yes. Actually, on the bottom of the *www.AdSecrets.com* page there's something called "Books and Tapes." You can get a lot of the classical marketing books there, along with other similar products.

TC: We're talking about how one begins, and I'd like to put in a plug for the classic marketing books. Back when I got started in 1993 and 1994, there was no such thing as an Internet Marketing Conference. I learned everything from those classic marketing books... Then little by little I applied what I learned to the Internet. You couldn't build on any more solid base than the classics.

A FREE Gift...

CG: Like you, Ted, many of the people now on the Internet learned a lot of their marketing from things that were written in the early 1900's as the principles are basically the same.

Claude Hopkins would have gone crazy on the Internet because he always said he never sold anything, he only gave things away and let people sample them. His idea was that when people found out how good his products were, they'd be back and buy more on a regular basis. He kind of pioneered the whole coupon industry and the idea of giving away free samples. That's basically what a lot of the people are doing on the Internet now. Giving something away for free, building a relationship with customers, finding out the customers' needs and wants, then building a pipeline to deliver that.

TC: And the good thing about giving away something for *free* on the Internet is that - digitally delivered - it is absolutely FREE to you, the merchant, to give away. That's never happened before.

Something delivered in a file form, an e-book so to speak, doesn't cost you anything. Right?

RL: An e-zine alone is a free gift that doesn't cost you anything.

CG: Such products could be sold for a lower price and delivered instantaneously.

TC: Speaking of which, giving away something free... Isn't that a classic marketing device?

> *Once the list is there, the market is there. And once the market is there, the money starts to flow.*
> *- Michael Penland*

RL: Sure!

TC: What does it do? Why is that so effective?

MP: Let me tell you why I'm doing it, Ted. Just as Ron and Carl mentioned earlier, I use free giveaways to build my list - to increase the size of my list.

Once the list is there, the market is there - and once the market is there, the money starts to flow.

TC: Okay, and talking about the mountain climbing sport, a person that wasn't interested in mountain climbing would not download a free report on mountain climbing, so we've kind of qualified our audience when they opt-in, haven't we?

The P.T. Barnum's of Internet Marketing

We've had such a tremendous show today... Fast moving and very informative. We've had with us today the P.T. Barnum's of Internet Marketing - Ron LeGrand with the Internet BootCamp, Carl Galletti with the Internet Marketing Super Conference, Michael Penland with the Internet Marketing and Mail Order Super Conference, and your host and P.T. Barnum himself, Ted Ciuba, bringing you the *How To Get Rich On The Internet*™ BootCamp.

Men, thank you for taking time out of your busy schedules and for being here with us today. It was wonderful!

How To Get Rich On The Internet

All right, let's recap! If you discount what you've just learned as more "get rich B.S." or even something that will work for others but not for you, you've missed the whole point! This is all about YOU! All you need to know is how to get rich on the Internet and you've just heard from these Internet doers exactly how you can do that.

Yes, people can get rich on the Internet! There's plenty for you - especially the small entrepreneurs. We talked about Terry Dean who put out an e-mail blast at one of Ron's conferences and earned $33,000 before the eyes of every attendee there! We didn't even mention Corey Rudl, a personal friend of us all, who last year earned $5.2 million dollars. He started his Internet business by himself in his garage in cold and snowy Canada.

That's the whole thing... Michael Penland reminded us that Internet marketing is a people business, not a technology business.

Ron LeGrand talked about how, if we want to make money on the Internet, we've first got to go to the people who are actually doing it. Beyond that, Ron shared that basics apply equally on the Internet and offline because the Internet is a delivery mechanism. He called it a "cash cow on-going money machine." That sounds good to us!

Carl Galletti shared a smart-bomb secret with you – if you were smart enough to catch its significance! If he has seen that the people who are willing to invest some big bucks to attend a conference are "a cut above" those fools believing that a $29.95 manual is going to turn it all around for them...Which crowd do you think you should join?

Michael identified something that seems pretty important, and that's marketers have to let go of a crippling consumer mentality. He also compared marketing to playing baseball, where you're working with every move to win the game.

It seems our panel of experts has recommended that you get started - find someone who's doing what you want to do, copy from them and learn from them.

When you go to apply this, find a market, listen to that market, create a product or license a product, write the copy (sales letters, web pages, ads, publicity) and start building your list.

Building that list is the most important element of your Internet success.

The next time you have an opportunity, whether it's a joint venture product someone approaches you with, or your own product, you can just press "Send" and sit back and possibly earn your own $33,000 before the weekend's out!

Special thanks to the contributors to this show...

Ron LeGrand - *www.GlobalPublishingInc.com*
Carl Galletti – *www.AdSecrets.com*
Michael Penland – *www.StrategicMarketingSecrets.com*
Ted Ciuba * *www.InstantInternetMarketing.com*

To always get up-to-the-minute news on seminars, tune to *www.GetRichOnTheInternet.com/seminars*

Other resources to supercharge your progress!
www.GetRichOnTheInternet.com
www.GetRichOnTheInternet.com/seminars
www.AutoPilotRiches.com
www.KillerWebCopy.com
www.ProtegeProgram.com
www.MailOrderInTheInternetAge.com
www.LowCostInternetAdvertising.com
www.PrePaidLegal.com/go/parthenon

Technology
Marketing To Get
More Leads,
More Sales,
And Make
More Money

Chapter 7

Ted Ciuba *Interviews Marlon Sanders*

Marlon Sanders is one of the Internet's oldest success stories, having started pretty early in the nineties. He's also one of the most controversial success figures, maybe because he's got some psychological training. You know, attorneys and psychologists... There are a lot of jokes about those two professions. But quite literally, that training has helped Marlon in his sales letters. He's an excellent salesman and writer, which is important today in writing a web page.

YOU Can Cash In On The Internet!

Ted Ciuba (TC): Without further ado... Good day, Marlon Sanders!

Marlon Sanders (MS): Hi, Ted. Thank you for inviting me to be on the call. I'm excited to be here today and let me tell you why. I want to talk about a broad umbrella of Internet marketing. I want to talk about how the average Joe can make money on the Internet. Maybe they have a business wholesaling and need to stimulate sales from buyers and rotate new buyers and their base.

Maybe they've got a retail store and need to get some new customers. Maybe they're a real estate agent so they're in the service business or a mortgage broker who needs more sales to become profitable. Maybe they sell products on eBay, or have a mail order business and want to leverage their results on the Internet. Maybe they're a manufacturer who needs to recruit, train, manage, and motivate wholesalers and jobbers.

Perhaps you're a professional, a dentist, doctor, chiropractor, or consultant and you need patients or clients. Maybe you're a salesperson and are sick and tired of making those cold calls - you want to generate leads. Maybe you're in network marketing or Multi Level Marketing and you want to create an automated recruiting system or maybe you're a stockbroker and you're tired of people hanging up on you.

If not any of these, maybe you're "just" a business owner who wants to get more leads, more sales, make more money - you want to generate people raising their hands and saying, "Hey! We're interested!"

Well, Ted, that's what we want to talk about. This just isn't about a business opportunity for people who don't have a business. What I'm saying is, whether you've got a business or whether you don't, either way we can show you how to leverage your results and cash in on the Internet.

TC: Marlon, if you can deliver one piece of what you just broadcasted, we're going to have our ears glued to you!

Leverage Is The Key

MS: Well actually, Ted, we can. Let me set the big frame for today, because really, the bottom line here is what I'm about. The bottom line in today's world is: you've got to have *leverage*.

Archimedes said, "Give me a lever big enough, I can move the world." That's really what this whole deal is about. I think most people in business and most Internet marketers really don't get it. They don't grasp that single concept - the power of the Internet, the power of technology is that you *leverage yourself*, you multiply yourself, you clone yourself.

Ted, how many times have you heard someone say: "If I could just multiply myself, if I could just clone myself, if I could just be in a hundred places, or a million places at one time, then I'd have the key!" Well, that's technology and that's what the Internet can do for you -

and today we're going to talk about that.

Whether you're in real estate, sales, or own a business or would like to start a business, we want to give you a few ways to get you started making money, cashing in, leveraging yourself, leveraging your time, cloning yourself, multiplying yourself, getting the deal going, and making money.

TC: Wow! That sounds great. Hey how do we start?

The Internet Can Work For You!

MS: Let's talk about a few of the advantages of being on the Internet and using cutting-edge technology. I want to show the average person how to apply this for themselves.

We've heard about the *dot.com* crashes, the companies going down and the companies having problems and many have bought into all that hype and nonsense. Maybe you think, "That's okay for other people, that's okay for the gurus, or maybe that works for the guys doing that, but it isn't going to work for my little business, my service, my gift basket business, my eBay business." Let me just prove to you right now that whatever you do, whatever you sell, the Internet can work for you. Just let me lay it out.

How To Leverage Yourself With Technology

I'm going to throw on the table right now some ways you can use technology, the Internet, to leverage your time, multiply yourself, and virtually clone yourself.

Here are some examples:

Number one: you can follow up automatically with your customers and prospects; you have timed sequence e-mail, faxes, even phone calls. Technology today allows you to do that.

Number two: you can obtain hundreds and literally thousands of referrals at a time. You can obtain automatic testimonials from people. We've seen several hundred pages of testimonials - you can get those automatically and use them to create word-of-mouth advertising. It doesn't cost you a dime regardless of what business you are in.

Let me ask you, what's your single, number-one best method of promoting your business? Word of mouth, right?

TC: I think that's what most people would say.

MS: Why would most people say, word of mouth? Because it's free! Word-of-mouth advertising is free and yet...

TC: It's ineffective, isn't it?

Generating Effective Word-Of-Mouth Advertising

MS: Word-of-mouth advertising can be very effective, but the problem is that most people don't have a way to stimulate and generate it. That's the difference, that's what the Internet can do. Let me get specific and give you a way to do just that.

How do you generate word-of-mouth advertising? While there are several ways, I'll just throw out one of our methods here. We use a little thing called a "tell-a-friend" script. You don't have to know how to do this yourself - I'm big on that. You don't have to be a computer nerd to be able to use the methods and techniques I'm going to give you.

> *Give people something for free - give them a bonus, enter them in a drawing for telling their friends about your website.*
> *- Marlon Sanders*

TC: Marlon, for a tell-a-friend script and most web-related jobs, people can go to an incredible site where experts are bidding for the low price to do these jobs, can't they?

That's *www.Elance.com*

Tell-A-Friend Scripts

MS: That is a *major* secret! You can go to that web site and find someone who can do this for you. You don't do this by yourself, you go to this site and pay someone $25 or $50 so you can get a little thing on your web site called a *tell-a-friend script*. That's a little button that says, "Click here to tell a friend." Right then, visitors to your site can click and automatically send a little e-mail to their friends to tell them about your web site. If you want to supercharge this technique, one of the things that you can do is give people something for free - give them a bonus, enter them in a drawing for telling their friends about your web site.

Incentivize Prospects To Get Their Contact Info

You should always be trying to get more names on your Internet list. Another way to do that is to use a free report. Let's say you're a real estate agent and you need to generate leads, or you're a stockbroker and you need to generate leads from your web site so you don't have to cold-call people.

What you do is offer a free report on your web site by saying, "Free Report Reveals How To Stock Up On Foreclosed Properties In Your City Before Everybody Else." For a stockbroker, "Free Report Reveals How I Generate Money Automatically Every Month In The Stock

Market Without Taking Big Risks." Anybody interested in stock trading will grasp that free report.

For Internet marketers, this is a one-two punch. You combine these methods for what I call *multiple stacking*. Your deals stack on top of each other. Here's how the deal works... People come to your site and request a report. We've already talked about the tell-a-friend script, so when they request that report, we're going to e-mail that report to them. What do you think is going to be at the bottom of that report - which of course is an e-mail sent by autoresponder?

TC: It wouldn't be a "bribe" to get them to give you more names and e-mail addresses, would it?

MS: It's going to say, "Win Free Cassette Recorder," "Win a Free Book," - win something free, some bonus, some incentive, for telling your friend about this free report. Once they click on that, they send a little e-mail over to one of their friends - "Hey, you too can get this free report by going to this web site. You know I thought it was really good" - blah, blah, blah. Enter them into a monthly drawing and each month hold a drawing that gives people an incentive for telling their friends about your site.

I just taught you two things, how anyone can generate leads from their web site and how to quit cold calling by getting people to request free reports using a tell-a-friend script. Ted, those are just two examples of Internet marketing.

It's Not Just About The Internet

TC: Generating leads is the biggest problem most salespeople and professionals seem to have.

MS: Yes. It's interesting because business owners think the Internet doesn't work... Blah, blah, blah... Those dot.com companies fell... Well, the dot.coms fell in most cases because they didn't have a product and they didn't have a buyable business. But if you have a business, a network marketing business, or some kind of a business - you already have an advantage. One of the first things you can do is run little ads offering a free report in e-zines and e-mail newsletters; "Free report reveals blah, blah, and blah." You could even run classified ads in a newspaper. I know people in different industries who do this. If you're a mortgage broker you could run an ad in the local paper that says, "Free Report Reveals How To Save Two Points On Your Loan Right Now."

TC: Marlon, now you're saying that you can combine offline and online methods...

MS: That's exactly the point. I'm about *technology marketing*, Ted, not just the Internet. We combine all these techniques and stack them - it's about the concept of stacking. We stack the Internet with other technologies, online, offline, multi-media, phone, fax - we just integrate them all into one big bundle.

TC: I love that distinction!

MS: Put them all together. We're implementing a system right now so when people come to our web site and sign up for the mailing list, they'll not only get an e-mail from us, they'll not only sign up for our weekly little tips, they will also get faxes and a phone call - all of which happens automatically. It's all technology; it's all automated. The way we use and envision the Internet is as the launching pad. Isn't that awesome?

The Internet is the launching pad of all these different marketing methods. Here's the beauty of it, Ted; it's elaborate. I can have faxes sent without having to stand over my fax machine feeding the paper in a page at a time. I can have e-mails going out offering special deals, helping others sell closed-out merchandise, slow-moving stuff they have to get rid of. I can have e-mails going out offering free reports and get people to call me up, e-mail me back, generating leads. I can have all this kind of stuff happening *automatically*. That's the beauty of it.

Your Lifestyle Will Improve, Even Without
Making More Money

Let's say you already have a business, Ted. Even if we couldn't make you rich in your existing business, there's a flip side to using this technology. The flip side is saving you stress and time, helping you make the same amount of money you're making - but with less effort.

TC: That's definitely another angle to consider. Marlon, you've grasped the concept of the Internet lifestyle more than most anyone else I know. Have you seen a lot of other people do it? Basically, you work when you want and don't when you don't want to. Have many other people have been able to do that?

MS: We've been talking about getting more results with less energy and less effort. You can do both. On one hand, you can elaborate your results, get more and make more, do more and accomplish more. On the flip side, you can actually work less, with less stress and less trouble. Whether you are operating an Internet business, or any kind of business, these marketing tools can work for you.

Wealth Accumulation On The Internet

Here's another good question, Ted. How do you create cash flow on a web site? It's about cash flow, seeing your web site as the part of your business that's going to funnel money into your retirement, into your wealth accumulation. This plan has got to be headed somewhere - it's not just, "Let's run real hard on this mouse wheel and in ten years we're going to end up where we are today." Let's make your business go someplace; let's get this wealth accumulation.

I see my web site as a cash funnel. At the bottom of that cash funnel, at the bottom of my web page, is an order button. When people click on that order button, it spits cash into my wealth accumulation funnel. That's really what this deal is all about.

Let's not just make money, let's not just have a business. Let's put systems together and make this business go someplace.

It's Easy To Get Started With E-Mail Strategies

TC: Marlon, what do you say to the average Joe who wonders if the Internet will work for him?

MS: Ted, what do you think is the number-one thing the average Joe would ask you? What do you think is the number-one question on peoples' minds?

TC: I hear it all the time. People are asking, "Can I really get rich on the Internet?" - but that's not the real question because they already know that answer. What they're really asking is, "Will it work for *me*?"

MS: In other words, "I know people are getting rich on the Internet. I know *other* people are doing it, but the question is, can *I* do it?"

TC: Exactly, and that's the question that comes up whether they're a beginner and don't have a product, or whether they've been in business for twenty-five years.

MS: That's the interesting question and the way I would answer it is this: You will know when you *do* it. I could talk all day long about how great an Internet business is, and what I do, and how I know a lot of people who do extremely well with Internet businesses or by using the Internet as an adjunct to their business to generate leads, make sales, multiply income, etc.

The bottom line is, you've got to do it yourself. Here's what I say, Ted. Take just a few of these methods, a few strategies, a few techniques, and get started with those.

Let's talk about e-mail. E-mail is a great way for people to get started. Let's say you're a florist and someone walks in to your retail florist shop and signs up for your "free weekly flower special." They are then automatically entered into an Internet marketing program anyone can run... Even a ten year old.

You type in a sequence of e-mail messages that will go out every seven days. Every seven days you have a special - and boom! - everyone who has come into your flower shop gets the e-mail telling about your special. And Ted, how much time does it take for you to send out those e-mails?

TC: Absolutely zero!

MS: Absolutely zip, that's the beauty of it! That's what I said about cloning yourself, multiplying yourself. You don't have to sit at your computer and send out those e-mails.

Not All "Experts" Practice What They Preach

I'll tell you something really funny. I was talking to a book author the other day who wrote a book about follow-up marketing. This is a book author, somebody that supposedly knows what they're doing and talking about, right?

His specialty is follow-up marketing, yet what do you think he does? Every week, or every month, he sits at his computer manually - by hand - sending out e-mail after e-mail because he doesn't know how to use the technology to do it automatically!

TC: There's no excuse for that because it's so simple, isn't it Marlon? We ought to let him know about the *AutoPilotRiches.com* system.

Leveraging Communications From The Web Site

MS: You got it! You know, every business - retailer, wholesale, manufacturing - everyone has to communicate, right? Communications - *relationships* - are the bottom line of every business.

That's one of the beautiful things about the Internet. You can leverage your results by using e-mails and faxes. Ted, most people don't know this but you can even have *phone calls* go out automatically. There are so many options, so many ways you can leverage your time, your energy, your money, and your efforts using the Internet. It's cutting-edge technology and it's phenomenal!

Get Rich With Leverage

TC: Marlon, give us your take on getting rich - I mean the title of our show is *"How To Get Rich On The Internet."* Let's address that for a moment.

MS: I'm not a big get-rich person. I don't talk a lot about getting rich, but let me tell you my insight and the one secret to getting rich on the Internet. I'm absolutely positive that every rich person in the history of the world has done one thing, and that one thing, Ted, is *leverage.*

You can't do it all yourself; even an employee is leverage. Just like Henry Ford; what did he do? He had machines and people building thousands of automobiles, right? Look at Microsoft's Bill Gates. He's got thousands and thousands of stores around the United States selling his software and his products. That's his leverage. He's not out at the local computer store in Dallas or over in the Philippines trying to sell his software package. You don't have to talk to Bill Gates about Microsoft Office. He leverages the people and the places. The whole world is selling Microsoft Office for Bill Gates. He's got all these computer manufacturers putting Windows in the computers, and he's getting paid every time.

> *I'm absolutely positive that every rich person in the history of the world has done one thing, and that one thing is leverage.*
>
> *- Marlon Sanders*

That's leverage, Ted!

Sounds Great, But Will It Work For Me?

TC: Marlon, we have Marty on the line, and he wants to ask you a question.

MS: Hi Marty, what's your question?

Caller: I have a service business, I'm in the carpet cleaning business. Do you think it's going to work for me?

MS: Marty, I appreciate your calling in. Let me answer that question for you. In your carpet cleaning business, how do you personally multiply and clone yourself using both the Internet and cutting-edge technology?

There are basically three things you've got to do in your business, actually, in any business. *(1)* You have to generate prospects or leads.

(2) You've got to convert those leads into customers and get them to buy. *(3)* You've got to get repeat business and get those people to buy from you over and over. Those are the three ways I want you to use technology and the Internet in your business.

Generating Leads

Number one is lead generation. How do you use technology to generate leads? You run a yellow page ad and put your web site in the ad. You could also offer a free report in your ad. For example: *"Warning! Do Not Call Any Carpet Cleaner Until You Read This Free Report! Send E-Mail to warning@carpetcleaner.com"* (or whatever your URL is).

You're probably already running ads in your local paper or sending out value packs or those kinds of things. Put your web address in there and offer a free report.

We love offering free reports. One free report that works great in any service business is that free report, *"Warning: Do not call any carpet cleaner until you find out these seven common scams."* You can run little classified ads in your local newspaper and offer a free report. That's how you're going to generate leads.

Turning Leads Into Customers

Your second goal is turning your leads into paying customers. And just how do your do that? Get those people to your web site *www.[whatever your domain is].* com Try offering a couple more free reports at your web site: Give a free report on how to save twenty or fifty percent on carpet cleaning, or reveal seven ways carpet cleaners take advantage of people.

Here's the key. To get that free report, visitors to your web site have to type in their name, address, and phone number. The free report is just the incentive or the motivation to get them to give you their address and phone number. What do you do once you've got their address, phone number, or fax number? You go ahead and send them something in the mail. You can also have people ask for your free report via e-mail. Put them in your e-mail sequence that we talked about earlier and send them an e-mail about your special offers once a week or once every quarter.

That's how you convert these leads into customers using technologies. There's other ways that you can do it, also, but these are just a few ideas.

Maximizing Repeat Business

The third thing that you've got to do is get repeat business. This is where technology is absolutely phenomenal! You can literally send out - once a month, once a week, once every three months - an e-mail offering to every one of your customers. Offer a "Special Deal," "One Half-Price," "Buy One Get One Free," or whatever, but always follow up with your customers.

The key is to reach customers not only with e-mail but also automatically with fax. Use a contact manager to track when it's time to contact each customer and automatically fax them your special deal including a phone number to call. Now you're reaching people with more than just one tool. You're doing your follow up.

Leverage Yourself, Clone Yourself, Multiply Your Energy!

Now you've got leads coming in, you're converting the names on your web site, and you're using different tools to get repeat business from the customers.

There are a lot of other things that I could tell you, Marty, but in a capsule, those are just a few of the ways you can leverage yourself, clone yourself, multiply your energy.

You don't have to send out the e-mails yourself; technology will do that for you. You don't have to get the people to your web site, your ads will do that for you. All you've got to do is use your ads, leverage the ads you're already running, and maybe run some classified ads in different newspapers offering free reports, etc.

Leverage yourself, leverage your advertising, leverage your marketing. You can even leverage people and personnel by having people designated to follow up on the leads you generate. That's it in a nutshell.

Caller: Thanks a lot!

The Money Is In The Follow Up

TC: Truer words were never spoken. Marlon, you keep talking about leveraging and following up. There's one important statistic regarding follow up that our listeners should know.

According to the Society of Sales and Marketing Executives International, 81% of all sales are made on the fifth contact or thereafter. It takes *five-plus* follow-ups for the average person to make a buying decision.

MS: Ted, I'm glad that you brought that up because that's true. One contact is *not* enough.

Let's use Marty as an example. Let's say Marty gets a call from his yellow page ad. The first time the customer talks to him, they might not schedule an appointment. They might not want to buy at that time but he still sends them follow-up letters or e-mails. They start hearing from Marty five, six, seven times and multiple contacts are occurring. He might call them again in a month or maybe in a week, whatever his system is. The point is, you get a system together and keep following up, because the money is in the follow up!

> *If you're only capturing easy business that comes in the front door, you're losing eighty percent of your business, because you're not following up.*
> *– Marlon Sanders*

If you're only capturing "easy" business that comes in the front door of your shop, you're losing eighty percent of your business, because you're not following up.

TC: In the old days, if you had to send a salesperson out, that was pretty cost prohibitive. You had to have employees, a car, time. Today you're talking about systems that don't require anything more than set up.

MS: Even salespeople can earn more money, a lot more money, just by leveraging themselves. A salesperson can literally have ads in different magazines, publications, on the Internet, off the Internet, in newsletters. The goal is to get people to e-mail them, go to their web site, or call them - and *now* they've got leverage. All these little ads and all of these things going around generate leads to businesses.

Writing Articles As A Marketing Tool

TC: Marlon, do you have a powerful Internet-only, free technique people can use? I always get that question.

MS: There are thousands of e-mail newsletters called e-zines on the Internet. You can write articles and send them once a week or once a month to a whole bunch of these e-zines. Many of these e-zines publish good articles for free; they don't charge you for it. At the end of the article, include your information and web site address. This is also the ideal place to offer your free report. What's the cost of this dynamic marketing tool? Zero! That's the beauty, *zero!*

TC: I know you use it, and I also use it.

The strategy of writing articles is really gangbusters because one of the things that happens is, once you're published, people suddenly see more credibility in you, and they're more inclined to do business with you.

MS: That's absolutely true.

Systems - The Ultimate Form Of Leverage

TC: Marlon, you've spoken so eloquently about multiplying and cloning yourself, about leveraging yourself to success. Could you give our listeners one last tip?

MS: What we've done is put everything into a *system*, the ultimate form of leverage. That's what we do. We create systems that people can use to make money and to leverage themselves.

The key is, we're doing it in *systems*. We have a system for writing sales letters, for lead generation, for getting referrals, for building relationships, and systems for recruiting hot new employees, workers and talent at fair or even bargain basement prices - automatically. We have systems for all these things - that's what we help others do. We plug people into systems and that's really the key to this thing.

How do you leverage yourself? You leverage yourself with people, marketing, technology, and systems - that's how you do what we're talking about. That's how people get rich. They use marketing as leverage.

You can use personnel systems for hiring, training, manager training - we've got systems for everything now. It's the McDonald's thing. Ray Kroc wasn't the best hamburger cooker in the world but he found guys and he sold the system. That's what this deal is all about, it's about systems, leverage, the Internet, technology. We've got systems for tracking sales letters, systems for your marketing, systems for all these things, Ted.

TC: Thank you so much, Marlon. You've shared some hard-hitting, insightful info.

MS: Thanks for inviting me.

How To Get Rich On The Internet

TC: Thanks for tuning in to "*How To Get Rich On The Internet.*" We've had with us Marlon Sanders, one of the most beneficial, hard-hitting Internet marketers on the planet.

He's a leading Internet marketer yet he's not stuck on the Internet. He was emphasizing *technology marketing*, combining tools, *leverage*. Snag leads and customers, follow up to make more sales, but *don't* make those phone calls yourself and don't stand over the fax machine yourself. Get the simple tools that can do the work for you.

Don't know how to do it yourself? Go to *www.Elance.com* where you can find someone to help you set things up.

Marlon revealed universal formulas and strategies that everyone can use - from wholesalers and retailers to professionals and real estate agents. Basically, he showed us how to get leads, how to convert them into customers, and how to sell more. He showed us how, with follow-up e-mail, automated fax, and automated phone calls, *you* can do that.

It's all about leverage. Using systems.

Multiply yourself, clone yourself, leverage yourself – get more leads, more sales, and make more money!

Special thanks to the contributors to this show...

*Marlon Sanders * www.AmazingFormula.com*
*Ted Ciuba * www.InstantInternetMarketing.com*

If you enjoyed this interview, there's more just like this!
Tune into *www.InternetMarketingInterviews.com*

Other resources to supercharge your progress!
    www.GetRichOnTheInternet.com
    www.GetRichOnTheInternet.com/seminars
    www.AutoPilotRiches.com
    www.KillerWebCopy.com
    www.ProtegeProgram.com
    www.MailOrderInTheInternetAge.com
    www.LowCostInternetAdvertising.com
    www.PrePaidLegal.com/go/parthenon

The $100 Million Round Table SuperConference On Internet Marketing

Chapter 8

Ted Ciuba *Interviews T.J. Rohleder, Russ von Hoelscher, Jeff Gardner, Chris Lakey & Don Bice*

Good day, listeners, and welcome to *How To Get Rich On The Internet!*

The group of guests we have today is known as The $100 Million Round Table. They are, in fact, a working MasterMind group, and one I'm very honored to be participating in!

These members all have mail order background and have accomplished outstanding Internet success. Today, working as MasterMind partners, they are creating new products, new Internet sites, and new Internet promotions. They are helping one another individually, helping themselves as a group, and always contributing to you, the listener.

It gives me great pleasure to welcome the members of The $100 Million Round Table: Don Bice, Jeff Gardner, Russ von Hoelscher, Chris Lakey, and T.J. Rohleder!

All: Thanks for having us, Ted!

Ted Ciuba (TC): All right, let's get right into the meat of today's topic.

"How Do I Get Rich On The Internet?"

TC: Here's the big question. Most of our listeners send e-mails asking, "How do I get rich on the Internet? What are the secrets?"

> *There's a lot of success in Ready, Fire! Aim...*
> *- Ted Ciuba*

Everyone knows there are secrets.

Don Bice, what's your secret to helping our listeners get rich on the Internet today?

The Five-Step Internet Profit Formula

Don Bice (DB): Well, Ted, I have what I call "The Five Step Internet Profit Formula." It's a sure fire way to get started fast and to get profitable.

First of all, you need to identify a market that interests you, one that's large and can be reached online and offline. Working on- and offline is very important since you primarily want to build traffic to your site but you also want an easy way to reach people who are not presently on the Internet.

Secondly, you need to construct a simple web site that uses good, strong selling principles. I've always contended the best web sites focus on selling one product in the beginning. That's what I suggest listeners do.

Offer an information product on that site that attracts your target audience so you can start the interaction.

Let's say that you're marketing to ski enthusiasts. A report titled "How To Save 25%-50% On Your Lift Tickets" would appeal to anyone interested in skiing. You could offer this information as a free report or you could offer it for sale on your site.

You want to generate income by selling a report on your site for instant downloading, or you can give a report away in return for a name and e-mail address.

The third step toward creating Internet success, of course, is to use your site to build a list of names of people who have interest in your product area. The income from the sale of the initial information is great, we all want that. However...

Using your web site as a lead generator to follow up with e-mail that sells higher priced, more specialized products, means the real value comes from collecting *names*.

Step four: Once you've collected the names of people who are interested in your product, you're going to contact them over and over again. Your primary job will be to look for products you can use to create a joint venture - products you can get wholesale, or products you create for your target group - so you can market to your list again and again.

> *There's no contradiction between learning the moves of chess, or of business, in 90 minutes and then spending the rest of your life mastering the game.*
> *- Ted Ciuba*

Use your web site to generate prospects to sell in regular mailings. That's the real secret... Develop a list of people you can go back to over and over again.

Step five in the success formula is duplicating your success. Take exactly what you've done and do it again in another subject area. Build a whole series of web sites, multiple streams of Internet income, and sit back and enjoy the profits. It's a very repeatable formula and a very simple way to get started on the Internet. You can start small and grow as fast as you want.

TC: Wow, that is truly a fantastic five-step process, it covers a lot!

It ends with perhaps dozens of auto-pilot web businesses spewing in $100 dollar bills every day!

AutoPilotRiches

Jeff Gardner, I know you've got some secrets for us, too. How do listeners get rich on the Internet?!

Jeff Gardner (JG): One of the things that I love about the Internet is the ability to do automatic follow up.

For years direct-mail marketers and direct-response marketers have realized that to get the most out of your list, you need to do constant follow up.

That means after the first sale, or even if you're just working leads of people who haven't purchased anything yet, after sending out your first sales letter, you need to contact those same people again and again and again to get sales to come in.

Sending printed pieces, sales letters, and postcards is a lot of work! There are also a lot of costs involved, like printing and outrageous postage! What I absolutely love about doing business on the Internet is the ability to create *autoresponders* that do your follow up automatically!

> *It's absolutely wonderful to realize that 24 hours a day, people are getting follow-up messages from you about new products and new offers and that's making you additional money... And you don't have to mess with any of it!*
> *- Jeff Gardner*

That's so exciting because you can have someone visit your web site and, even though they don't purchase anything, they can sign up for an e-zine, or request a free report. Once they're in your autoresponder system they continue to get information about your web site or products, weeks, months, and even years later - and it's all done automatically!

Want something even better?! A good autoresponder system, such as *AutoPilotRiches.com* will let you personalize your messages! Instead of displaying the message "Dear Friend," your e-mails go out actually giving the person's name - "Dear Jane," or "Dear Jeff."

It's absolutely wonderful to realize that 24 hours a day, people are getting your follow-up messages about new products or new offers. That makes you additional money - and you don't have to mess with any of it!

TC: You don't have to worry about printing or shipping, the work, the hassle, or the outrageous costs, do you? Automated Internet systems do it all for you.

JG: Yes, and you can use autoresponders for literally pennies a month! The technology is so reasonably priced it's insane not to use these follow-up systems. It's a great way to get a lot more money with a lot less work.

TC: That's a big secret, Jeff, guaranteed! As anyone who has your experience with mail order, the hassle and the money knows... It pays to use autoresponders. That's how to make an Internet lifestyle, isn't it?

JG: It really is. Using this technology gives you back a lot more time. I mean, you're making the same amount or even more money, but it gives you back the time to do the things you really enjoy.

Mail Order In The Internet Age

Russ von Hoelscher, tell us more on getting *rich* on the Internet!

Russ von Hoelscher (RVH): I don't want to sound like a broken record after Jeff Gardner, but I agree that e-mail is the biggest breakthrough of all time. Those of us with backgrounds in mail order businesses know that postage is your number-one expense.

E-mail is so fantastic because you can send out all the mail you want, virtually free.

The biggest point I would make is to learn everything you can about e-mail because it's such an effective way to reach people. Use it constantly, non-stop, and set it up so it can be done automatically. If you use e-mail consistently and with precision, you're doing the best marketing you can at the lowest possible price, virtually free.

That's the biggest secret of our time... Get involved with e-mail where you can reach hundreds, thousands, even millions of people at virtually no cost.

TC: That's a good one, Russ! As a matter of fact, a recent guest, Jay Conrad Levinson, shared a story that fits in exactly with what you're saying. He related an incident where they did $625,000 worth of business with zero advertising costs using e-mail.

RVH: Fantastic!

TC: Good advice! Thank you, Russ.

Chris Lakey! How do our listeners get really rich on the Internet?!

Follow The K.I.S.S. Formula

Chris Lakey (CL): Thanks, Ted. There's a lot of wisdom in following the K.I.S.S. formula. Translation? *Keep It Simple, Stupid!*

Start with a simple product - one product. Create a simple mini-web site - make it short. It shouldn't have a lot of graphics. You want your web page to load pretty quick so people can come to your site, see what you're offering, make a decision to buy, and get on.

People don't have a lot of time to sit and read through pages and pages - there are other places for that. You can create other types of web sites after they buy.

Whatever you put on the Internet creates your first impression.

When someone comes to your website, at the very beginning, you need to keep it short, sweet, and to the point. That way they can get in and make the decision to buy without having to wade through a lot of clutter.

TC: Listeners, pay attention!

And now, T.J. Rohleder from More Incorporated. T.J., welcome!

Don't Get Bogged Down In The Technical Crap

T.J. Rohleder (TR): I'm glad to be here, Ted. I think everyone would be better served if they let other people do the technical stuff leaving them to focus on marketing. Running a business on the Internet is just like running a regular retail business on Main Street. You can spend all day getting bogged down with all kinds of little crap...

> *The way to make money is to focus on the things that make you the most money. It's always in the marketing.*
> *- T.J. Rohleder*

The way to make money is to focus on the things that make you the most money. It's always in the marketing.

Marketing is where you make all your money. I see way too many people get bogged down with all the technical crap. They spend all day behind a computer and never make the kind of money they could if they'd just let someone else do all of the work. Focus on the marketing side of it.

That's the biggest secret I have to share.

I practice what I preach too, because I barely know how to turn the computer on.

TC: No kidding? And you've designed, marketed, and sold hundreds, if not thousands, of web sites and promotions that have been on the web.

TR: And let other people do all the work!

TC: It sounds good to me! Now that's rich!!

The $100 Million Round Table

T.J., people are always asking, "What does this *$100 Million Round Table* thing mean?"

TR: As for the one hundred million part, it really should be called the $200 or $300 Million

The $100 Million Round Table

We're a group that gets together to help each other make more money. That's something all our listeners should do, or have a goal to do. Create your own MasterMind or Round Table group, or join one that's already in existence.
- T.J. Rohleder

Round Table because collectively, our group has amassed that much money for ourselves and our clients. But the Round Table part is so cool.

It has to do with your whole MasterMind principle. We're a group that gets together to help each other make more money. That's something *all* our listeners should do, or have a goal to do. Create your own MasterMind or Round Table group, or join one that's already in existence.

TC: Excellent, and do you think that if people can't join or form a group listening to gurus, reading their materials, and applying their materials is the next best way to get going?

TR: That's exactly true.

The ideas that you need to get rich - or richer - are out there, people are already doing it. The more you expose yourself to those ideas through audiotapes, seminars, and books, the more you're actually putting the MasterMind principle into action.

Start Right Where You Are

TC: MasterMind partners, you've shared some fabulous secrets here. But is that all there is?

TR: Of course not! You could spend your life studying this. The truth is, realizing success on the Internet can be simple, but it can also be very complex at times. Those of us who are involved in it are constantly learning something new every day.

CL: There are occasions when someone says, "Here's what you need to do." Then you need to learn how to do it.

The Complex Moves Of The Simple Game Of Chess

TR: In theory that's simple, but remember, you can learn all the moves on a chessboard in about ninety minutes, then spend the rest of your entire life mastering the game.

DB: The secret is to just get started - you can figure out everything as you go along. Learn a few secrets, like some of the things we're showing and teaching you here. These are the ways to get started, but the whole process is just that - a process. It's a game. It's something you never really master.

Ask the richest people in the world if they're done learning and they'll tell you, absolutely not. The same applies to making money on the Internet. You learn enough to get started. Don't ever wait around until you know everything, because you'll never know everything. It just doesn't happen, you are always learning.

TC: Yes, I plead with people to GET started.

There's a lot of success in "Ready, *Fire!* Aim..."

Get started today - engage yourself. Thrive as a student of the game. There's no contradiction between learning the moves of chess or business in ninety minutes then spending the rest of your life mastering the game.

Adjusting, experimenting, trying out the successful ideas of competitors and partners... Business is a moving target. After all, sales are driven by what consumers want. Laws change, moods change, customers always want something novel, new, and better. They buy one thing and discard the old, but their interests stay the same. How you reach them with news of different products that alleviate their hunger briefly is the game. That changes too.

The Internet Is A Softer, Kinder Medium

You can make money while you're getting started, even from the point of learning how to turn a computer on. That's on-the-job training, isn't it?

TR: "Earn while you learn." The best way to do that is probably to use e-mail. Even if your letters are not that good, or if you don't make a ton of money the first or second time out of the box, you're dealing with a media that costs you very little. If we make mistakes running ads in publications, we can get hurt to the tune of thousands of dollars when the ad doesn't work. When you use Internet marketing (e-mail marketing) you can make a ton of mistakes and still not get badly hurt as you learn and earn.

How To Succeed By Modeling Your Competitors

JG: I think one of the best ways to learn on the Internet is to search around and find your competition, people doing what you'd like to do, and see exactly what they're doing.

That's one of the best elements of the Internet. You can find companies out there doing exactly what you ultimately want to do and you can see exactly how they market, the design of their site, and the exact prices of their product. You can even purchase a product and see what their back end (follow up) is. It's all laid out there in the open. You can learn simply by connecting to the Internet and doing some searching to find out what everybody else is doing.

There Are Great Ideas Out There On The Internet

TC: Jeff, I guess we should take this to the logical end... Have you ever "robbed" a good idea that you saw one of your competitors doing and put it into action in your own business?

JG: Oh, definitely. There are great ideas on the Internet and you've got to pick them up and use them in your business. That's how your business grows, and that's what we're talking about - learning by doing.

> *The results are exponentially better – in a fraction of the time – than if any one of us were working on the project individually. There's magic in a MasterMind group. The whole is greater than the sum of the parts.*
> *- Ted Ciuba*

You start at a base point and when you see others doing things, you take the very best of what *they* are doing and put it in *your* business. That's how you really start to make a lot of money on the Internet.

TC: Quantum business.

TR: Continuing with that same thought, Ted, we all "steal" from each other. I mean, we all take different ideas that everyone else is doing and we try to find unique ways to combine them in new ways. To me, that's the heart and soul of capitalism. Everyone is basically taking ideas and concepts that other people use and finding ways to incorporate them for themselves.

RVH: Learn to ask good questions. Ask, "How can I adapt what is working for this person to my situation?" Asking that simple question can give you all kinds of money-making answers.

TR: Too many people are out there scratching their heads. They're sitting around trying to figure out how to make money, and they're so confused and frustrated...

All of the answers they need are out there right now. All they have to do is what we call "stand on the other side of the cash register." Instead of thinking like a consumer, start thinking as an *entrepreneur*. Ask the question Russ recommended...

I mean, isn't it that simple, guys?

JG: It really is. When you think like an entrepreneur, you're thinking of all the ways you can take ideas from others. We don't steal ideas word-for-word, or absolutely block-by-block. When we talk of "stealing" someone's ideas, we mean taking their best ideas, incorporating them with our ideas, and creating a better product, service, or marketing effort.

MasterMind: The Whole Is Greater Than The Sum Of Its Parts

TC: Being a member of this MasterMind Group, one of the things I've always liked most is when we get together and contribute different ideas, then build on the ideas or plans we've decided on.

These ideas relate to everything concerning our businesses – from direction and resources, to creating and pricing products and making souped-up marketing promotions and materials. The MasterMind effect kicks in and the results are exponentially better – in a fraction of the time – than if any one of us were working on the project individually.

There's magic in a MasterMind group. The whole is greater than the sum of the parts. 1+1 doesn't equal 2, it equals 11! 7+7 doesn't equal 14, it equals 77!

DB: One of the great things about a MasterMind group is that people share the results of their own research, their own experience. It means you don't have to keep making the same mistakes yourself. When someone says, "Hey, I tried this, and these were the results that I got..." You know you're dealing with someone you can trust. If they got good results, you can model it and apply it to your situation.

> *All the millions and millions of people out on the Internet, they're all searching for something!... And if you can deliver that something that they really desperately want and desire, you can make a lot of money.*
> *- Jeff Gardner*

If someone's plan didn't work, we discuss as a group why we think it didn't work then someone else tries it and reports on their results. It's a very informal process.

Experience Gives You Confidence

TR: You constantly learn and grow, and you gain tremendous confidence. If you're new to this Internet game, you probably won't have a lot of confidence in the beginning.

I want to assure you that all millionaires and billionaires had to start somewhere - and they gained confidence as they went along. Confidence comes with experience and, unfortunately, the only way to get experience is to get out there and get your butt kicked.

TC: T.J., the first time you ever put $300 of your own money down to buy an ad, how confident did you feel?

TR: I was terrified to the point where I was living in fear. That was all the money I had at the time... And spending $300 back then was like spending $30,000 now. The longer you play the game, the more you can take big risks without fear.

The Internet Has Slashed Costs

TC: Of course today we don't have that same problem. When all we had for marketing options were magazine ads and mail, which cost a fortune, it was life and death.

Now we can put our full story on our web site and all our ads have to do is direct people to our web site.

TR: Which is very easy to do, by the way. It's very easy to drive people to a web site.

People On The Internet Are Searching For You!

JG: Think about all the millions and millions of people on the Internet. They're all searching for something, and if you can deliver that something they desperately want and desire, you can make a *lot* of money.

Like T.J. said, it doesn't take a lot to get people to a web site. That's because if you can deliver what they want, they're going to search you out - they're going to find you. People go to search engines looking for a certain something. If you have that something, they're going to pay you cash to get it.

Internet For Any Business

TC: Jeff, here's a question a lot of listeners ask, "Will this work for my product? Will this work for my business?"

JG: Take a simple look around to see the companies that are using the Internet! Some people say, "That works for hard products that you actually ship..." Or, "It works for information products, but it might not work for a dental hygienist." "It may not work for a cosmetologist..." "It may not work for anything..."

> ### Internet Profit Alert!
> *You can find companies doing exactly what you ultimately want to do and you can see exactly how they market, exactly the design of their site, exactly the prices of their product. You can even purchase a product and see what their back end or what their follow up is. That's all laid out there open for you so you can learn just by connecting to the Internet and doing some searching and finding out what everybody else is doing.*
> *- Jeff Gardner*

It really does work, though. For example, my wife is a veterinarian and works at a vet clinic. The guy that runs the clinic put up a web site. He didn't do that to generate new clients and customers - what he did was create customer contact over time to create a better relationship with the company. Now when people visit the site, they get a great feeling about it. The clinic owner can e-mail specials to customers and bring them back in. He's making a good income off his web site.

The point is, he does it to create a relationship with people he's already had coming through the front door. It's a powerful secret. You don't have to use the Internet just to generate that new traffic - you can also use it to create relationships.

Giving Away FREE Stuff Can Make You Millions

TC: Why does each of you offer so much free stuff when you're in the business to make money?

RVH: It's a tactic that works.

TC: Free information is a tactic to get the prospects to come and see what you have. I like it!

How To Get Rich On The Internet

We've had an exciting hour with the members of the $100 Million Dollar Round Table. What did they share? Well, of course, you know it — how to get *rich* on the Internet. Let's review what we've learned from our experts.

Don Bice shared his five step process for getting rich on the Internet: *1)* Find your market first, *2)* construct a simple web site, *3)* build names - that's really important because you want to, *4)* go back to the people again, then, *5)* duplicate the success, and do it again.

Jeff Gardner talked about the tremendous opportunities of autoresponder follow up. The best system I know for that is found at *AutoPilotRiches.com*

Russ von Hoelscher shared the incredible potentials of e-mail. No cost, low hassle, high sales! It's a future whose time has come.

Chris Lakey shared a secret that's a big stumbling block for a lot of people... He said, *Keep it simple.* Put up a mini-web site with one product and get it working before you go on to anything more complicated. Get your feet wet making money on the Internet! People want the simple and direct.

T.J. Rohleder reminded us you don't have to get bogged down in the technical stuff. A lot of Internet marketers, including myself, think you need to have some basic confidence, but every single one of them agrees... It's not the technical stuff, it's the *marketing* stuff that makes you money! It's not the engineers, it's the entrepreneurs who are making money on the Internet. That's a very important secret.

We talked about a lot of different ideas, comparing learning in this business with being a chess player and learning on the job. You get money, you make money, you learn, and you improve. You make *more* money.

We also talked about the importance of competitive intelligence. You should know what your competitors are doing so you can craft and adapt their ideas in your own business. And the incredible thing is it's all laid out for your view and modeling on the profitable world wide web!

Review your notes and put what you heard today into action.

You *CAN* get *rich* on the Internet!

Special thanks to the contributors to this show...

Don Bice – www.DonBice.com

Jeff Gardner - www.TopBizOpps.com

Russ von Hoelscher – www.rvhfreegate.com

Chris Lakey – www.FreeInternetMarketingCourse.com

T.J. Rohleder - www.TheWorldsGreatestInternetBusiness.com

*Ted Ciuba * www.InstantInternetMarketing.com*

If you enjoyed this interview, there's more just like this! Tune into *www.InternetMarketingInterviews.com*

Other resources to supercharge your progress!
www.GetRichOnTheInternet.com
www.GetRichOnTheInternet.com/seminars
www.AutoPilotRiches.com
www.KillerWebCopy.com
www.ProtegeProgram.com
www.MailOrderInTheInternetAge.com
www.LowCostInternetAdvertising.com
www.PrePaidLegal.com/go/parthenon

Guaranteed Internet Profit$

How To Buy A Web Business, Finance It With Its Own Cash Flow, And Sell It In 18 Months For An $11 Million Gain!

Chapter 9

Ted Ciuba *Interviews* *Kirt Christensen*

Today's guest, Kirt Christensen, from Provo, Utah, and Beverly Hills, California, runs a number of web sites, including *ScientificMarketing.com* What's really got my attention about this young man is that I've seen him take struggling Internet businesses, I'm talking businesses no one would want, and make massive money off these struggling businesses. He takes them, amps up their marketing procedures, then turns around a few months later and sells them for outrageous, obscene profits.

Ted Ciuba (TC): Kirt Christensen, welcome to *How To Get Rich on the Internet*.

Kirt Christensen (KC): Thanks, Ted. I'm excited to be here!

TC: Tell us a little about who you are and what you've done.

A Lifestyle Of Freedom

KC: Ted, I'm 28 years old and I've been doing Internet marketing almost exclusively for about four or five years, since I graduated from college. To tell you the truth, I've never had a real job where I have to punch the clock and work 9-to-5, that sort of thing.

TC: You might not be able to relate to some of our listeners.

KC: I can still relate; all my friends have jobs.

The real power of not having a job, of having an Internet business, is that you have a chance to live your life, live the lifestyle you want, and not be tied down to a paycheck or the daily grind. You've got loads of money. You can go on vacation when you want, do what you want, and basically live your life in a fashion that's agreeable to you.

A Revolutionary Product, Perfect Timing... Poor Sales

At the beginning of the Internet boom - that would have been '96-'97 when I was still in college - there was a little company in my town that was barely launching an Internet product. I helped them start it up and was one of the first seven in the company. They developed a piece of software that allowed web site owners to build an entire web site from scratch, using just a browser. Users didn't have to know anything about HTML or anything like that, so at the time, it was quite a revolutionary piece of software.

But listen to this. We had this revolutionary piece of software, perfect timing, a lot of energy, and some really sharp programmers who were working on the software. Guess how many units of the software they were selling per week?

TC: I would imagine, with a product like you described, a ton of them.

KC: They were selling exactly *three* copies per week - at $150 a copy.

TC: Kirt, you said this was a product whose time had come?

KC: Right! The next comparable thing to it on the market was probably in the $2,000 to $2,500 range.

TC: So you're telling me, if I'm reading you right, that having a super product is not going to get anybody rich?

KC: That's exactly right. Just having a product doesn't mean jack squat. The famous saying, "Build a better mousetrap and the world will beat a path to your door," is absolutely wrong.

Build A Better Marketing System

What you need to do is build a better *marketing* system for that mousetrap, *then* the world will beat a path to your door.

It's amazing how many people get caught up in the technical side of Internet business, the actual knowledge about the product, and things like that. That's important, and it's super critical to have a great product, but it's even more important to have fantastic marketing.

Starting With Three Simple Strategies

TC: I'm assuming you ramped up sales so the company started selling more than three a week?

KC: Back then I was just barely getting started in Internet marketing, and was still learning all the stuff that you teach. I really didn't know a lot, but I knew a few things, so I just did those few things.

First, I wrote a sales letter describing exactly what the software did. The letter contained a story about a guy who was selling computer parts and wanted to sell them online, and how he built his online store in fifteen minutes, etc. That real story was the basis of the sales letter. Looking back on it, I'm sure that sales letter was horrid. I'm sure I would laugh at it now, but the point is, I *did* something. I took a massive action - I tried.

The second thing we did was set up a simple system so that when anyone inquired about the software at our web site, we followed up with them by e-mail three times. That couldn't be simpler, Ted. We used an autoresponder, like at *AutoPilotRiches.com*

Third, we offered a 30-day, money-back guarantee on the software.

That's it, we didn't do anything out of this world, nothing crazy, no stroke of genius, just basic common-sense Internet marketing - tools people can use to sell products no matter what industry they're in.

TC: You mentioned three very important points which affected a turnaround. You wrote a sales letter that had a story in it - which is very powerful. You installed an autoresponder with sequential follow ups where you kept contact with prospects. Then you offered a 30-day guarantee.

KC: Exactly.

TC: These are all standard, basic mail order ideas moved over to the Internet, right?

KC: Exactly. Nothing original, nothing novel. This was just stuff

I'd read in books by the masters, people who had actually been there and done it. They said, "Write a sales letter," and I did it. They said, "Follow up with the customer," and I did it. They said, "Offer a money-back guarantee," and I tried it. Listen to how well it worked, Ted.

Then We Raised The Price

Oh, we actually did one more thing, we increased the price. I thought people were going to look at that low price and think, "It can't be any good because it's only $150." So, we increased the price of the software to $750.

Unit Sales Tripled, Revenues Skyrocketed

Within a couple weeks we were selling ten copies of the software per week at $750. To put it in round numbers, we increased our revenues by sixteen times, just by doing the four simple things we mentioned.

TC: In a few weeks you pushed software sales from $450 a week to $7,500 a week?

KC: Exactly.

TC: And you haven't even shared anything super sophisticated yet.

KC: There's nothing I did for that company that any Internet marketer couldn't do. The possibilities are astounding. It's simple, common-sense marketing.

You Can Do It, Too

TC: A lot of our listeners are in a position similar to where you were when you first got started. They're wondering what to do. In fact, many of our listeners aren't even making $450 per week from their web site.

What you're saying Kirt, is if they'll get up, start following instructions, and start *doing* things, something will happen?

KC: Exactly. You've got to take action. There's nothing like taking massive action and seeing what the results are. Remember the sales letter I mentioned? Originally, it did all right, but over time I revised it. I tested and tested and tested to see what else I could do to make it work.

Reaping The First Rewards

As time went on, the company did really well, and eventually we got an offer for a buyout. When I started with the software company they were making $450 a week in revenue - obviously not even covering basic expenses. We ended up selling that "measly" little software company in May of 1998 for 11 million dollars.

I was the director of sales for that company so I only got enough money out of that sale to make me hungry for more. It was enough to more than satisfy my desire to move up a little in life - and remember, I was still in college. I made more money off that one sale than most college graduates make in five or six years.

> *I made more money off that one sale than most college graduates make in 5 or 6 years.*
> *– Kirt Christensen*

The Source Of Success: Direct-Marketing Gurus

The company I worked for thought I was a genius. They thought, "Man, he's coming up with this stuff left and right!" All the while, whenever I needed to come up with an idea, what did I do? I went back and read the direct marketing manuals by the great names like Jay Abraham, Gary Halbert, and Ted Nicholas. That's how I came up with all my ideas. I didn't mention *that* to the company.

TC: No, always keep your sources protected!

Get Involved With An Existing Business

KC: That's one simple story. I guess what I want listeners to take away from this is that there are a lot of people who know a little bit about Internet marketing. Maybe they've dabbled in it, read a few books on it. The real problem people have in Internet marketing is getting something going - getting from zero to point A, where they have a web site, a product, are getting some traffic and a couple of orders here and there.

For some people, the best idea would be to use their Internet marketing knowledge and acquire, buy, or partner with existing companies that already have some sort of Internet track record. The company owners might say, "For every one hundred visitors we get at our site, we make one sale. Can you help us do better?" You can then use your Internet marketing knowledge to help that company. That's totally different than starting from scratch, wouldn't you think, Ted?

TC: I couldn't agree more. It hurdles right over those big old problems like, *What do I do about a product? Is it proven? Will it work? Do they want it?* Blah, blah, blah.

That's a good idea. Get involved with a company that's already established and amp up their marketing.

KC: Exactly.

TC: Who better to share those insider secrets than Kirt Christensen? Kirt, you've had some marvelous success at buying small, struggling businesses, ramping up their Internet marketing proceduress, and selling them off for fortunes.

The E-Myth Archetypes

You have a unique point of view on business. You go where the profit potential is instead of being in love with a product and trying to make that work. You were a diamond broker for a while. Can you tell us a little about that experience?

KC: The diamond business was one of my favorite things so far. Have you heard of the book, *The E-Myth*, by Michael Gerber? If your listeners haven't read that book, they really need to.

There are two types of people in the world: *entrepreneurs*, who are concentrating on the business processes and marketing, like we all should be, and *engineers*, who concentrate on the product and the interior working of the business, the accounting, and things like that. Both are needed, but only one of them actually makes money, and that's the entrepreneur.

Buying A Business On eBay

The reason I say that is, one day I was looking on eBay for businesses for sale - that's going to sound ludicrous to most people, but I find a lot of the businesses I end up buying just by looking on eBay.

TC: I'm glad that you recognize that. That does sound a bit ludicrous because we all have access to eBay.

KC: When I tell people that the first time, they look at me and their eyes just kind of go blank.

There are actually two different ways to find businesses on eBay. You can either search under *Businesses for Sale* or *Web Sites for Sale*. Either one will pull up a list. There's a category on the front page of eBay where you can click on Business Equipment. There's a category under there called Businesses for Sale. If you click on that category at any one time, you'll find about thirty pages of businesses, quasi-businesses, or people saying their business is for sale.

Diamond Brokers With A Broken-Looking Web Site

Last year I was looking on eBay and found an online diamond brokerage. All they did was sell loose diamonds over the Internet. Here's the interesting thing, they showed their site right there on the eBay ad.

I looked at the site and about fell on the floor. It was awful. It was probably the ugliest site I've ever seen - and I've seen a lot of ugly sites. The site was downright, outright bad.

TC: And they probably wondered why their business was suffering?

KC: Here's the crazy thing, Ted... The year before, they had done over $600,000 worth of business off that site!

Let me repeat that again, they had a crappy little web site that was bringing in over $600,000 in business.

> There's so much money on the Internet it's unbelievable!
>
> *Let me repeat that again, they had a crappy little website that was bringing in over $600,000 in business.*
>
> *- Kirt Christensen*

TC: There's so much money on the Internet it's unbelievable!

KC: It gets even better. Originally, they were asking $120,000 for the business. I talked to them back and forth through e-mail a couple times. I finally decided to talk to the owners on the phone and it ended up that the people who were selling the business lived in the exact same town that I live in. That doesn't happen all the time, of course.

TC: That *is* a coincidence...

Missing The Marketing Mentality

KC: Quite a coincidence. I met with the owners in person a few times and discovered they strongly fit into the E-Myth engineer mode. They knew all kinds of stuff about diamonds and were experts on diamonds. In fact, the man had worked as a manager in some of the top diamond stores in my region.

They knew everything there was to know about diamonds, all about the cuts and everything like that, but they were quite horrible at Internet marketing, getting traffic to the site, and actually selling diamonds. It was just one of those things where they happened to be in the right place at the right time. Their web site got a decent amount of traffic and, once they got customers to call, they made a decent amount of sales to the tune of $600,000 per year.

TC: That's pretty good. What you're saying is they did that by knowing their business really well, but they didn't know how to *do* business.

KC: Exactly. They didn't know what to do to get more business; they had no idea at all.

For example, here's a funny story... They had an 800-number, of course, on their web site. That was good - but the people who owned the web site also had what I would call a "real" job. Flat out: they had jobs that required them to be gone during the day, so the phone would just ring to a voice mail.

Good Internet Marketing - More Than Internet Alone

Even after I gave them free advice, they didn't do anything to correct this mistake. I told them, "You know, during the day when you're not there to answer the phone, you can route calls to a live answering service who will answer in the name of your company and at least take a message for you." They just saw that as a cost - it was going to cost them about $50 a month to do that.

TC: So when you got the business, I'm assuming that's one of the first changes you made?

KC: Exactly. It was one of the very first things I did.

TC: Kirt, we're talking about marketing on the Internet, but now you just brought in the telephone and a bad telephone answering system. Is that Internet marketing, too?

KC: Sure, it all ties into Internet marketing. If someone in the UK sees your web site and picks up the phone to call your number, most of the time they don't stop and think, "Wait a second, it's the middle of the night in the United States!" They just want to talk to someone.

We would get all kinds of calls from Saudi Arabia, India, Europe, in the middle of the night. Our answering service would very politely answer, "E-Diamond Brokers, how may I help you?" When callers said, "I'm looking for [some specific type of diamond]," the answering service was trained to ask them "diamond questions:" How big? What shape? What color? What clarity? That information was instantly forwarded to us by e-mail and we would get on it as soon as we possibly could the next morning.

TC: Excellent! Tell us what else you did - we want to know how this victory turned out.

The Price Was More Than Right

KC: As I said, the sellers originally wanted $120,000 for the business. That was probably a decent price, considering that it was basically one year of profits from the business. At that time, a 20% profit margin in the diamond business was common. The owners were doing $600,000 a year, and basically asking for one year of profits, which isn't that bad.

Think about it though. I knew they would (and were) having an incredibly hard time selling their business with that ugly web site. They had a few other minor glitches - like they didn't have a very good accounting system, everything was done on paper... Several things like that.

Everyone else who looked at the business just saw all these problems, but I thought, "How long does it take to put up a new web site?" My experience and intuition whispered back, "A couple minutes."

I knew I could put up something better than what they already had within a couple minutes and work on it over time to make it better and better.

I asked, "What's the absolute least you'd take for this business? I'll write you a check right now." I ended up buying that business for $29,000.

TC: That's a *big* difference.

KC: Yes, the selling price went from $120,000 to $29,000 simply because the owners were so desperate and because everyone else could only see the problems.

Simple Strategies To $18,000 Per Month In Profits!

Immediately after I bought the diamond business, the first thing I did was install a twenty-four hour answering service. I put some good sales copy on the web site with a headline that read something like, "Discover How to Buy Top-Quality Loose Diamonds At Up To 34% Off Of Retail." That's a common-sense, direct-marketing headline.

I wrote a seven-day course on how to price a diamond without becoming a gemologist and offered that free on the site to get people to sign up. I followed up with all the leads that signed up for the course, then I started using a program called *Zeus* which does an incredible job with linking strategies - getting other sites to link to you. That's about all I did.

TC: What did you sell that business for, and after how long?

KC: I sold it seven months later for $110,000 cash.

TC: Wow! So in a few months you made $80,000 part time?

KC: Actually, I made $80,000 on the sale of the business and another $50,000+ selling diamonds.

TC: That's $130,000 in seven months, part time! That isn't bad, Kirt Christensen!

You Really Can Do It, Too

Kirt, I'd like to change the subject a bit... And it's almost a joke in light of what you've just shared. It's just that...Very often people say, "It's not possible to earn $100,000 on the Internet!" What's your opinion on that?

> *It's very easy to earn $100,000 a year on the Internet.*
> *– Kirt Christensen*

KC: My opinion is that it's very easy to earn $100,000 a year on the Internet - you just have to be in the right place at the right time. By saying that, I'm not saying that you have to be lucky or anything like that. Simply put - the people who are out there taking action are going to be able to cash in on the great deals like that.

Two Months To A $50,000 Profit

Just a very quick example: Six weeks after I bought the diamond business, I got a funny little e-mail from someone on AOL. The e-mail said, "Hi, I'm interested in looking at either of these two diamonds." The first diamond they listed cost $220,000. The second one was $250,000.

TC: A quarter of a million dollars! You'd had this business six WEEKS?!!

KC: We're talking about a five- or six-carat diamond. That's about the size of a quarter. Within two weeks we had sold the $250,000 diamond and pocketed 20% of that, or about $50,000.

If You Do The Work, The Opportunity Shows Up

Some people would say that's flat-out luck. I would say - and I'm sure that you would agree with me, Ted - that luck is simply being in front of opportunity. It's about being in there, taking your licks, and doing the real work so you can be there when the opportunity comes up.

TC: I couldn't agree more wholeheartedly, and you were there!

> *Instead of working all those hours, toiling away at a job and getting a certain amount of money, invest your time in something that has the potential to make you a vast fortune.*
> *– Kirt Christensen*

KC: Exactly. Obviously, I can't say that everyone who starts an Internet business is going to make that much money that fast. But Ted, I have more friends than I can count who make well over $100,000 a year on the Internet - simply because they were willing to put in the time and effort, and do something ever-so-slightly more risky than having a job.

Instead of working all those hours toiling away at a job and getting a certain amount of money, invest your time in something that has the potential to make you a vast fortune.

> *Make more money, work fewer hours, and have more time to spend with the people that you love - your friends and family.*
> *– Kirt Christensen*

Even The Downside Is Up

TC: Most of the Internet marketing friends I have earn more on a good morning than their friends earn in five months on the job. It only has the perception of being more risky than a job in the beginning, correct? Or do you think that's always true?

KC: No, I think you're exactly right. If you think about it, what's the worst thing that could happen for anyone who takes the initiative and starts doing some venture on the Internet?

Say you try it for a year or two and it doesn't work, then what? You can go back and get an even better job than you had before because you have so much entrepreneurial experience that people will be falling all over themselves to hire you. That's the worst-case scenario!

TC: That's not such a bad case - but just think what happens if the business takes off! That might be *exciting!!!*

KC: If your business takes off, you're going to make more money, work fewer hours, and have more time to spend with the people that you love - your friends and family.

Linking - Higher Rankings & More Visitors

TC: A lot of people tell me, "I've heard that there's no such thing as free marketing on the Internet any more." What's your take on that?

KC: I hear that a lot. The thing is, there *is* still free marketing on the Internet only it's not what people think. It's not anything fancy or razzle-dazzle or anything like that, it's not one of those new-founded programs that you get by bulk e-mail.

One of the vast and most effective ways to make money on the Internet is by using a concept called *linking strategies*. I've actually written a whole course on this based on things that I've done. You can check it out at *LinkingStrategies.com*

There's a piece of software called Zeus that you can download from my site at *ScientificMarketing.com/zeus* This software enables you to get hundreds of other sites in your same category to link back to you, all for free, and the software handles almost 99% of the work.

TC: Why would someone want other sites linking back to them, Kirt?

KC: One of the huge benefits of having sites link back to you is that you get the traffic from those links, right? That's the obvious thing.

The second thing is that most of the search engines, especially the big search engines like Google and Alta Vista, now rely on a thing called link popularity. When they get two sites submitted to them, site A and site B, they have no idea which site is better - in whatever subjective terms "better" means. All they can do is look at each site and calculate how many other sites are linked to it. Whichever site has more links must be the better site, right?

TC: Well, it sounds logical.

High Ranking Doesn't Require Big Money

KC: It's easy search engine logic. As an example, one of the most common phrases people use to search for diamonds on the Internet is "loose diamonds." For my diamond brokerage business, my site was ranked number two on the Google search engine under the phrase "Loose Diamonds" for about six months. The thing is, I never even submitted my web page to Google. They found it by themselves through all the links I had out on the Internet.

TC: I know people who spend $2,000 to $20,000 a month just to keep their site in the top search engine rankings.

KC: For a while, the site that was number three on the Google listing for that exact phrase ("loose diamonds") was a company called *BlueNile.com*, which is funded by $20 million in venture capital. They do exactly the same thing that I did, they sell loose diamonds on the Internet.

Better Service From The Little Guy

TC: So you're telling me the little guy really can compete with huge companies and make a big fortune on the Internet?

KC: Exactly. The Internet is a fantastic opportunity for the little guy, the mom and pop business, to compete with the big guys.

TC: Why is that so? This is especially important, since most of our listeners actually are little guys.

KC: For the most part, people like buying from little guys, from the mom and pop businesses that specialize in one specific thing instead of trying to sell everything under the sun. Most mom and pop business owners are not trying to be like *Amazon.com* They're just trying to sell one specific thing and they know everything there is to know about that thing.

If you go into a Wal-Mart and want to ask a specific question about a product they carry, no one in the store that can really tell you anything specific about that product.

On the other hand, try asking questions at a store that specifically sells only one thing. For example, if you go into a custom-tailored suit shop and ask a question about suits, you can bet they're going to have more answers than you want to hear. They'll have all kinds of information about what you need to know about that suit, why one suit is better than the other, all that sort of thing.

Good Service Leads To Repeat Business

TC: So you're saying people like to buy where they feel like they are a significant factor, or they can get service, or get a high touch?

KC: That's exactly what you do on the Internet. You get repeat visits, and repeat traffic from buyers.

TC: That's repeat money, isn't it?

KC: Exactly.

Buy A Business, Not A Plan or "Potential"

TC: Kirt, we'd like to keep you here until we get your juiciest secrets that could help us do the same thing - buy a struggling business for pennies, amp it up with some common-sense Internet marketing, and sell out quickly for a small fortune.

You said earlier we should go to eBay, but what do we look for? How do we size up a prospective purchase? Have you got any advice we could use to make sure we're getting a good deal?

KC: Of course. Here's the biggie... Make sure you're actually buying a *business*. You don't want to buy a copy of a business or some information about a business. A lot of people on eBay sell what I call "template businesses." They have some successful business and they're trying to sell you their business plan.

You'll want to buy a business that's up and running and making money. Watch out for the *P* word, "Potential." A lot of times people try to sell things or businesses based on potential. They say, "This has the potential to make hundreds of thousands of dollars a year."

What do we care about that? Jack squat. You want to buy a business that's already up and running and making money. That's a critical piece of advice.

Where To Find Information And Businesses For Sale

Check out eBay, *Businesses for Sale*, or *Websites for Sale*. There's a few other web sites that you can check out. A really good one is *BizBuySell.com* That's more of a business brokerage listing but it has a really cool feature which allows you to search for businesses that are relocateable businesses - meaning it doesn't matter where you live. Those are usually Internet businesses.

As a last resource to getting your feet wet, consider chatting with some people in the industry of buying web businesses. *GetHighForums.com* has a discussion board where you talk back and forth about buying web sites and purchasing different online businesses.

TC: Of course, as a first resource, everyone should check out your own web site, *www.BuyingWebBusinesses.com*

KC: Yeah, you better!

Purchase Price Should Be Based On Net Profits

There are some really critical points to remember, besides the obvious ones I told you before. What you're looking for, and this may sound ludicrous but time will bear it out - is to purchase a business for an amount equaling four to six months of the net profit of that business.

Anything over that, with the current economic climate we're in, and you're paying too much.

That said, it's not like you're going to go out and be able to buy a hundred of these businesses. You're going to have to do a little bit of foot work. There are hundreds of businesses out there that you can purchase for an amount equaling four to six months of their net profit.

Do you know what that means, Ted? What if you don't change anything on their site? What if you don't do a single thing different than they've been doing? How long will it take to earn your money back?

TC: I like your strategies, Kirt. Four to six months!

KC: Four to six months!!

TC: Then you'll be in the green stuff.

KC: Right. If you're too scared to even try changing anything, that's fine, don't. Make all your money back in four to six months, then, after you own the business free and clear, experiment all you want.

Product Pricing

That rule will save you all kinds of frustration and agony. There are a lot of different things you should be looking for when you buy a business. One of the things you want to look for, ideally, is a business with a high-ticket product that sells for over $100. A product that sells for under $100 and requires shipping can be kind of a drag after a while. It's ideal if you have a product that sells for over $100, or even better, something that's downloadable like software or an information product. Those are perfect.

TC: There's no shipping on that. No handling? No hassle? Right?

KC: Exactly.

How To Get Rich On The Internet

TC: Today we've enjoyed talking with our guest Kirt Christensen, a young man of 28 years, who has made a lot of money by buying struggling Internet businesses, applying some common-sense marketing procedures, then selling them for tremendous amounts of profit in a very short time.

What did he share that you could learn from? He shared that a lot of his big successes came when he wrote a sales letter, or improved a sales letter. He mentioned changing a headline and increasing the percentages. He even mentioned raising the price on a product to make the value perception consistent with the product description. He talked about sequential autoresponders, e-mail that goes out automatically after a person has made an inquiry or joined an e-zine list.

> *Most of the Internet Marketing friends I have earn more on a good morning than their friends earn in 5 months on the job.*
> *- Ted Ciuba*

Kirt also talked about playing with the elements of the offer. His software sales jumped after he added a thirty-day guarantee, meaning people were afraid when no guarantee was offered. He talked about the importance of using a 24/7 live answering service instead of forwarding all the calls to voice mail. For a few bucks a month - that's another valuable Internet marketing technique.

Kirt talked about designing a course, which for his business was how to select diamonds, used in conjunction with an autoresponder that gives you the opportunity to stay in contact with customers. He also recommended using a linking strategy, and doing it scientifically and easily with the Zeus software he mentioned, so you can increase incoming traffic to your site and get higher ratings on the search engines.

Kirt wrapped it up by giving us the real benefit of his expertise - how to buy Internet businesses, what percentages and ratios to look for. The important thing is not to purchase a business for an amount exceeding four to six months of the net profit of that business.

This might be your new angle for you to get rich on the Internet. Instead of starting up a business and suffering through the development period, buy a struggling business that you know has promise, optimize the marketing, then make some very good money - very quickly!

If you buy a business on eBay, please let us know how you did.

Special thanks to the contributors to this show...

*Kirt Christensen * www.BuyingWebBusinesses.com*
*Ted Ciuba * www.InstantInternetMarketing.com*

If you enjoyed this interview, there's more just like this!
Tune into *www.InternetMarketingInterviews.com*

Other resources to supercharge your progress!
www.GetRichOnTheInternet.com
www.GetRichOnTheInternet.com/seminars
www.AutoPilotRiches.com
www.KillerWebCopy.com
www.ProtegeProgram.com
www.MailOrderInTheInternetAge.com
www.LowCostInternetAdvertising.com
www.PrePaidLegal.com/go/parthenon

Information Marketing
The Secret, Easy, Insider Way To Wealth
On The Internet

Chapter 10

Ted Ciuba *Interviews Jonathan Mizel*

Everywhere you turn people are getting rich on the Internet!

And It's Not Just The "Giants" Like Microsoft

Jonathan Mizel was in direct response marketing before the Internet burst onto the scene. He was there; he saw the Internet happening, he caught the vision, he jumped into the play, then he started teaching others how to do it.

As a matter of fact, he has instructed and guided some of the largest companies into their Internet success. I'm talking about companies you recognize, like Microsoft, Intel, American Express. If those heavyweights go to Jonathan Mizel to get the goods on winning Internet marketing techniques, I think you and I are in for a good show on how anyone can get a strategy to create income online!

Ted Ciuba (TC): Jonathan Mizel, welcome to *How To Get Rich On The Internet.* We are so excited that you're here.

Jonathan Mizel (JM): I'm really excited to be here. You said something a minute ago that I want to expand on. A lot of people think they need to be the size of Microsoft, Intel, or American Express to make money on the Internet. The fact is, it's usually the big companies that spend years losing money on the Internet before they finally turn a profit.

How You Can Make Money Quickly
Without A Big Investment

A lot of what we do and teach has to do with teaching companies and existing businesses how to put their business online, how to increase their profits.

I'm going to talk about something I think everyone will be very interested in, how anyone can start marketing on the Internet quickly and easily by selling a specific kind of product. I'll tell you, it's *information products*, information-based products. That's how I got started and how many of my friends got started.

Frankly, if the big companies had started out using the techniques we're going to talk about today, they would have reached profitability a lot sooner than they did. A lot of businesses, such as WebVan and others, spent billions and billions of dollars and couldn't pull out even one dollar of profit. We're going to talk about how you can spend almost no money and start making a profit very, very quickly. Does that sound good?

TC: I think everyone listening is on your side.

Anyone Can Get Started Marketing On The Internet
Quickly And Easily

JM: Okay, good. It's not even about making big money - billions or even millions. A lot of people are just looking for an extra $500 or $1,000 a month. A lot of people who have jobs are making $2,000, $3,000, or $5,000 a month. It's not a very difficult process to come up with that much income and that much revenue every month. Man, if you make $5,000 or $10,000 a month that will change your life in and of itself. You know what I'm saying?

TC: I think most of our listeners would agree with you on that one, Jonathan.

Direct Response Marketing: Generate Leads, Work With Interested Prospects

JM: Let me tell you how I started, just to give you some background. Like a lot of people, I had a job. In 1987 I was selling life insurance and other insurance to lawyers and doctors. We used a process called "direct marketing" to do that. Instead of picking up the phone or going out and knocking on doors, we would send out letters to people. Anyone who called us was already interested.

That's the key to direct marketing: developing hot, qualified leads who are already interested when they call you, visit your web site, or request your information. That's a very important concept to remember.

I did not like the corporate world, so in 1989 I started selling information products. My very first book was one I wrote myself; it was about 40 pages long. I made about $10,000 my first year. It wasn't a big seller and it did not change my life, but, you know what? It got me started.

I Don't Like To Work, Do You?

Now, Ted, I must confess that I don't really like to work. That's why I was not cut out for the corporate world, getting up every morning, going into the office, putting on a suit, doing the meetings.

TC: Well, you ought to have a lot of company in our listening audience, because even though most people have to work, they don't want to.

> *Make $5,000 or $10,000 a month and that will change your life in and of itself.*
> *- Jonathan Mizel*

JM: You've got to do something; you've got to contribute to the world. There's that universal thing. I think Napoleon Hill said, "You can't get something back unless you give something."

I just choose to give something in a highly-efficient manner that suits my lifestyle as opposed to my boss' lifestyle.

Some people call me lazy. Frankly, I like to save my challenges for things like ski slopes and scuba diving. I'm calling from Hawaii today, where I can see whales out my window. I could never do that when I was stuck in a cubicle working my butt off.

You Can Make A Genuine Contribution To The World In Your Own Business

Running an Internet business has really been a wonderful process for me, my family, and the other people I love and work with. Even more so, it's allowed me - and this is a very important thing - it's allowed me to contribute much more to the world than I was able to do before. Not only am I making good money (and we make way more money than we need to live on; we live in Hawaii in a big house overlooking the ocean; it's not cheap to live here) but also, the impact that we have on people - and the impact that anyone of you who are listening to this could have on a large group of people - is significant.

If you're going to a job everyday, all you're doing is pleasing your boss. When you set up your own business where you are pleasing hundreds or thousands of customers, instead of having a boss whose butt you have to kiss, you create a process where you are building something really significant. The number of people you are affecting, whose lives you are changing, who you're giving information to... You're having an impact on people that's far more significant than you have with a job being an anonymous wage slave every day.

TC: Significantly...

Information Products Are The Way To Go

Okay, Jonathan, give us the low-down on *Information Marketing*.

JM: There are a lot of things you can sell on the Internet. If you have an existing business, you should probably be on the Internet generating leads and making sales. If you don't know where to start, if you have a business and you're looking for something else to do, or if you don't even have a business and you're just looking to get started, in my opinion, the very best thing you can sell is information. Let me explain why.

Information Products Are Easy To Create

First of all, information products are very easy to create. All you do is pull out your brain and your typewriter or computer, whatever you use to write, and start writing. It's not difficult. This is what we call "intellectual property," because it's something that you create that comes out of your head.

If they're not a good writer some people will be saying, "I can't write. I can't do that." We hire people to write for us. We sell a couple products, actually five, and two of them I didn't even create. I came up with the outline and put together the marketing plan for them. As for the product itself, I just paid somebody a few hundred

> *It's not difficult to come up with a product idea. I'll even tell you how you can get a product idea for free.*
> *- Jonathan Mizel*

bucks to write for me. It's not hard.

There are also products that you can get the rights to or products that are in the public domain, like books that are over 75 years old or information put out by the government. We've got a client who sells government information that he gets from that Pueblo, Colorado place. He packages that stuff up, wraps it up in an e-book, and sells that. So, it's not difficult to come up with a product idea. I'll even tell you how you can get a product idea for free.

You Can Live Wherever You Want!

Second of all, you can live and work anywhere in the world. People sometimes tell me they have to live in California or Ohio or New Jersey. I like all those places, there's nothing good or bad about any of them, and I don't want to make any judgments. What I hate is when people say they *have* to live there.

TC: You left that behind a long time ago with the cyber lifestyle, didn't you?

JM: It bugs me when people say, "I *have* to live here because that's where the jobs are, that's where the customers are, that's where my boss is, or that's where my company is."

> *It doesn't matter where you live; just that you have an Internet connection!*

TC: It seems to me that you'd rather live in Hawaii, eh, Jonathan?

JM: I'd rather live in Hawaii.

We were going to head to Europe and live there for a few years, but when we came to Hawaii on vacation last year, my girlfriend said, "Hey, let's move here." Just like that we said, "Okay, let's do it."

Why not?

My servers are in Maryland, my order processing center is in Washington State, some of our technicians are in California, and we've got people in Colorado. I've got people all over the world who are working with us - programmers in England and other people in Sweden. It doesn't matter where I live; all that matters is that I have an Internet connection.

TC: Exactly.

JM: That's the key. Right now, while I'm doing this interview, I'm looking down at the ocean and know that my girlfriend is out there swimming with dolphins. She couldn't do that unless we lived here in Hawaii.

Make Money Like A Rock Star

TC: Jonathan, I saw you at an Internet marketing event a couple months ago. I heard you wow the crowd, talking about making money like a rock star.

JM: Let me explain what I was talking about. It goes back to selling information products. If you look at what rock stars do, they really sell information products. Now, they sell it in the form of CDs and stuff like that, but they only have to produce the CD one time. That's really the key. Produce your best-selling product, whether it's a CD, a book, an information product, a software or whatever. Maybe it's something you just got the rights to....

Produce It Once, The Money Rolls In Daily

The point is, you can produce it one time and sell it for years. That gives you what we call "leverage," financial leverage, marketing leverage. Instead of having to wake up and figure out what you're going to do today, or having to kiss someone's butt, or even worse, having to work a service trading dollars for hours, you just wake up and you have more money than you had the night before.

> **Make Money Like A Rock Star**
> *Produce it one time and sell it for years.*
> - Jonathan Mizel

AutoPilotRiches! You Don't Even Have To Go To The Bank Anymore!

We've all heard the phrase, "Make money while you sleep." It's true. Another funny thing is the phrase, "Laugh all the way to the bank." Well, you don't even have to go to the bank anymore! The money comes in automatically now. In our office, we just laugh, then we go down and swim with the dolphins.

TC: Wait a minute! You said you woke up and had money. You said during the break you checked your orders. They must be those automatic deposits processed through your merchant account. You don't even have to go to the bank because it's all electronic. Is that right?

Digital Delivery - The Ultimate Way To Make Money Quickly

JM: That's right, Ted. Let me explain how it used to be, then it will probably make sense. In the old days, if we wanted to do a promotion we'd have to call a magazine and try to get a good price on an ad.

We'd send our ad to the magazine and two months later they'd run that ad. Thirty days later, we'd get a bunch of leads then we'd send out a bunch of direct mail. Maybe we'd get some sales, maybe some orders. It just didn't jive with my lifestyle because it took too long.

To me, the most valuable thing is not money, it's *time*. I can't stand to waste time! What's beautiful about the Internet is that you can deliver your product digitally. In other words, customers buy your products and enter in their credit card information. You don't even have to deal with bad credit cards since they simply don't go through. When the card is good, the transaction goes through and the customer is automatically taken to a page where they get to download your product. It's automatic, digital delivery, and it's an unbelievable way to not only make money, but make money quickly.

Test Your Markets Quickly, Easily, And Inexpensively

Here's an example. We recently launched a new product using one of the new pay-per-click search engines called *Overture.com* Using this search engine, we generated a bunch of traffic and determined in only four or five days that this product idea was good - instead of the four or five months it used to take.

What the Internet has done, especially for selling information products, is give you the ability to move very quickly and to test a bunch of ideas at once to see whether or not they work. Not everything you try is going to work right away, some need a refinement process. The problem with the old system was that if something didn't work, I couldn't change things for two months. I had to wait to put another ad in the magazine and see if that one worked.

> ### No Place But The Internet!
> *I sent out 35,000 e-mails... I sent them an e-mail – it cost me nothing. Now think about that trying to be able to contact 35,000 people for free, in any other place, besides the Internet.*
> -Terry Dean

TC: Not to mention that it costs a fortune to buy a magazine ad.

JM: Ted, what you wrote in your book, *Mail Order In The Internet Age,* made those differences clear! That's a great book, by the way. I love mail order. As you say, all we've done is taken those tried, tested, and proven mail order principles and applied them towards the Internet. That's really the key.

TC: I couldn't agree more wholeheartedly.

People Don't Want To Buy A Book

Jonathan, what makes Information marketing so lucrative, especially on the 'Net? Can't people get everything they need by visiting a bookstore?

> *The point is, they want information, they want it quickly, and they're buying it on the Internet.*

JM: It's interesting how many products people are buying digitally right now because going to the bookstore is a pain in the butt, you have to wait in line.

People want their information *now*. I think what's important about information products is that people want convenience. They're not looking for a book. Nobody wakes up in the morning saying, "I need another book today." If they wake up saying anything, they're saying something like, "I need bigger muscles" or "I need to stop this arthritis pain." They don't care how they get the information. They'll take it in an e-book, they'll take it in a report, they'll take it on a web page. The point is, they want information, they want it quickly, and they're buying it on the Internet.

Get Started Quickly With Affiliate Programs

Let me talk about how you can start selling an information product. There's a very easy way for anyone to start selling online. A wonderful new process came out a few years ago called affiliate programs. An affiliate program is a reseller or distributor type of program, if you want to call it that, only it's all done on the Internet and they're almost always free to join.

TC: Go to *InternetMarketingInterviews.com* There you can sign up for our affiliate program. Sign up and see how it works. It's free.

The Power Of "Pay-Per-Click" Search Engines

JM: That's great! This is the case with our affiliate program and almost every other affiliate program out there... They are free to join. The affiliate gives you a web page and all you do is advertise that web page. The affiliate program takes the orders, sends everything out, does the customer service, and processes the credit card. You don't need to do anything as a reseller or as an affiliate, except send traffic to your site. You can do that through *Overture.com* or *FindWhat.com* or one of the other *pay-per-click search engines* that actually allow you to buy traffic for pennies then earn twenty, thirty, or forty cents a visitor. There's some significant money to be made.

Living From Affiliate Programs: The Aussie "Hermit"

One really great site is called *AssociatePrograms.com* Have you ever been there?

TC: I recommend everyone visit it!

JM: This is a funny story. Allan Gardyne splits his time between Australia and New Zealand. I think he's only been to the States once or twice. He's a very nice guy who had an idea to put this web site up. I don't know how much money he's making, but I guarantee you it's in the six figures annually.

TC: Exactly, and he's well respected in the United States.

JM: He's very well respected in the US, but see, he just had an idea. He decided, "Man, associate programs look like the way!" (Or something like that...) He put up the site which was just a listing of sites with affiliate programs.

At that time, there were only five or ten sites with affiliate programs. Mine was one of the ones he put up, and let me tell you, Allan's idea just took off. He gets thousands and thousands of visitors to his site each day. He's got a very big newsletter, he's well respected, and even more important, he gets to live where he wants. He lives in Northeast Australia which is apparently some desert-like area. He likes to be alone. He doesn't want to live in a big city. Allan has the time of his life, and *that's* the kind of lifestyle we look forward to when we start selling information products.

TC: And that's exactly what he's selling. He's selling information, his ideas, opinions, and some gathered information. He's just selling that, isn't he?

JM: That's exactly what he's doing, and it's so easy. What's so beautiful is that he's promoting products. He's got a list of people who come to his web site, he promotes the products, and he doesn't do any work except cash the checks.

Internet Insider Secret

A Quick-Start No-Fail Way To Enter The Internet

TC: A lot of people have gotten started with affiliate programs, and it's an excellent way to get started.

I also encounter people who say, "I have a product idea. I've already got a market." Do you have any advice to help people who have their own product?

JM: Yeah. I'm going to make it real simple, because you can spend a lot of time, energy, and money developing sites and getting set up with e-commerce. I'm going to tell you the absolute easiest way to get going.

Before I explain that, I want to go back to affiliate programs for a minute and tell you a little story about why I like to use affiliate programs, even before I develop my own product.

Sometimes when we develop a product or come up with an idea, as I've said before, it's not a winner right out of the gate. It takes a while to get an offer "tight," as we call it. You've got to get the right offer and the right audience. It's got to look good. There are actually a hundred things you've got to do right, as opposed to just starting out trying to get all those things right.

That's why I like to use an affiliate program. Let me explain. We have a product which you can check out at *PersonalAndPrivate.com* It's a book and a software package on how to protect your privacy on the Internet. That was a significant project for us to come out with. We had to develop the product, develop a sales letter, and deal with the e-commerce and all that stuff. I wasn't really sure the market was out there. That's the case with a lot of products. People think their idea is great, but then they launch it and it doesn't make a million bucks. By then they've put all their time and energy into it.

What I like to do before launching a product, and this is what we did with the *PersonalAndPrivate.com* site, is go out and find similar products. In other words, we found products that were already developed. The product was done, the sales letter was done, the e-commerce, order system, and all that stuff was done. All we had to do was drive traffic to that web page and see if people bought the product.

Select Your Test Marketing Sites

Believe it or not, we found about one hundred products with affiliate programs similar to the one we wanted to sell. We took the best five and test marketed them by using some of our traffic-generating techniques. Using search engines, newsgroups, and e-mail and stuff, I drove traffic and visitors to someone else's web page to see whether or not the idea I had would fly. We were using someone else's product, and - even better - somebody else's dime. I was not about to spend whatever it cost, probably a couple thousand bucks, to launch a product unless I knew I was going to make my money back. I think it was Mark Twain who said, "I'm far less concerned with the return *on* my investment than

I am with the return *of* my investment." Before we invest any money, we need to make sure that we have a pretty good chance of succeeding.

Coasting Into A Homer

Once we had determined ... *Yes, this is a good idea for a product... Yes, this product will sell... Yes, here's the way we generate traffic... Then* I spent the time and energy to actually roll out my product. And it happens to be a great product.

TC: The important thing here is the "affiliate testing *process*" you followed *before* you invested substantial time, energy, and money in a product that may or may not have produced a substantial return.

At the point you entered with your own product, you *knew* it would work.

Make Sure Your Good Idea Is a Product People Want

JM: There are a lot of great products sitting on shelves. The important thing is, do people *want* those products? Before you develop your own product, find a similar product and test it. You can search for similar products at places like *AssociatePrograms.com - ClickBank.com - IBill.com* or any search engine. Enter "affiliate," "affiliate programs," or "associate programs," and you'll find hundreds and hundreds of sites that have affiliate programs and products you can plug into without any risk or money. That's what we recommend before launching a product.

TC: That really is a stroke of genius, listeners, made possible by the Internet. I hope you heard what Jonathan said. He said you can find someone in a comparable market, with a comparable product, and *test* your idea, quickly and cheaply. You're getting real insider info. It's great! Jonathan, thank you for sharing that.

JM: We do it all the time. Look, there are a lot of great ideas for products, in fact, I see them all the time. There are so many e-books and information products out there. Just try it out beforehand. If the test works, go ahead and put the time and energy into your product. If it doesn't work, thank God all we had to do was spend twenty or thirty dollars and a few days of testing. I'd rather spend a few days and a few bucks than a lifetime falling in love with my product only to discover there is no market for it.

Quick-Start To Internet Million$:
A Web Host And An Autoresponder

Suppose you want to set up a site, you already have your own product, you've done some testing and determined people might be interested in your product, and it looks like you could write a similar sales letter - you could create a similar process with e-commerce and all that stuff, test it out with an affiliate program, and *if* it works, move forward.

I'm going to show you the easiest way to do that. It's so simple.

There are really three things you need...

The first thing you need is a web host account. You need somewhere to put your web page. I recommend either Verio or any big hosting company. The cost is usually about twenty to thirty dollars a month.

Second, you need an autoresponder. Let me tell you what that is. An autoresponder is automatic e-mail that follows up with customers over a period of days, weeks, months after you collect their information.

TC: Let me give an example... If you go to *www.InstantInternetMarketing.com* you'll get an offer to subscribe to an e-zine, which is our free online magazine. You will immediately get a personalized response from the *Internet Insider's E-Bulletin*.

I don't have to send the response, it's done automatically and it automatically sends follow-up messages out over the next ten or twelve weeks.

JM: It follows up with customers automatically, so you've got to have an autoresponder.

Getting Set Up: Use ClickBank For Easy E-Commerce

Third, here's the real quick-start secret:

Forget all the stuff you learned about order forms and expensive e-commerce. ClickBank. That's all you need to know - *ClickBank.com* It costs just fifty dollars to get set up and it's so easy and cheap.

There's more! *ClickBank.com* has a whole bunch of resellers ready to sell your product and they have a system where you can actually recruit people to sell your product through their software and their system. They charge fifteen percent. Whenever we have a product that just needs to be launched, because time is really of the essence - and that's the key, Ted, you've got to move quickly - I say ClickBank. Go to *ClickBank.com*

You can also use another company called *iBill.com* which is similar to ClickBank. The point is, use one of these third-party services.

To Be A Guru, Delegate The "Techie"

If you are writing a book about how to lose weight, you don't want to be an e-commerce expert, you want to be a weight loss expert. Right?

TC: That's absolutely right.

JM: If you want to be a gardening expert or a cooking expert, or whatever the subject matter is about, *that's* what you want to be an expert in. You don't want to be an expert at e-commerce. Let someone else do that.

Once you know your project is going to work, you can very easily set everything up and spend the money to promote your product. But I say spend the money *after*, not before. Spend it *after* you know your idea is going to work.

How To Get Rich On The Internet

TC: Though he never used the words, it's obvious where Jonathan Mizel comes from... He has taken us to the heart of the "Internet Lifestyle."

Sell *information products*, deliver them digitally over the Internet. Test you ideas quickly for chump change, roll out the ones that work. Work online a little bit, earn an obscene income. Live where you want, how you want.

It's a formula for a life of fulfillment and contribution.

At the basis of his marketing plans is a solid grounding in direct response marketing: generate leads, work with interested prospects. Online is the easiest, quickest, cheapest marketing arena on the planet today. It can make you a fortune quickly. A marketer's paradise!

He revealed how you can *know* in a matter of days for $30 if a project you're considering investing time, energy, and money in will pay off or not. This is a major secret, revealed from the mind of a scientific marketer with experience.

It's the *Information Age*, and you don't really need anything other than what you received in the interview to get started. Jonathan revealed how you can get started tonight, surfing *ClickBank.com*

Apply what you learn here and you, too, can get rich on the Internet!

Special thanks to the contributors to this show...

*Jonathan Mizel * www.CyberWave.com*
*Ted Ciuba * www.InstantInternetMarketing.com*

If you enjoyed this interview, there's more just like this!
Tune into *www.InternetMarketingInterviews.com*

Other resources to supercharge your progress!
  www.GetRichOnTheInternet.com
  www.GetRichOnTheInternet.com/seminars
  www.AutoPilotRiches.com
  www.KillerWebCopy.com
  www.ProtegeProgram.com
  www.MailOrderInTheInternetAge.com
  www.LowCostInternetAdvertising.com
  www.PrePaidLegal.com/go/parthenon

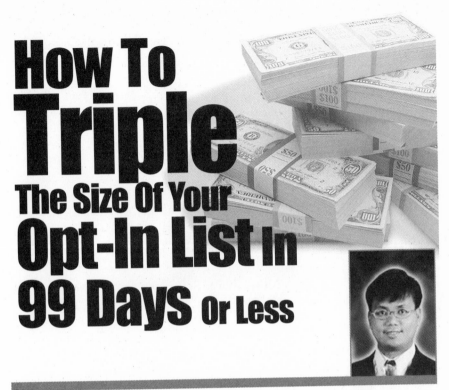

How To Triple The Size Of Your Opt-In List In 99 Days Or Less

Chapter 11

Ted Ciuba *Interviews* Joel Christopher

I first met our next guest at Carl Galletti's amazing *Internet Marketing SuperConference*. For the story on that one see *www.GetRichOnTheInternet.com/imsc* He was running around, meeting gurus, meeting other people, exchanging numbers, exchanging e-mail addresses, talking, getting ideas. He had hunger in his eyes.

I *do* recommend that same strategy for *you*.

Why? Perhaps the next episode will clarify...

Joel and I shared the stage a few months back at *TheInternet BootCamp.com* He didn't get there by accident. He was listening to the people who knew what to do and how to do. He took what he learned, implemented it, gained a quick success thereby, and showed up on stage.

Today Joel Christopher is an up-and-coming marketing star. He developed a system to make his own money and his own Internet revenue. He had such tremendous success that he developed a system so *you* can triple your online mailing list in ninety-nine days or less. Phenomenal! That's what he's presenting to you today.

By the way, that's how easy it can be to develop a product. Solve a problem and systematize what you did. Bingo! Presto! Follow the leader!

> *He took what he learned, implemented it, gained a quick success thereby, and showed up on stage.*
> *- Ted Ciuba*

Ted Ciuba (TC): Without any further ado, Joel Christopher, welcome to *How To Get Rich On The Internet!*

Joel Christopher (JC): Thank you, Ted. I appreciate your inviting me here.

TC: Joel, you've got a lot to share. Before we get into how to triple your list in ninety-nine days, which is a phenomenal feat, tell us a little about who you are and how you actually got started, and even why you wanted to get started.

"If I Can Do It, Anyone Can"

JC: Thank you, Ted. I'm a perfect example of "If I can do it, anyone can." My background is a far cry from marketing, a far cry from computers, or the Internet.

I was a touchy-feely, non-techie physical therapist for thirteen years. My biggest goal back then was to retire by the age of forty-five. I knew I needed to have a business of my own to make real money, so I started my own therapy business. I quickly discovered having my own therapy business, where I had to be there to make money, was *not* the way to go.

Using the Internet, I found a way to own a business that I can run from anywhere, whenever I want. I don't have to have any overhead or employees, and I don't have to travel. I can stay at my house. I'm actually an alien from the Philippines whose second language is English, so if I can do it, anyone else can, too.

> *Using the Internet I found a way to own a business that I can run from anywhere, whenever I want. I don't have to have any overhead or employees, and I don't have to travel. I can stay at my house.*
> *- Joel Christopher*

TC: Very inspiring. You knew you wanted to be free from hassles and restraints, and make a lot of money quickly. So the Internet was your logical choice.

Build Your List And They Will Come

JC: Absolutely. Two years ago, when I started, I was looking for a web site that spoke my language as a newbie netpreneur. I couldn't find one, so I started one. I even started a list of my own, which is the smartest thing I've done in the last two years. Since then, I've built the list to about forty-thousand.

In the last two years I've been to eleven live Internet marketing BootCamps and seminars. The goal for that is to cut down my learning curve and learn from the experts themselves firsthand. I've learned from them.

The number-one thing the experts told me was "build a list." *Build a list.* What was interesting was that I didn't find a system that was simple enough to allow any newbie to start, grow, build, and explode their list. About one hundred and twenty days ago, I gave myself a ninety-day challenge of doubling my list from ten thousand to twenty thousand.

Let me give you a little background before I continue. I did a survey to my list, which at that time was ten thousand, and I asked what their biggest challenge was. Sixty-seven percent responded with "How to build a list." I went to another BootCamp, a Hawaiian lifestyle summit, and talked to the pioneers of Internet marketing – Corey Rudl, Jonathan Mizel, and Stephen Mahaney.

Do you know what they said? If their business burned down that day, the only thing they would take from the burning building or house would be their database. In fact, Corey Rudl said he values it so much that if any of his employees steals his database, he'll sue them for $25 million. That's the value of his list.

I took the challenge and I gave myself ninety days to do it. Luckily enough, and with persistence, I found a way to actually *triple* my opt-in list in ninety-nine days. I'll tell you more about that later.

TC: That's a phenomenal accomplishment, Joel. By the way, I want to make sure that people catch the significance of your survey. You asked your list *what they wanted.* When you decided to provide the information they wanted, you already had buyers. You knew who wanted your information product because you'd asked them. That's a great way to make a product, my man.

JC: Yes, sir. That's it.

TC: Then how *do* you build your list?

The Six Benefits Of An E-Mail List

JC: I'm going to share the twelve list building steps. Before I do that, though, let me explain the six important benefits of having a list; why it's valuable.

The first benefit of having a list is, as you said, *free market research*. The beauty about having a list is that instead of spending a lot of money on mailing and waiting a long time for the results, you can get results instantly. I did a survey recently and within an hour, I had hundreds of replies. My customers, my subscribers, told me what they wanted to buy, how much they're willing to pay for it, and when they'll buy it. That's absolutely amazing.

The second benefit that I found in building or having a list is that you build your *credibility as an expert* in your field or niche market.

The third thing is that you build a *strong relationship with a huge number of people, almost instantaneously*. Relationships are very, very important. That's part of the key to making a lot of money on the Internet. Before anyone will buy from you, they have to know you, like you, and trust you. Having a list is your key to building a strong relationship.

The fourth benefit is you are creating a *system to generate and follow up on leads or prospects, which are your subscribers, and convert them to paying customers*. That's what it really is about. It's about making money and building this relationship with your list.

The fifth benefit is making even more money. We do that by developing *multiple streams of income*, as Robert Allen would say.

Robert talks about creating multiple streams of income, usually by selling your product in ventures with other product owners, doing affiliate programs, and reselling rights.

For me, the most important part or benefit is the sixth benefit. When you have a list you are ensured of a *guaranteed monthly income as long as you regularly provide good content and good offers to your list.* You're virtually guaranteed a permanent monthly income.

For example, our friend and my mentor, Terry Dean, who has been your guest on this show, made $33,245 in seventy-two hours - three days. Another of your guests, Robert Allen, made $94,532 in twenty-four hours, and that was by contacting only 11,000 subscribers!

That's the value of having a list.

TC: You're saying that both Terry's accomplishment and Robert's accomplishment came about because they mailed an offer to their list?

JC: Absolutely. That's exactly what they did. They made an offer to their opt-in list, which is permission-based marketing. The members of their list gave them permission to send them offers and good content.

TC: Oh, by the way, Terry did it again... Even better this time. On stage he pulled in $72,930 in twenty-four hours. An ex-Little Caesar's delivery driver.

TC & JC: Amazing the power of a list!

How to Build Your E-Mail List

TC: Those are exciting benefits. We're really anxious how to build our list.

JC: Let's get started.

First, you've got to know *how to target your market*. How do you do that? The first thing you do is look inside yourself and determine what your passion is - what you're interested in, what you're an expert at as compared to the average Joe.

For example, let's say you like golf and you like making money. That would be an interest. Do market research and see if there's money in that market. Go to *Google.com* and search for the keyword "making money online," or "golf," or "left-handed golfers." That's your passion. After you've done that, see what products are available with that keyword. After you've collected the keywords, go to *www.WordSpot.com* where you can subscribe to their free service. Using their service, look for the high-ranking keywords. From there, you can basically know that your target market is a paying market, it's a hot trend.

Another way to do that is to find the books and the topics that are being discussed at *Amazon.com* and other places like that, like *Borders.com*

When you do that, what you do is start with the first item which is targeting your niche market. You come out with a catchy name for your list or your newsletter. That's really what you're trying to do, Ted, come up with a newsletter... Come up with a catchy name. For example, my domain name is *SuccessAccess.com* And because at the time, coming up high in directories was important, I reversed the words and called it *AccessToSuccess* e-zine.

The next step, which is also part of part one, is to come up with a tag line, what Jay Abraham calls the Unique Selling Proposition (USP) that brands your web site or your e-zine as unique.

TC: If I remember correctly, your tag line was "No nonsense net guide for newbie netpreneurs." Is that right?

JC: You got it, sir.

TC: Quick, short, sweet, and has the benefits... Identifies it... Good... Captures and keeps your target market's attention.

JC: Number two: after you are done targeting your market, you now want to capture the attention of your target market, which also captures their wallet, which is what you're really after.

What you do is you compel and convert them from lookers to *subscribers* or *prospects*. How do you do that? What you do is three things: Number one is write a 15-word description of your list, of your e-zine or newsletter. The next step you do within that big step, number two, is write a 30-word and then write a 100-word benefit-laden description of your e-zine or newsletter. You'll need to do them all in this step, because you're going to need them later on in the succeeding steps.

Now, you build on your USP. For example, my USP is "*Access to Success E-Zine - No-Nonsense Net Guide For Newbie Netpreneurs, The Ultimate Internet Business Success Guide For Internet Marketing Beginners.*" It's targeted, it's benefit-laden.

After you've done that, you go to step three. This is how you learn how to keep your target market in your profit pipeline. Robert Allen calls this the *wealth funnel*. I call it the *profit pipeline*. Same thing. What you do here is choose the format and frequency of your contact follow-up system, which is really what your list system is. You decide if you want to have a regular e-zine, a weekly or biweekly newsletter where you write articles every week or two. You can also do a pre-written evergreen e-zine in a box, where you have pre-written e-mails, e-zines, or mini e-zines set up for fifty-two weeks, and you upload it to an autoresponder. Because after you've written it out, you have nothing to do but rake in the money.

The third thing, which to me is the easiest way to do it, is the report or lead generation system. What you do is you take a sales letter, cut it up into seven to ten parts, and upload it to a newsletter. This one is more product-specific or business opportunity-specific. My e-zine is more of a combination of regular newsletter and the puritan evergreen e-zine in a box. Once you've decided on your format, you write three to seven follow-up e-mail messages sent by a sequential autoresponder, according to a pre-set schedule. You have to have a super autoresponder system, and I recommend *AutoPilotRiches.com*

You do this because you want to welcome your new subscribers... You want to start to build relationships with your new subscribers. There's that word again, *relationships*. Of course, you want to do this because you want to initiate the sales process by offering your lead product.

That's step three of our 12-step system, which is how to keep your target market in your profit pipeline.

Harness The Contact-Drawing Power Of Your Web Site

The fourth step, Ted, is how to harness your own web site traffic to build your e-zine list, your contact list. How do you do that? Number one, you put a sign-up form on your web site. Some people have a whole page for their e-zine sign up alone, even though it's a free offer. They still try to sell the benefits to people in terms of joining their list. I have one like that. You can even do a whole web site focused solely on your e-zine, if that's what you want.

Another variation of this is the *pop-up box*. A pop-up box is very effective for marketers to use to capture the leads or the subscribers. If you've been on the net, you've probably seen this. In fact, go to *InternetMarketingInterviews.com,* and when you leave the site a small box in your browser comes up. That's why it's called a "pop-up."

That is a sample of an exit pop-up. Now an entry pop-up is something that is displayed up-front. An example of this is actually a neat gadget that reads the e-mail and the name automatically without the visitor typing it in. It's a software that just came out called *OptInAutomater.com* A friend of mine, Ryan Deiss, from Austin, created that. That's a powerful way to build your list. So, using a sign-up form or a pop-up box is how you harness the traffic of your own web site.

Follow Up To Make More Money From Your List

The fifth step is how to make even more money from your list. Part of the basic foundation of building a huge list is doing steps one through five. It is very important to start with one through five *before* you launch your newsletter. The fifth step is how to make even more money from your list. You do that by writing three to seven subscriber follow-up e-mails for your newsletter once they subscribe. Just load them up in your autoresponder and they go out automatically.

You can also maximize your list by giving them an offer in your follow-up series. For example, the first e-mail would be a "thank you for subscribing." The second one would come out two days later, thanking them for subscribing again, and giving them the bonuses. Then third or fourth, which are sent a week later, can be an offer.

Upsell: Do You Want Fries With That?

Another way to upsell is actually on your order page. Let's say they order an e-book for $19.95 then click on "order." At that point you give them a special no-can-resist offer for the gold version. This is what we call the "Do you want fries with that?" option at *AutoPilotRiches.com*, where you sell them another e-book for a 50% discount off of, let's say, $39.95. That's a 100% increase in revenues! That's how you upsell and make more money from your list.

TC: Well, I think our listeners would identify with that pretty easily. After all, who hasn't called a $19.95 infomercial "800" number only to end up subscribing to a *monthly* auto-ship program, plus 2 free bonus videos that come with the $99 super kick-start regimen?

You catch my drift?...

JC: Absolutely.

TC: That's the great thing about the Internet. It's possible to take the greatest, most effective sales mechanisms that have ever been developed, no matter what the medium, and adapt them for the Internet.

> *It's possible to take the greatest, most effective sales mechanisms that have ever been developed, no matter what the medium, and adapt them for the Internet.*
> - *Ted Ciuba*

There's no extra effort. It's really easy to do an order upgrade on your order page and in your confirmation e-mail, and it's all automated and *personalized*. All at *no extra cost*! So you can really make more money by selling more stuff to the same customers. That's *leverage*.

And that's, of course, a principle we need to drive home to our listeners... What we're all talking about and doing about is selling more. You've got to get the first sale. But then, of course, what you're doing is saying, "Hey, there's more." Part of that "more" can actually happen, as you're describing right here, at the time of the sale.

JC: Exactly. And it's easier to sell them *now*.

TC: Because they are motivated. They're *hot*. They've already made a positive buying decision. In short: they're *sold*!

JC: Absolutely.

TC: Joel, you've just laid the foundation of what we need to build our lists. Now give us the inside scoop on actually getting those numbers into our own subscriber lists.

Reveal to us what you promised... How any of us can triple our opt-in list in 99 days or less.

JC: All right, Ted! As I said, the first five form the foundation of success in building and really expanding your list.

I compare it to a rocket launch. Most of the energy is spent in launching it. Once launched, however, the going is easy... Like friction free. That's what's going to happen with list building, so spend a lot of time on steps one through five...

Then you're ready to launch with step six. This is how you can harness the visitors of dozens of high-traffic web sites and lists, and acquire subscribers for *free*. You will notice that steps six to twelve will be free or low-cost ways to build your list, build it massively, and build it quickly.

In step number six you announce your list, your e-zine, to many web sites and announcement lists in e-zine directories. You can do that by manually submitting it to different directories but there's about 8,400 of them, which makes it a tedious process. But one smart guy named Jason Potash created a software that actually automates the whole process for you, so you can submit to all these dozens and dozens of directories. Go to *www.EZineAnnouncer.com*

In the next step, step number seven, you learn how to effectively attract thousands of targeted subscribers to your e-zine or list for free, while building your credibility at the same time. This is probably the best way to target serious customers, serious buyers, not just freeloaders. The reason for that is because when you do this step, you'll be recognized as an expert in your niche market or chosen field.

Write A Short Article Focused On Your Niche Market

Write a 300-500 word article that's focused on your niche market and is benefit-laden to your niche market. You can do this manually, as I said, to different publishers. Terry Dean, my friend and mentor, wrote the e-book *Internet X-Factor*, which includes a list of 500 publishers. For that alone, the price of the book is easily undervalued.

Remember the EZineAnnouncer in step number six? Well, guess what? They have 509 publishers that you can automatically send your articles to. That software will help you submit your articles to these 500-plus publishers.

TC: So *EZineAnnouncer.com*, that same software you said we could use to announce our e-zine to the world, can also be used to submit the 300-500 word articles we write up?

JC: Absolutely.

TC: By the way, just so nobody thinks 300-500 words is too terrible, about how long would that be on a double-spaced, typewritten page?

JC: That's probably not even two pages. It's easy to write, and here's what you do. Let's say you want to write 300 words... Just think of three benefits you want to talk about to your niche market, then write approximately fifty words to introduce the topic, fifty words for each of the three points in the body, and fifty words to finish it off. That's approximately 250 words... That gives you a little leeway to say a few additional words on any of the point you want. There's nothing to it!

If you want to have a 500-word article, just write five points.

TC: It really is that easy.

JC: Now you want to harness the traffic these directories and submissions are bringing you.

Do you remember the USP and the 15-word description you wrote in the first two steps? Well, guess what? You're going to use it here at the bottom of your newsletter.

> *Send one or two articles a month and it will grow your list effectively and massively in a short period of time.*
> *- Joel Christopher*

You write what we call the "resource box." It's a short paragraph that comes after your article that points readers to your web site. People read your article, see you as an expert, go to your web site, they sign up for your list, and they order. *You can do this.*

Send one or two articles a month and your list will grow effectively and massively in a short period of time. That's how I got started two years ago.

After you're done submitting articles, you're ready for step number eight. Actually, this is a group of steps that I clump together as more free ways to build your e-zine or opt-in list.

TC: By the way, Joel, since I saw you at *TheInternetBootCamp.com* - I noted that steps one through six are linear steps, but seven through twelve are not. They are different techniques that people can use to build their list – but they could actually be done in any order, couldn't they?

What you label as "steps" seven through twelve, for the clarification of our listeners, could really be called "ways," couldn't they?

JC: Absolutely! Thanks for bringing out that point of clarification, Ted!

Always Use A Sig File At The End Of Your Messages

On with number eight: The first component of number eight is real simple... Create a *sig file* in every e-mail you send. You should also have a sig file you can use when you post your messages in a discussion board. A sig file basically includes your name, e-mail address, a benefit-laden statement, and a link or e-mail that will subscribe someone to your list or send them to your web site. Four to six lines... That's a good sig file.

An example of that is, in my case, "The best of success, Joel Christopher, *Joel@SuccessAccess.com*" My benefit line is, "My free, downloadable co-brandable e-book is now yours to give away for free." Then I list my URL and phone number.

TC: It's that easy? Just a salutation, your e-mail, a benefit line, a URL, and a phone number?!

I count *three* ways to contact you!

JC: And make the sale!

TC: This, too, is a basic *mail order* principle, isn't it? Make sure that they've got a way to get a hold of you, have your contact information printed on everything that goes out of your office!

JC: Yes sir, absolutely.

TC: You give them *reasons* to get a hold of you.

JC: Exactly. With e-mail you're *only a click away*!

Build Your E-List Through Viral Marketing

Another free way to build your list is through *viral marketing*. What you do is give away a free co-brandable e-book, using software called *eBookGenerator.com*, created by our mutual friend Armand

Morin, who was at the BootCamp with us recently.

Using this software, you create a book and *give* it away to your subscribers.... But you also take it to the next level. How do you do that? You allow them to give it away on their site!

Why would they do that? Because you allow them to put, or embed, their own web site address on your e-book so they have a reason to give it away – it has *their* link in it!

TC: That not only builds *their* traffic, it builds *your* traffic! And everybody profits!

Word-Of-Mouth Marketing With Electronic Referrals

JC: The next idea is a little-known free service, which is really a free subscriber referral program at *ListPartners.com* It's a free, web-based software that's easy to manipulate and use, and actually allows your subscribers to refer other subscribers. You reward them by offering free ad space, money - like ten or twenty cents per name they refer, or products, such as a free special report.

What's good about it? Well, what's the best method of marketing online?

TC: It would have to be the same as offline as online. That would be word-of-mouth advertising, wouldn't it?

JC: Absolutely, and wouldn't you say that these are high-quality referrals?

TC: The best. They come pre-sold, don't they?

JC: Yeah.

Take Advantage Of Low-Cost Advertising

We're up to number nine, how to build your profits while building your list.

For the first time, I'm going to mention low-cost advertising. The concept is this: you do some low-cost advertising, using e-zine ads, solo ads and top sponsor ads, and pay-per-click search engines. How do you do that? Remember the ad copy you created in step two? You can use it here, which is the 15-, 30-, and 100-word description. When you do that, you also send visitors to your site. Now, 90% to 97% may not purchase on the first exposure, so how do you capture them? Through the pop-up box.

TC: I'm assuming you're saying the concept is when you advertise, make sure you have a way of offering people a second chance to be in your list if they don't purchase? Then your system will follow up and sell them your product later on...

JC: Absolutely!

TC: The major pay-per-click search engine, though a search would turn up others, is *www.Overture.com*

Use "Co-opetition" To Achieve Fast List Growth

Step number ten is how to build your list fast through co-registration by cooperation. "Co-opetition" is what I call cooperation with your competition. In my opinion, there is no competition on the net. There's only cooperation with the biggest cooperative network. That's why it's called the Internet – a network of computers hooked together. You do this by going to different sites, and in their thank you page or their subscription e-zine, cooperate with them and have them offer your free e-zine to their list.

You, of course, reciprocate in kind...

JC: Another way to do that is to go with a pay-per-subscriber directory, where you can purchase subscribers or leads for between fifteen and thirty-five cents a name. My favorite site is *List-Builder.com* You go there and basically buy subscribers and pay for it either in time, effort, or money. The best option is to pay for it in money because it's cheap and you don't want to waste a lot of time getting subscribers.

The eleventh step is a powerful and *FREE* way to build your list cheaper and faster. Remember the example of writing articles? You can do this by creative co-opetition and dramatically increase your marketing reach. Partner with another article writer. Team up with them... Double up with them so that the sig file at the bottom of both your articles will have both your name and his or her name, so you're doing a double whammy in terms of marketing reach.

Another way of doing creative co-opetition is by going to co-registration sites and partnering with one or two other marketers in the same niche market. Instead of paying twenty-five cents a name, divided by three, you're paying *only eight cents*! That's a cheap way of increasing your subscribers really fast!

The ultimate step, number twelve, I call the *ultimate co-opetition* because it combines building your list and automatically getting customers at the same time!

This will create absolutely unlimited profits to you at no cost. It's affiliate marketing. Two-tier affiliate marketing is probably the best way to go, and I know, Ted, you have a two-tier affiliate marketing at *www.InternetMarketingInterviews.com* - so that's a perfect example.

The key to this step is going for the super affiliates. I use a software called *InternetSuccessSpider.com*, created by Neil Shearing from the UK. It shows you a system and the software to find, approach, contact, and build relationships with key influences in your niche market.

From Unknown To Number One

Two guys who I found and befriended did this massively. They created a cooperation with at least twenty-five publishers who owned a big list and I was one of them. Fourteen of us sent an e-mail endorsing their book. This is the story of how two young, first-time, self-published authors went to number one on the *Amazon* big list in less than fifteen hours, with zero advertising costs, no press release, no offline publicity campaigns, no book signings, not even public speaking to promote their first book, and they created it all in seventy-six days.

Guess what? They didn't even have to write the book. It's called *Conversations With Millionaires* by Mike Litman and Jason Oman. They went to number one in fifteen hours bypassing John Grisham. They sold more than 2,000 books at $15.95 a pop. You do the math. That's about $32,000.

TC: That's about $32,000 in *fifteen hours*.

JC: Yes sir, a world record feat. It cost them nothing, and you know what they did? They just cooperated with major publishers online and got them to send an endorsement of their book.

TC: Anybody could do that, couldn't they?

JC: Yes. Jason Oman and Mike Litman went from unknown to number one and a small fortune in 15 hours on the Internet.

TC: Because they harnessed the incredible power of *lists*.

How To Get Rich On The Internet

We have had with us today Joel Christopher talking about how you can triple the size of your opt-in list in 99 days or less.

He's not talking about buying CD's loaded with useless, ancient, harvested spam addresses, he's revealing the hottest secrets about current time, aggressive, effective, opt-in list building.

He started off with a six-step prelude, outlining the benefits of an e-mail list. These major benefits include the fact that it mushrooms your credibility, your follow-up ability, and the money you make. As

Joel says, when you have a list, "you're virtually guaranteed a permanent monthly income."

That's one definition of getting *rich* on the Internet, isn't it?... Repeat that several times... Let the words roll around inside and outside of your body... *A permanent monthly income*!

How do you feel? Who are you with? What is going on? How are they congratulating you?...

Say, *Yes!* to getting *RICH* on the Internet!

Yes!

After getting your greed glands sweating like an Arkansas razorback hog in the summer swamp, Joel jumped feet first into the twelve steps to building your own powerful list.

He showed you where to go to find your market, how to prepare for your onslaught, and then how to gather in the leads.

One of his big ideas was to create articles, send articles, and include your resource box in the conclusion. Want an accelerated technique? He talked about cooperating with another marketer, both of you putting each others' blurb and info in each others' resource boxes and instantly *doubling* the number of signups you're getting. A 100% increase!

Another accelerated technique? He spoke of buying leads from co-registration companies. And he talked about how you can slip yourself into the ultimate list-builder system, your own affiliate program.

You definitely should. Review this chapter.

Follow Joel Christopher's expert advice - **build your list** - and *you*, too, will get rich on the Internet!

Special thanks to the contributors to this show...

*Joel Christopher * www.SuccessAccess.com*
*Ted Ciuba * www.InstantInternetMarketing.com*

If you enjoyed this interview, there's more just like this!
Tune into *www.InternetMarketingInterviews.com*

Other resources to supercharge your progress!
    www.GetRichOnTheInternet.com
    www.GetRichOnTheInternet.com/seminars
    www.AutoPilotRiches.com
    www.KillerWebCopy.com
    www.ProtegeProgram.com
    www.MailOrderInTheInternetAge.com
    www.LowCostInternetAdvertising.com
    www.PrePaidLegal.com/go/parthenon

The Amazing Internet And Your Dreams Come True!

Chapter 12

Ted Ciuba *Interviews* Mike Litman

Our guest today is really an interesting guest. He's a young man who published a book recently – self-published it with his co-author. The story of how he put that book together is going to have you fascinated. But that's not where it ends, or he might not be on our show, *How To Get Rich On The Internet*.

With no advertising budget, no offline publicity campaigns, no public speaking, and no book tours, he took his first book to #1 on the Amazon big chart.

That should get your attention. But when he gives the secrets to us, we're going to get even more than that, because there's more than just the sales of the book. You're going to have to run down and get this book, I guarantee it. You will see how he coordinated not only his online Amazon sales, but how he coordinated his web site in that activity with his book to really pull off something Internet spectacular!

Ted Ciuba (TC): Mike Litman, welcome to *How To Get Rich On The Internet.*

Mike Litman (ML): Ted, it's an absolute pleasure to be with you and to shake-n-bake with your audience today and to be able to deliver some great information that people can use, apply, and do some extraordinary things with.

Offline World, Online Revenues

TC: Mike, you're no stranger to radio, you happen to be a radio show host yourself, right?

ML: I am a radio show host, as well. On my show, we talk about personal development, we talk about marketing, we talk about sales. Radio's a great way to be able to help people, to be able to deliver value to people. I'm excited to do just that today on *How To Get Rich On The Internet.* So thank you, Ted, for having me on today.

> *We've been number one on Amazon three other times and, as you said, have spent no money on promotions... No publicity, no big PR agents. The power of the Internet was solely responsible for our explosive growth.*
> *-Mike Litman*

TC: Thank you for sharing with us. We really want the information that you have. Tell us a little bit – I did not mention the title of your book – tell us what it is, and bring us up to speed before we go into some other techniques.

ML: Let me give you a little bit of a rundown. My show is the Mike Litman Radio Show. I've been doing it over two years out of New York. On that show, I've interviewed people like Famous Amos, Mark Victor Hansen, Robert Allen, Jimmy Kane, who is the CEO of 1-800-Flowers, the *Rich Dad, Poor Dad* authors, all these exciting entrepreneurs doing extraordinary things.

So what we did with my book is, I said, "How could I best deliver this information I've collected in a different form and in a different way to help people?" I asked myself, "How can I help the person looking to make more money, the entrepreneur, who's not listening to my radio show?"

What we did is we took the top nine conversations I'd had with some of the people I mentioned, and put it into a book called *Conversations With Millionaires.*

In it, you learn what millionaires do to get rich. You never learned about that in school. As you mentioned, it's been a number one *Amazon.com* best seller. Since then, we've been number one on Amazon three other times and, as you said, have spent no money on promotions... No publicity, no big PR agents. The power of the Internet was solely responsible for our explosive growth.

How To Have A Best Seller Without Writing A Single Word

TC: That is really tremendous.

It seems like everybody wants to write a book. I'm sure you've discovered that. Correct?

ML: Absolutely.

TC: Well, one curious thing about your strategy is you didn't even write this book...

ML: Yeah, people think writing a book could take a year or two... Could take all this time. *How do I write a book? How do I begin? How do I start? How do I end?* All that kind of thing, Ted.

What we did is we *leveraged content*. Let me say that again. I was doing these radio shows anyway. They were done and over with, I had the recordings gathering dust in my basement. So why not take that *content* that was done years ago, and use and apply that in a different form?

So, in my number one best-selling book I haven't yet written a single word.

"I Have This Idea"

Let me take it up a step higher, because people are listening, Ted, and they're saying, "But I don't have a radio show. I don't know how to do this."

Let me tell you this. Let me tell you about a genius who I think is one of the biggest geniuses out there right now. Let me tell you about someone who never had a radio show, never wrote a book, never had anything to do with the content of a book, and right now he is the co-author of a number one best-selling book. Meet my partner, Jason Oman.

He came to me over a year ago and said, "Mike, you have all these old radio shows. You have these new radio shows. I have this idea." Let me say it again. He said, "*I have this idea.*"

He laid out the concept, laid out the idea. These tapes were laying in my basement, gathering dust. He said, "Let me take these tapes. Let's get them transcribed, let's get them put together in a book, and let's put a book together where we can share the information about what millionaires do to get rich that you never learned about in school."

So, *listen*, my partner Jason *didn't do anything*. He didn't write anything. He had an idea. *He had an IDEA*!

We're talking *Internet time*! Things can happen fast! He brought me an idea. Now we're 50/50 partners, now we're number one best-selling authors, now we have the foundation for growing an empire.

So I might sound like a smart guy... I didn't *write* the book.

More importantly, my partner didn't even do the radio shows!

There's so many opportunities. They're grand, great, glorious opportunities. Put your mind on focus, start looking, start thinking. There's so much out there to do.

TC: Wow! That is inspiring, and I wholeheartedly agree.

People who approach any issue with a *solution* in mind rather than focusing on "problems" usually find the going pretty quick and easy.

Isn't The Internet Available To Everyone?

When we bring up the issue of opportunity on the Internet, isn't success readily available to everyone? I mean, we're not talking about producing a radio show, we're talking about creating a file on a laptop computer that we post to nine dollars worth of server space.

ML: The truth is, if you have a goal and you have a dream, the Internet is an incredible, vital, low-risk, low-cost way to get going fast.

Ted, what you're doing is exposing people every week to what's possible and available on the Internet. It is an amazing thing. However, to make things happen, you need to have a dream, a plan, a goal, and then you have to get out there and shake it.

I think you need to exist, then persist. Find your passion, then let the world know. The world needs to know you exist, that you're alive! Let the people who can help you know you're there. Persist, persist, persist. Anything is possible.

> *If you have a goal and you have a dream, the Internet is an incredible, vital, low-risk, low-cost way to get going fast.*
> *- Mike Litman*

Tests Were Never So Much Fun In School!

TC: That's really, really great. Listen, we've established that your book is a great seller. By the way, I do recommend everyone pick up *Conversations With Millionaires*.

We've also established that you and your partner, Jason Oman, published your book without writing it. Now tell us, how did you go on from that? You had tapes originally gathering dust and that *great idea* which is always the spark of genius and wealth. You got the tapes transcribed and found someone to put them between some book covers.

Did you print up thousands and thousands of books? Or how did you go about it?

ML: Only a fool prints up thousands and thousands of a book without knowing how they're going to sell it or what they're going to do with it. What the Internet allows us to do, what technology allows us to do, is to *test* things. Let me say that again. The Internet allows us to test things for relatively no money, very quickly.

Build An Empire Without Spending One Penny

I'll give you an example. Let me tell you about eBay. Everyone's heard of eBay, right? Auctions, sell things, etc. We had this idea for *Conversations With Millionaires*. Instead of spending all this money that we didn't have nor want to spend without knowing if we were going to be even close to succeeding, we put up this idea. We started selling the tapes and selling the idea, the concept, and the information on eBay for free.

> *We started selling the tapes and selling the idea, the concept, and the information on eBay for free.*
> *- Mike Litman*

You pay like two dollars to post something. The feedback was extraordinary.

We knew we had a viable product, and we didn't spend any money on that. That was testing the idea.

Secondly, we said, "Hey, this sounds good. Let's get up the money! We've got the momentum, the foundation of a business. We'll start getting more feedback on the book." We turned it into an e-book and sold thousands of copies of the book electronically using *ClickBank.com* That means we didn't even have our own merchant account! A merchant account is a way for a business owner to take credit cards and process orders. In this case, *ClickBank.com*

We were able to get the book going, test the book, see what people liked, and get testimonials. Then we put up a web site. A web site only costs a few bucks to do. Don't spend thousands of bucks on a glorious web site. Get something out there that can persuade people that what you have is viable to them.

We started at eBay and were number one for the first time on January 18.

This whole thing was an idea using eBay, then an e-book, then we went to digital printing. With digital printing, you can print 25-50 copies at a time. Then you build, you expand.

When people go out there looking for all this to be put together for them, it might cost $8,000, $10,000, $15,000, $30,000, $40,000, $50,000, or even $60,000 to get a business like this.

I'm not saying it wouldn't be worth it… I'm saying *think*!

Think and invest in yourself. There are ways to go about it to find out the viability of an idea, to find out the viability of a concept, without putting up a pretty penny of your own.

Fortunately, the Internet allows you to do in one day what would have taken a year or two years to do only five or ten years ago. There's so many possibilities.

Loverage Is 21st Century

TC: Tell us, how could you possibly… Since you didn't at that time have the fame of the other big, number one names, how you could possibly, coming from nowhere, put this book at number one on *Amazon.com*?

ML: That's a great question. The first thing I want to say, before I mention some of the really successful things that we're doing and have done, is that the real key is to *believe* first that you can get there and that you can take the action steps if you have the desire. Success-minded principles are really the foundation of getting going, rocking and rolling, and shaking and baking on the Internet.

First and foremost, you asked about how to get to number one without spending money, no publicity, no PR, all that stuff.

I'm going to walk you through what we call *loverage*. We're sharing with the world a

> *What the Internet allows us to do, what the technology allows us to do, is to test things. Let me say that again. It's to test things relatively for no money, very quickly.*
> - Mike Litman

concept called loverage. *Leverage* was 20th century. *Loverage* is 21st century.

I don't have enough time today to go through this whole thing, but I'm going to throw out a few elements. I'll give you a few points, a few factors of this concept, and an idea of some of the things that anyone can do.

Loverage. We used loverage to go to number one at *Amazon.com* Loverage can be used to start a business, to grow a business to any level you want. It's the world's most powerful force for achieving your dreams, and it can only really work in this day and age. Let me tell you why.

Your Network Equals Your Net Worth

One of the first cornerstones, the first elements of success with our book and everything else is something anyone can do. It costs no money and it's so easy to do on the Internet.

It all starts with creating *relationships*. Creating relationships is the network. Your network equals your net worth.

If you're not sure what business you want to be in, or if you're just starting, you need to make cash flow. As important as cash flow is, you need to start by adding people to your network, people who will be able to help you, people who are potential joint venture partners. Add people who can be evangelists for your product or service.

It's so important, so critical. The key is to go out there and create relationships. There has never been an easier medium for doing that than the Internet. The Internet makes it so easy to get out there and meet new people that it's almost a joke.

Joint Venture Partners By The Thousands

TC: Mike, can you give me a concrete example about what you're talking about?

ML: Sure! Let's say that you come out with a new book, a new gardening book... Let's use that as an example.

What I would do - what I *did* and still do - is go to *Yahoo.com* or to your favorite search engine and put in the keyword "gardening," or "gardening books," or something like that.

What you get out of that is tons and tons of people and websites that pertain to your target market. These people have existing businesses that can help you, that can mentor you, that can share your product with their customers. There are just endless amounts of possibilities.

Your Action Strategy For Quick Results

I would go to ten of these sites a day. I would find ones that I really connect with, that I like, that I really enjoy, and I'd look for the e-mail address of the person who owns the site. That information is usually at the bottom of the site. I would say, "Hey Jane, Hey Joe, I just came across your site. I love your site. It's got an amazing amount of information. Your products seem so good." Something like that...

If you enjoy their product, come from the heart, be sincere. I would say, "I have a strong passion for gardening as well..." or "I'm the author of this book... "or "I'm starting this business..."

Lead By Giving

Here's the key. This is the sentence heard around the world. This is the most powerful sentence I know. You want to end your e-mail with this. Write it down... "If I can help you in any way, please let me know."

"If I can help you in any way, please let me know."

The start of achieving greatness in anything is a four-letter word that starts with G and ends in E, and the word is *GIVE.*

You want to lead by giving. It's common sense. If you want to go out and create awesome relationships, you want to lead by giving to them. Say, "How can I help you? How can I help you?" You might have something about you in your signature file of your e-mail.

Lead through helping.

They'll e-mail you back and say, "Oh, that's really nice of you. Maybe we can do this, maybe we can do this." Then you pick up the phone and call them.

The point of the matter is that you want to make a note every day to start with doing this to five people. E-mail them sincerely... People that you want to connect with, that you want contact with, that you want relationships with.

TC: Mike, such sound wisdom! You sound like Earl Nightengale... Add people to your network. Do it everyday.

ML: No matter where you start, my experience indicates that you'll soon be flooded with money-making contacts!

Go The Extra Mile

Another part of the formula of giving is that you need to start going the extra mile for these people.

Take my *Amazon.com* experience, for example... How do you do this without any money without doing all this stuff? What we ended up doing...

I'm going to bring it to the fast-forward then rewind back.

Fast-forward: We had all these people – all these contacts, these people that I gave to first, the people who went the extra mile to help me. They told their newsletter lists about my book, all free, all online, all through e-mail. They told all these people to go out there and buy my book.

We had hordes and hordes and hordes of people buying my book.

Rewind: How did we do it? It all stems from loverage, about creating new relationships, loveraging, leveraging those relationships, going the extra mile.

Oh we have a good, a *great* product, don't get me wrong. But when you talk about loverage, it's talking about using love and leverage to help others help you. The concept is not only big, it's enormous. It's really the foundation of how we went to number one at Amazon, and how you can take your own product or service to number one on the Internet as well.

TC: Wow, that is fascinating. *Loverage.*

Mike, I know that normally when someone approaches others on the Internet, as you suggested – that's a very good e-mail strategy, by the way – they'd normally say, "Hey, join my affiliate program and you'll make 30%-50%" or whatever they're offering.

Going through *Amazon.com*, you didn't actually have that in your control. What did you do? How did you solve that one? Or did you find it an issue?

ML: Ted, when you have a great relationship with someone, money does not come into play at all. It's not an issue. How much people could make from it or this or that wasn't an issue for us. Most of the people that helped me when we blasted news about the book didn't make any money off of it. They did it for me for free because I had delivered.

I had already given so much in value. I went the extra mile from my heart for all these people because I love these people. These are people providing great value, providing extraordinary value for my target market. I love people who do that. I had all these people, on the same day, send an e-mail to their list recommending the book, and... *Miracles happen.*

The Loverage Continues

TC: Indeed! Mike, I noticed that at the bottom of every page of your book and in one of the first pages in the intro, it says, "Get two free, valuable gifts…" It says that on every page.

I know, Mike, that beside being a good guy there's a reason why you're giving free gifts away. Can you tell us what you're doing there as an Internet marketer?

Business At The Speed Of Light

ML: If you talk about the Internet, you're talking about being able to reach people at the speed of light. It's just absolutely amazing what can happen. The goal of our business and the goal of our book is to provide extraordinary information that can powerfully impact and progress the lives and futures of people who read the book all over the world. The book's already translated into Korean. Japan and China are on the way.

The point of the matter is this: on the bottom of the book, in *Conversations With Millionaires*, we say, "Go to some web site." What we do is we offer free gifts, so we're extending the value past the book.

Why do we do that? For the marketing angle, put on your marketing mind. For the marketing mind we do that because we're capturing the buyer, we're capturing the name and e-mail address of someone who bought the book.

Someone might say, "Mike, don't you know who buys your book?" The answer is, *no*. When they buy through Amazon, a bookstore, or when a friend gives the book to another friend, you have no idea who your buyer is.

If you can capture the e-mail addresses of the people who buy your book, you'll be able to bring people into your funnel, into your pipeline.

Start by giving them *free* information then, more importantly, you can proceed to sell them additional products and services that you have.

They win because they liked the book enough to go there and get more free gifts. They like what you do. You're able to help them with their financial success education by bringing products to them that can help them and take them further.

Build Your List

When you're a marketer, especially online, getting a list, reaching people quickly and effortlessly for zero cost, having an e-mail newsletter list, you want to figure out how you can capture the name and e-mail address of that person.

If you have a web site and you don't have a newsletter on your web site, you ought to have your head examined. Get a simple e-mail form on your site. Always offer something for free. Give them an incentive, something extraordinary. Give them a reason to *do* something: *Get my free e-book, get my free this, get my free that, give me your name and e-mail address*!

What you do, over time, is build your list. Start with one name. Don't get frustrated. Then you go to two, then three. Before you know it you'll have 100 names on your list, then 500, 700, 3,000, 5,000, 8,000 names. Some people even have 500,000 names on their list.

> *It's easy, it's simple, but you need to educate yourself.*
> - Mike Litman

The point of the matter is, if your goal is to get rich on the Internet, or even if your goal is only to make an extra $3,000 a month on the Internet, the key is utilizing e-mail to capture names of customers and prospects, providing value to them, and selling them additional products and services.

It's easy, it's simple, but you need to educate yourself on the power and the possibilities of this technique.

TC: That ties in real well with our recent guest, Robert Allen. What he said sounded surprising to some people, I'm sure, but it's the same thing you're saying. He said, "The web site is not really where we do our selling." That's what *you* just said, isn't it?

ML: That's exactly what it is... And most people can't see it.

The Keys To Success

You need *education* to see it. Actually, there's two things you need.

First, you need education. You need to listen to shows like Ted's show. You need to buy books. You need to educate yourself on your industry, on marketing, sales, persuasion, building your business, systems, all this kind of stuff.

Secondly, you can have all that education, but if you don't have a vehicle to apply that information to produce revenue and income for yourself and your family, it's all for naught. Find what you're inter-ested in. Find your passion. Find something that you want to do.

Start part time if you have a job right now. Do it three or four hours a week. You have to go the extra mile. Put yourself in a situa-tion where you're uncomfortable, force yourself to leave your comfort zone.

If these concepts I'm talking about today sound foreign to you, or you feel unsure, that's fine. I was there, too, not too long ago. The point of the matter is you need to make a commitment. Read a book a week, read a book a month, read three books a month, buy some audiotapes. The key is not to say, "Oh, Mike Litman knows this stuff, he's a number one best-selling author." The key that I'm saying right now is *educate yourself*.

There's so many things out there, free and paid for, that if you want your dream, if you want the end result that's been in your heart for-ever, you need to find what's inside of you and turn up that desire. You need to crank up that ambition. You need to go out and educate your-self.

The Internet is an amazing landscape for dreams to come true.

What Two People With A Dream Can Do

TC: I couldn't agree more wholeheartedly with you, Mike. The route you followed, isn't that the same thing you just described? I mean education and *following your dream*. I mean... Seventy-six days from the time you announced your book to #1 on *Amazon.com* – you were screaming!

ML: Yeah, seventy-six days is the number that will go on and live in book history. Think about it. If you want to make your book num-ber one on The *New York Times* list, there's so many factors that go into all that stuff. Put that aside.

TC: It would be very, very expensive, too.

ML: When you talk about seventy-six days, you're talking about two people with a dream. It was our lifetime dream, Ted, to be able to have our book a number one best seller.

When you self-publish a book these days, if you know what to do, self-publishing and using digital printing is easy. It's like taking a bath. It's cake.

The point of the matter is, when you're a self-published author, you need to make things happen. You don't have Harper-Collins or

Random House or a big publisher helping you out. You need to make things happen. You need to be focused, to be determined, to know how to accomplish your goals and have a plan.

The point is we had it. If you're out there doing a business by your-self, you can do amazing things. But be open and open-minded to hav-ing the ability to bring someone in with common goals, common interests, common visions to share with you. One and one does not equal two, my friend. It equals 11.

In seventy-six days from our book's release, we went from ranking two million at Amazon to number one. We threw John Grisham off of number one. Seventy-six days later we opened the gates to getting in all the stores. The book is sold in airports and all the bookstores now.

> *The Internet allows you to fast forward and shortcut the path to living your dreams.*
> *- Mike Litman*

The Internet allows you to do so many things. Check this out! What's the creditability? What is it worth to be a number one best sell-er on *Amazon.com*?...

The Internet allows you to fast forward and shortcut the path to living your dreams.

Flow: The Optimal Experience

TC: Well said. Listen, Mike, that's exactly why I wanted you to be on this show. So many people want to write a book about whatever their topic is, but you took it from an *idea* as an entrepreneur, self-published, and now you've got your product in the bookstores and airports across the world. You've mentioned that you're now licensing various rights in different countries. Can you tell us a little bit about that? Was that a big, big challenge to do?

ML: You know what's funny? I want to bring this up. The most incredible thing is – and I'm repeating myself, so be it because success is so much based on repetition – but when you have something that's extraordinary, things happen by themselves! We get offers from for-eign publishers daily. *Daily*. First was Korea. Now we have offers from Japan and China, the Czech Republic.

Is it easy? We haven't done anything. I don't even know how to contact a publisher in another country. I don't know how to find a guy in the Czech Republic or China or Japan. These people see the excite-ment, they're clamoring to see the book.

My point is when you do something, when you take massive,

focused action, these types of things happen. In less than three months, we're having offers from all of these countries come to us.

For people that don't know, when you license a book to a foreign country, they give you money up front, then offer you royalties that continue for the length of your contract.

> *On the Internet like an old book about seeing opportunity called Acres Of Diamonds by Russell Conwell –right in front of you are the tools and the strategies and the people and the technology to do anything you've ever dreamed about.*
>
> *- Mike Litman*

Anything Is Possible On The Internet

There's just so many things. On the Internet – like an old book about seeing *opportunity* called *Acres Of Diamonds* by Russell Conwell – right in front of you are the tools and strategies and people and technology to do anything you've ever dreamed about... Anything you've ever seen in your mind's eye.

Get out there and turn it into a reality.

Authors Write Books, Entrepreneurs Sell Books

TC: Mike, you've been extraordinarily successful, extraordinarily quickly. What's the most important thing you've learned about being an author?

ML: There's a key point in what you said. While we are authors, while we are number one best-selling authors and all that kind of super-duper, awesome stuff, the key really is... Authors *write* books. Entrepreneurs *sell* books.

You need to think of yourself as an entrepreneur. Eighty percent of the process is sales and marketing. Be an entrepreneur. I am an author, but I'm an entrepreneur. Be an entrepreneur and the world will open its doors of abundance for you.

TC: That's definitely a very valuable point there. It would seem that every author should be an entrepreneur. Along those same lines, Ted Nicholas said he had written a book that had about 10,000 words and had written about 70,000 words in different ads to sell it.

ML: So true.

The "Tell-A-Friend" Script

TC: Mike, you've shared a lot of things that have contributed to your success...

One of the things that I noticed prominently on one of your web sites is that you use a *tell-a-friend script*. Go ahead and give us a little bit of info for our listeners as to how that ties in with your overall objectives.

ML: I would love to. It's an amazing thing, like so many of the free scripts out there. What the tell-a-friend script is... You've seen it on peoples' site, they say, "Do you like my site? Tell a few friends." They put their name in and they send out a message to their friends.

> *Authors write books. Entrepreneurs sell books. You need to think of yourself as an entrepreneur.*
> *- Mike Litman*

Forced Word Of Mouth

What we did is we take that a step further. If you have a product, an e-book, a tape, whatever, you have a business. We amplified the whole process.

You can just take this strategy, copy it, steal it, and imitate it yourself. It works. Embed in your product a reason for people to go to a web site.

Our book says, "Go to this web site and get some free gifts." When they get to the gifts, we give them the gifts and say, "You want more?" Most people want more.

Here's the pitch... "My goal is to share this book with millions of people. If you help me tell people about this book, I'll give you a few more additional free audios, $20 value each one."

They put in three and four other peoples' addresses. They hit *submit*, and a message goes to these friends and says, "I'm your friend, Don. Jane, this is a great book, go check it out." Those people get more free gifts.

> *Embed in your product a reason for people to go to a website.*
> *- Mike Litman*

It's the most innovative thing we've pretty much ever seen. We're creating *forced word of mouth*. We have people in the world sharing our book with others. We're creating forced word of mouth where we're making a win-win equation using the tell-a-friend thing, the refer-a-friend thing, and we take it another step further.

When you talk about creating forced word of mouth in the book industry, in any industry, you're talking about an innovative concept.

TC: You sure are. We all know that word of mouth is the best advertising you could possibly get. I'm glad you shared that.

How To Get Rich On The Internet

Mike Litman, I'm glad you could be with us today, broadcasting *How To Get Rich On The Internet*!

ML: I'd like to dance again with you, Ted. Thank you very much for having me on the show today.

TC: Well, listener, did we do it? Did we bring you a tremendous MasterMind meeting, where you've got all kinds of executable ideas that you can put into motion, whatever your business, whatever your product, whatever your passion? Can you now go and make your own fortune on the Internet?!!

Mike Litman shared a lot of good stuff with us. Let me give you just a few, brief rundowns on it.

He told how he put nine conversations with millionaires in his excellent book, *Conversations With Millionaires*. He recorded them, transcribed them, had a book..

Want one better?.. His co-writer, Jason Oman, just brought the idea up and became a co-author. "Let's get these things transcribed and we can do it."

There is no shortage of opportunity and you don't have to be an "author" to be an author. In fact, Mike made a point that being an entrepreneur, someone who works on *marketing*, may be more important to the success of a book than the person who writes it.

He was talking, and I think it hit home with a lot of us, about personal development... How we can take the genius of these geniuses, get that into our consciousness, then we can move forward.

Did you hear the positive energy exuding from him? Of course, he said, "What's one of the secrets? One of the secrets is believing that you can do something, then you go to work to do it."

So dream, make goals, plan, and then take that step we're talking about and execute the thing.

Listen to this, too. He stair-stepped his publishing venture so that he never had to invest any money, never had any risk. He started by selling a few of the tapes on eBay. Will they sell? They sold. They got good feedback. He wrote an e-book, a digital product that had no cost of delivery. Did it sell? It sold real well.

He then said, "We're going to do some physical books." He took it in and did what they call "publishing on demand," digital printing in the print industry. You can buy one, two, or three books at a time. He was buying twenty-five books at a time. Now, of course, he's rolling out thousands at a time.

You can take that same strategy, adopt it, and adapt it to whatever your passion is.

Mike also talked about his idea of *loverage*, developing *relationships*. He attributed his number one spot one on *Amazon.com* to building relationships over the preceding months. When it was time to release his book, he said, "Hey, tell your listeners, tell your fans."

> *You can take that same strategy, adopt it, and adapt it to whatever your passion is.*
> *- Ted Ciuba*

I'll tell you what, he laid out the plans… Contact ten people a day, and you'll be going.

The most important thing you can do on your web site is capture the name and e-mail of the buyer or the visitor. Key strategy: build a list. With that list, you can go forward and mail repeatedly to your list.

Our guest, Mike Litman, has really showed you that anything is possible on the Internet. Go out and act on your dreams, because you can get *rich* on the Internet!

Special thanks to the contributors to this show...

Mike Litman * *www.MikeLitman.com*
Ted Ciuba * *www.InstantInternetMarketing.com*

If you enjoyed this interview, there's more just like this!
Tune into *www.InternetMarketingInterviews.com*

Other resources to supercharge your progress!
 www.GetRichOnTheInternet.com
 www.GetRichOnTheInternet.com/seminars
 www.AutoPilotRiches.com
 www.KillerWebCopy.com
 www.ProtegeProgram.com
 www.MailOrderInTheInternetAge.com
 www.LowCostInternetAdvertising.com
 www.PrePaidLegal.com/go/parthenon

How To Make $94,532 In 24 Hours On The Internet

Chapter 13

Ted Ciuba *Interviews* Robert Allen

Our guest today is none other than the very famous *New York Times* best-selling author Robert G. Allen. He's the author of *Nothing Down, Creating Wealth, Multiple Streams Of Income*, and - the book we'll make special references to today because it directly concerns us - the big hit, *Multiple Streams Of Internet Income*, which, of course, you can find online at *Amazon.com*

Ted Ciuba (TC): Bob Allen, welcome to *How To Get Rich On The Internet*!

Robert Allen (RA): Hi, Ted. It's exciting to be here with you today and to share with your many listeners how they can benefit from all the wonderful things that are happening on the Internet today.

TC: I can't think of a better person who could tell us how to do that. Anyone who's heard anything about you knows you came from real estate. And, of course, they know you're very famous for your big challenges. For those who don't know you, can you give us some background?

Fame and Credibility From An Unusual Challenge

RA: Thank you. It's true, some of the listeners here probably have never heard of me and my world, where I came from. My fame really came from a lot of the challenges I did. I believe if you say you can do something, you really should be able to prove it.

When I was launching my very first major best-selling book, *Nothing Down: A Proven Program That Shows You How To Buy Real Estate With Little Or No Money Down*, a number one *New York Times* best seller, all through the 1980's, I set this challenge:

"Send me to any city, take away my wallet, give me $100, and in seventy-two hours I'll buy an excellent piece of real estate using none of my own money."

It was a very blatant, in-your-face kind of statement. The *Los Angeles Times* picked up on it and said, "Okay, Mr. Allen, we'll take you on. Let's drop you in the city and see if you can put your money where your mouth is."

They dropped me in San Francisco, took away my wallet, and gave me only five $20 bills. Seventy-two hours (actually fifty-seven hours) later, I had bought six properties - and later a seventh from that experience - and gave the guy back $20 in change!

> ## Wealth is Not Money!
> *Wealth is your attitude. Wealth is the ideas that you have. It's your courage, it's your commitment, it's your determination, it's your contacts, it's the information that you have in your head. It's all the intangible stuff. It's the invisible stuff that makes up the real wealth.*
> - Robert Allen

Wealth Is Not Money, Wealth Is Your Attitude

When they dropped me in the city, they literally took from me all the things that people associate with wealth. Most people don't understand wealth. They think it's physical assets, your credit rating, your financial statement, the cash you've got in the bank or the cash flow that's flowing into your life. They think it's money, and wealth is not money.

Wealth is your *attitude*. Wealth is the ideas you have. It's your courage, it's your commitment, it's your determination, it's your contacts, it's the information that you have in your head. It's all the intangible stuff. It's the invisible stuff that makes up real wealth.

What I was trying to do by having them drop me in the city was to prove that you could take away all the tangible aspects of wealth, you could literally leave me with only the intangibles, and I could create wealth out of nothing.

Rising To Another Challenge

My challenge was started that way and the *Los Angeles Times* printed the article. I'm looking at a copy of that article here on my wall. That was a proud day for me, on the front page of the Business section, standing with my arms folded in front of a beautiful property that I had bought. The headline reads, "Buying Home Without Cash: Boastful Investor Accepts *Times* Challenge and Wins."

> *There is no faster way to create wealth than on the Internet. It's just the flat-out fastest way to create wealth, period.*
> *- Robert Allen*

That started me on this challenge binge that I've been on ever since. Then I set a new challenge:

> "Take me to an unemployment line, let me select someone who's broke, out of work and discouraged. In two days time, I will teach them the secrets of wealth. In ninety days, they'll be back on their feet, having earned at least $5,000 cash, never to set foot in an unemployment line again."

We did that in St. Louis. They dropped me in the unemployment line, let me pick someone to work with. I worked with three people, actually, who had incredible stories to tell. Ninety days later, I wrote an entire book about that experience called *The Challenge*, which we subsequently retitled as *The Road To Wealth*.

Creating Wealth Quickly On The Internet, From Nothing

The point I'm trying make here is the first "Aha!" of wealth, the first thing that you've got to understand, is that you can create wealth starting from where you are.

I don't care what kind of financial circumstances you're in; it doesn't matter to me what kind of financial pressures you happen to be under.

And there is no faster way to create wealth than on the Internet. It's just the flat-out fastest way to create wealth, period. That's what we're talking about here today.

How did I find out about the Internet? Frankly, it was from one of my students, David LeDoux. What goes around comes around. David called me on the phone one day all excited. He'd gone to Tahiti on a retreat, and called me on the phone and said, "Bob, I'm on the Internet. It's working! I've figured it out! I made $13,000 in one day!"

I asked, "Well, how did you do that?"

TC: Good question!

RA: That's the first question that pops in your head. This was is the fall of 1998. I did not have my own web site and I barely used e-mail at all. I'd heard about it, studied it, talked about it, and bragged about it, but I had never done anything about it.

That's the way a lot of people are. They've heard about the way the money is made and they've tinkered with it, and they've tried a web site, but they really haven't gotten serious about it.

How Would You Like Your First Internet Profits Sixty-One Seconds From Now?!

The day that I got serious was when David said to me, "Bob, why don't I come to your house, sit at your computer, and make money for you in front of your very eyes?" That got my attention.

A few weeks later, he was sitting here at this chair, this office. On the computer here, he sent an e-mail message to 1,500 subscribers of a little newsletter he had created that attracted people interested in making money online. He'd been in the chat rooms and posted here and there, and he did all kinds of things to gather this little group of 1,500 people. They were opt-in. They wanted more information. They liked David, and every week he'd send them off a little blast on this or that.

Frankly, there's probably not a person who hasn't heard the word "e-zine." It's very, very prevalent today, but back then, it was still kind of new. He said, "I have these 1,500 names, these 1,500 people, these relationships I've developed. Whenever I send an e-mail to them, they listen. I want to bring them in front of you, Bob."

David sat at my computer and typed out this kind of message: "I'm here in Robert Allen's office, the famous millionaire-maker. I'm here for an hour. While I'm here during this hour, spending time with him, I'd like to make all of you an offer. If anyone would like to get one of Robert's tape sets," - it was my Nightingale-Conant tape set called *Multiple Streams Of Income* - "we'll give it to you for half-price, but only for the next hour. When the hour is over, the offer will expire."

He sent out the message, turned to me - I'll never forget - and said, "Check your watch." Sixty-one seconds later the first e-mail response came back and said, "Is it too late? I'd like to get that offer. Here's my credit card, here's my address, here's my phone number." This was all sent unprotected over the Internet. No security - we were worried about that. E-mails started pouring into my own e-mail box!

You Only Need A One-Percent Response

About an hour later, there weren't that many orders - about fifteen orders, or a one-percent response. But for me, being a marketer for many years, I know that I can have ninety-nine percent of the people never respond and still make a fortune on that one percent.

This Internet stuff is sweeter, sweeter by far! The difference is, I would have to do a direct mail piece to get that one percent. I'd have to send out a direct mail piece that would cost me fifty or sixty cents, sometimes a dollar apiece after renting the name. If you send a direct mail piece to 1,500 people, it's going to cost you anywhere from $1,000 to $1,500. If you get no response, you're out $1,000, $2,000.

Let's think sending 10,000 pieces in direct mail – I'm talking about snail mail with the post office. It would cost you at least $5,000 just to mail to 10,000 names. If I get a one percent response on 10,000, then I have 100 people who will respond. If I sell them a $100 product, that's $10,000.

TC: So you made a couple bucks there.

RA: Yeah, I made *some* money. But, if my response rate drops to half a percent, which is really more traditional, I'm only breaking even. If my response rate is a quarter of one percent, I'm out several thousand dollars. If there is a September 11th on that day and some tragedy in that city or something goes on, as it happens, you're out your $10,000, your full marketing budget.

Anyway, here I was, sitting at my computer, and with no money spent, my offer was instantaneously sent to 1,500 people at no charge to me. David was making money for me right in front of my very eyes. My light went on and I asked, "What do I need to pay you to teach me how to do this?" He said, "Six thousand dollars is what it will cost for me to help you get the web site all figured out." I became his student. I wrote him a check for $6,000 on the spot and said, "Let's go!"

Make Money Fast, And Fail Fast For Free

I knew I wasn't talking about 1,500 e-mails. I was talking about 15,000, 150,000, a million e-mails. If you gather a large list of opt-in, totally clean, totally legitimate e-mail addresses, and you get a one percent response rate, you're rich. You're rich *fast*.

That's got to be one of the best $6,000 bills I ever spent!

What I also like about the Internet is that you can fail fast for *free*. In the real world, you can't fail fast for free. You can fail, but it's usually slow and it usually costs you an arm and a leg.

TC: Like your example... You could lose your entire marketing budget of $10,000, say, and because mail is so slow and antiquated, you wouldn't even know it for 2 weeks! On the Internet you know inside of minutes or an hour – for *FREE*. Great difference!

Attracting People Who Are Interested In Your Offer

RA: Yes, on the Internet I can do the same kind of mailing and get instantaneous results, and it's *free*. That's *if* I'm using all of the vehicles we'll be talking about in this hour.

How do you attract people to your web site? How do you get them to sign up for your letter? How do you get them to stay there with you so you can communicate with them? All of that is part of the science of the Internet.

Just get the theory down: The theory is, we need to attract into our lives people who are interested in our subject matter, and we have to give the information to them for free. It is absolutely essential. That's the bait. The bait is good, solid, powerful information at no charge to your customer. When visitors come to your web site, they've got to see the word "free" plastered all over it.

Go to *MultipleStreamsOfIncome.com* - you'll see the word "free" plastered all over it. We want people to feel that they can be there without any charge. There's good stuff on that site.

Filling The "Maybe Pond" With Lots Of Fish

Now you have the opportunity to put them in what I call your "Maybe Pond." (Be aware, I use *pond* and *lake* interchangeably.) In the real world, doing a direct mail piece, there is no Maybe Pond. It's only "Yes" or "No." You send out a piece, it's a Yes or a No and that's it. Done.

In the Internet world, when I gather an e-mail address, create a relationship with that person and continue to send them information, I call that my Maybe Pond.

In other words, I don't want them to say yes. In fact, the last thing I want them to say is yes now. I want them to be comfortable with me. I want them to realize that I'm a good guy and that I've got good stuff, and that I'm going to take care of them. Therefore, I want to avoid having them make a "Yes" or "No" decision. I want them to just say *maybe*: "Oh, maybe I'll try this out. It's free, I can always opt out. I can always tell them not to send me any more stuff. Let's just taste it here. Let's just see how they're doing."

> *I'm just trying to attract lots of fish into my lake, realizing that every week a different one percent is going to be hungry.*
> *- Robert Allen*

A Mere 1%

Since they're in my Maybe Lake, they don't say "Yes," they just say "Maybe" and start to test me to see what stuff they get. The longer I can keep them in that Maybe Lake, the more profit can be earned. Only one percent is going to buy something, not the ninety-nine percent. I'm just trying to attract lots of fish into my lake, realizing that every week a different one percent is going to be hungry. This week it will be this one percent, next week it will be another one percent, the week after that will be another one percent. Does that make sense?

> ### Right Now!
> *There are literally over 100 million people online right now.*
> *- Robert Allen*

TC: That makes good sense! Every week, then, our listeners should be looking for a different one percent.

The Magic Number Of Fish For Your Ocean

Let's finish the theory of how you need to think differently from an ordinary, traditional marketer.

RA: Traditional marketing involves a lot of cost, a lot of direct mail, a lot of "ordinary" marketing. Online, it's a different animal.

The theory is, I have what I call the "great ocean of fish" out there on the Internet. (I like to create analogies so I can get it myself. I'm a simple-minded guy and if I can understand an idea, I find it easy to teach.) I see all those fish out there. There are literally over 100 million people online right now in North America and most of the world. Over 100 million people! That's an enormous amount of people.

Of this great ocean of fish, how many do you need to attract into your life to make yourself a fortune? The answer is about 10,000.

Passion Is Particularly Potent For Your Success

TC: That begs the question, *how* DO you attract 10,000 people into your lake?

RA: You need to start with the most important thing for your future. You need to pick a subject matter that you're interested in, that you're passionate about. If you're not passionate and you're just trying to make money, after a while your e-mails are going to be kind of thin. It needs to come from passion.

What are you passionate about? Spend some time figuring that out. I'm passionate about making money, about multiple streams of income. I don't care which multiple streams of income I'm talking about that day. Today, I'm talking about the Internet. Yesterday, I was talking about real estate. I've identified ten major streams of income that I focus on and try to teach to my students.

You need to pick something that you're passionate about - relationships, diet, health, a hobby that you have... Something that's empowering or impassioning to you, that really turns you on, then you need to find the people that are going to come into your sphere of influence.

You Don't Even Need A Web Site To Succeed!

You don't need a web site. It's nice to have one, but frankly, you don't need one. A lot of the marketing that gets done in your e-mail box right now doesn't have a web site attached to it at all.

A lot of you may think you need to have a very fancy, very expensive web site, but go to my web site. You'll find that it's very simple. There aren't a lot of bells and whistles; it's just pretty straightforward. Most of our marketing is done directly into peoples' e-mail boxes. Most of the people are not even going to go to my web site.

Six Major Ways of Attracting People To Your Web Site

Your target audience is a group of people out of the great ocean of fish who are interested in your subject matter. I'll use my subject matter as an example here because that's what I'm really familiar with. I'm just going to ask you to translate what I'm saying into *your* particular subject.

I'm looking for people in that great ocean of fish who are interested in making money. I'm going to attract them into my Maybe Lake.

I've got to get them to come to me. I've got to get them to agree to allow me to send them free stuff.

You're going to use one of the six major ways of attracting people to you or your web site. Many of these methods are traditional and you'll recognize some of the things I'm going to say, but some of them are a little less traditional.

1: Register Your Web Site On Search Engines

You're obviously going to use search engines, but you can't rely on search engines to build your business if you want it to be stable or consistent. You can be bumped off of search engines in a minute. I like paid search engines, such as *Overture.com* and a bunch of other ones where you can actually bid for a spot on the search engine. Therefore, you maintain a little bit more control. It costs you money every time someone clicks on that paid search engine. The person who's searching doesn't pay - they just get a list of twenty things they're searching for.

Remember though, these people are searching. They're looking for something, like people using the Yellow Pages. Which would you rather have, someone who's reading a newspaper, primarily interested in reading the paper and is interrupted by your ad, or would you rather have a person with a toothache who is looking for a dentist in the Yellow Pages? They're in search mode. They want a solution.

TC: That's the one!

RA: That is the massively different approach. That's how the Internet can be dramatically different. When people are searching, they want you and they want you now. Pay your way to a search engine. You get a much higher quality lead.

2: Give Your Visitors Lots Of Free Stuff

When people come through that search engine into your Maybe Lake, your web site, don't try to sell them anything. Instead say: "Here's some free information that will solve your toothache. All you've got to do to get this wonderful batch of great free reports and free stuff is sign in and agree to let us send you a regular bunch of this free stuff every single week." They'll sign in for it.

If they won't sign in for that, they don't get the free stuff. "Sorry, goodbye. I don't want to deal with anyone who is not willing to at least begin the dialogue." Unbeknownst to them, my free stuff costs *me* money. It's cost me 20 years of my life, millions of dollars worth of mistakes. It's free to them, but it's extremely valuable to me. I'll give you lots of free stuff, but you've got to play my game. You've got to agree to let me send you more.

3: Take Advantage Of Online Advertising In E-Zines

The other online lead source is running ads online, meaning that you can pay for an ad in e-zines. You can find a great source of e-zines at *DirectoryOfEZines.com* where my friend Ruth Townsend has gathered together information on well over a thousand e-zines that accept advertising. You can buy a full page from that list and send out a solo blast to their people with your ad in it, you can sponsor one of their e-zines, or you can place an ad buried into somebody else's e-zine. For very little money, you can run ads in e-zines. You're going to get a trickle of people into your Maybe Lake as a result of that process.

4: Use Offline Advertising, Too

The goal is to get six lines in the water.

The fish are out there. You've got to figure out what kind of bait you need to use to attract them up the river and into your lake.

Then you want to run ads offline. This is more traditional advertising. Everything you do you should have your website attached to it.

5: Don't Neglect Online and Offline Public Relations

Another way to attract people to your web site is to do a lot of PR, both online and offline. That's the free stuff that attracts people to you.

TC: I agree! The "free" stuff – because of the attached credibility – can be worth *more* than all you pay for!

6: Spread The Word!

RA: The sixth method is what I call "word of mouth." You need to do everything you can to get people to share your information. This is the stuff from Seth Godin's *Permission Marketing* and his *Unleashing The Idea Virus*.

That's great stuff you should all be reading. Go to *IdeaVirus.com* where you can download a segment of his book, *Unleashing The Idea Virus*. This is brilliant theory. You need to use that kind of theory to build your web site.

Finally, build your web site by putting your name on *everything* you send out, your brochures, your cards, etc.

Those are the six ways of attracting people to your web site.

TC: All right, Robert. Thank you so much for that.

How A Millionaire Maker Makes His First Million Online

You're a millionaire maker who has put a lot of emphasis on the Internet. You say ordinary people can make extraordinary money online…

I happen to know that, without a web site, you set up another challenge and succeeded in a big way. I know our listeners would love that riveting story. Could you fill us in on that and tell us how we can make money?

RA: Let's take it to the next step. Remember, I started off our conversation with the true story of someone sitting at my computer, making money in front of my very eyes. In 1998 I started to build my own web site. It took me about nine months to get it figured out. I'm a busy guy and doing all kinds of things. It took me another nine months to gather about 11,500 e-mail addresses from 11,000 people.

I used all six ways that I mentioned earlier to attract people to my web site and 11,000 people signed up. We had a list of people who were happy with the free information they were receiving. I had never marketed anything to them, ever. I just kept giving them free stuff. I still didn't know if there was any money in that list or not.

Remember, I said that you needed about 10,000 people on your list. You don't really need that many, but that's the ultimate goal. Obviously, you need to keep making sure that you have at least 10,000 people because there will be people coming and going from the list, some who aren't interested at all, and e-mail addresses that are no longer good. Today, our list is much, much larger than that. Back then, we had about 11,000 e-mails.

Robert Uses 11,000 E-Mail Lists For $1,000-Per-Hour Challenge

I used that list for one of my famous challenges…

> "Sit me in front of any computer with access to the Internet. Let me send off a message, and in twenty-four hours, I'll make $24,000."

That's what my goal was. I wanted to see if it was possible to make $1,000 an hour on the Internet, so we sent a message to the people we had already started a relationship with.

This is an important point: You have two ways of building a lake full of fish. You can build your own lake and attract the fish yourself so you own the lake and get to own the names.

That's what we call *list building*. You build your own list.

The other way is to go to other peoples' lakes. That's a nice way of saying you rent other peoples' lists. When you rent someone else's list, all you're really doing is going in front of their audience, at their lake, throwing your bait in there, and seeing if anyone's interested.

We decided to go the long route, the harder route, and gather our own list. We sent an e-mail around 12:37 in the afternoon. We were hoping to make $24,000 in twenty-four hours so we made several different offers to this group.

Churning The Waters: Advance Notice Of The Offer

We actually sent four e-mails to our list in advance of this day, churning the water a little bit, getting the fish interested and letting them know that the offer was coming. "Watch for May 22, it's going to be the day. Don't miss that day." We told them that we would even be willing to give them a lot of great free stuff if they would just check their e-mail on that day. In the first message, I promised them a free report on how to make $24,000 in twenty-four hours on the Internet.

The second message asked, "Why don't you tell me what you'd like me to sell you on that day?" I gave them a list of about ten different choices. I also did something that you cannot do in the real world: I asked them what they would like to pay. We asked them, "How many of you would like to spend three days with me? What would you be willing to pay? I'd spill my guts, share all my inside secrets, yadda, yadda, yadda. How much would you be willing to pay for that?" We gave them a choice: $500, $1,500, $3,000, $5,000. We said, "Just tell us, what do you think that's worth to you?"

We got an enormous response. Two thousand people took fifteen minutes of their life to tell me what they were willing to pay. Eighty people said they'd be willing to pay $5,000 for that experience. That really shocked me. Given a choice of spending $500 or $5,000, eighty people said they'd be willing to pay $5,000.

Successful Results Of The Challenge

Now I had the e-mail addresses of all of those people. We had the eighty people who said, "Yeah, I'll pay $5,000." Multiply eighty by $5,000, and you're talking about $400,000 from that one list. Remember, we were just growing into this. I didn't know as much as I know today about it, but for me it was a complete revelation.

We sent our mailing piece off exactly at 12:37 p.m. We offered some really great prices and special package deals, and ended up making $94,532.44 in twenty-four hours. That works out to about $3,500-$4,000 an hour in that one day.

TC: And you weren't even sure you'd really even make your goal?!!

RA: Exactly. When that happened, I said to myself, "This really *is* the goldmine I thought it was!"

Marketing Focus Is On The Internet

We have geared most of our efforts towards the Internet, away from direct mail. Direct mail is effective, but very expensive, and if you miss, if your marketing isn't good, it can be devastating. We put most of our efforts online. It only costs us about six cents a name to add someone to our e-mail list. We have several companies that help us do list building. There are hundreds of these companies out there, and we finally narrowed it down to a handful that really know what they're doing, ones who really deliver the goods. We are constantly adding names to our list.

We add one hundred to two hundred names a day to our list of people who are out there in the great fishpond of the Internet. By renting or buying this service from these various companies, we are sometimes able to add thousands of names a week to our growing Internet e-mail list.

TC: I'll tell you, it doesn't take too much intelligence to do a little multiplication and see what kind of money you could be earning now.

Strengthening The Bonds With Your Internet Subscribers

RA: Exactly. It's a *lot*, let's put it that way. We find that almost half of the names will sign up for a free teleconference with me. That's where we start to introduce a lot of our own products, services, and ideas. Most people stay on the list and agree to receive offers of free stuff. When you sign up for our list, basically you're going to get a lot of different offers. You're going to get a lot of different conference call offers. Come listen to this expert, come listen to that expert.

What that does is bridge the gap in this impersonal Internet, where all you've got is e-mails coming into your box. You don't know who the people on your list are. Conference calls bridge a person through the telephone. The telephone is a little more personal and that creates a warm relationship.

Actually, people on my list have heard me on the phone or they've heard some of our Multiple Streams of Income experts, and they've formed a stronger bond than the normal e-mail lists. With a lot of the e-mail lists, the bond is really thin; you can break that bond in a second.

If someone has spent some time with me on the phone, they realize that I'm doing what I'm talking about, I'm articulate enough to teach it, and they can learn from that. That's how we build our business today and it's extraordinarily possible, very successful. The Internet's changing all the time, but our goal is to gather a million e-mails by this time next year.

How To Use The Internet To Make Your Book A Bestseller

Now, I'd like to talk about exactly how to make a best-selling book on the Internet... How to drive a book to the number one spot on your best-selling list.

TC: I think everyone wants to know, and there's no better person than you to do that.

RA: Strategically, marketing is simply figuring out where to employ your resources in the most effective way. Obviously, I have certain goals that I set. One of the goals was to get *Multiple Streams of Income* and *Multiple Streams of Internet Income* to the best seller list. You want to be able to prove that, because once you hit a list like that, all kinds of other good spin-off things start to happen. So, the first goal of an author is to create that best seller cachet.

When we were promoting *Multiple Streams Of Internet Income* last year, we gathered a lot of friends together, people who have their own opt-in lists, people we know, and we asked them to do something special for us. On a specific day (I think it was April 19) we asked them to send a message to their list announcing that my book was available for purchase and that we would give them a special bonus if they buy the book on that day, and on that day only.

We wanted them to go to *Amazon.com* - obviously because it's the number one bookstore online, and we knew that it's one of the major sources the *New York Times* uses for their best seller list. It's a very important site, so we knew that if we could drive books to the top of that best seller list, we would get attention from the *New York Times*.

Test-Marketing For A Best Seller

About two months earlier, I'd done a little test. I was a guest on someone else's conference call with about three hundred people. I said, "Just for fun, would you do this for me? I'm going to give you an hour of my time, and it will be free for you guys. But if you like what you hear at the end of this call, I'd like you to go buy a copy of my book on *Amazon.com*"

At the end of that hour, these three hundred people who were online went to *Amazon.com* that very day and started buying the book. What I didn't realize was how few books it takes for you to drive a book to the best seller list, to the top of the list. You see, every hour *Amazon.com* refreshes this list. For instance, if you go to *Multiple Streams Of Income* on Amazon right now, at the bottom of the listing it tells you what the ranking is in that particular hour.

Anything under 1,000 is really good. Lots and lots of people compete for that spot. As I was speaking with this group, I watched my book, *Multiple Streams Of Income*, go from number five hundred-and-something to number one hundred, to number fifty, to number forty. I think we got down to like sixteen or something, and this was with three hundred people. I thought, "Gosh, if all of them bought a book, if every one of them did (which I knew they didn't) only three hundred books can drive a book to the top twenty on the best seller list." I said to myself, "Hmm...."

Success For This Best Seller Challenge And Others

When we got ready to do the real blast with *Multiple Streams Of Internet Income*, I knew we had thousands of names on our own e-mail list and I brought a lot of friends in to help me. We asked them all to buy the book on that day. In twenty-four hours we drove the book to number one on the *Amazon.com* business list and number two on the overall list. (Number one was a book called *Founding Fathers*. I still don't know who had this book, but we just couldn't dislodge it.)

I said to myself, "Wow! If you give a focused blast on one spot, you could hit number one on *Amazon.com*!"

We recently used the same technology to help my friend Brian Tracy drive his book, *The Power Of Focus*, to number one on the *Amazon.com* best seller list. We did a blast to our list and he did a blast to his list and a few other people combined. In other words, we have been able to prove it!

Focused Marketing And Creativity Are The Keys

What I'm trying to point out is that with focused marketing, you can literally create a best-selling book.

You just use a little bit of creativity, a little bit of focus, you can literally create a stream of income that will set you up for life.

TC: Bob, you hit the nail on the head there!... Our listeners all want *financial freedom* – on the Internet. All it takes is just a little bit of focus? A little bit of creativity?...

RA: Do everything to get that magic 10,000 people, like I said. Then, if just one percent of those people buy a $100 item every week from you, a $100 package of items that you put together, then you're making about $10,000 a week from your web site.

> *If you just use a little bit of creativity, a little bit of focus, you can literally create a stream of income that will set you up for life.*
> *- Robert Allen*

That's the secret here, to get that list of 10,000 and to take care of them, and to have the financial freedom you've always deserved.

TC: And doesn't $10,000 a week from your web site seem like getting *rich* on the Internet?!!

Special thanks to the contributors to this show...

*Robert G. Allen * www.MultipleStreamsOfIncome.com*
*Ted Ciuba * www.InstantInternetMarketing.com*

If you enjoyed this interview, there's more just like this! Tune into *www.InternetMarketingInterviews.com*

Other resources to supercharge your progress!
www.GetRichOnTheInternet.com
www.GetRichOnTheInternet.com/seminars
www.AutoPilotRiches.com
www.KillerWebCopy.com
www.ProtegeProgram.com
www.MailOrderInTheInternetAge.com
www.LowCostInternetAdvertising.com
www.PrePaidLegal.com/go/parthenon

5:00 p.m. Thursday

Start the stopwatch. Seconds whirr.

One hundred eighty-three pairs of eyeballs sizzlin center stage...

Tension trembles like an over-taut fiddle string, a cringe away from a scream...

The winner of the money-making web site hangs in the balance...

By popular acclaim the crowd chooses the elegant Dr. Emma Jean Thompson, from Integrity Church International, Washington DC. She ascends the stage, places herself in the momentous position, closes her eyes, turns away, and gives her right hand permission to enter the bowl, swirl, and hand me a number...

Which I hand off to...

Phil Huff, the Marketing Webmaster, partner in this special event, breaks out in goose bumps...

Articulates The Numbers Slowly And Clearly - Individually. Thunder In The Silence...

"4-7-5-3-9-9!!!"

A white-haired man on the left front table pop ups like a champagne cork!

"*Yes! We have a winner!*" I exclaim.

"*Everybody!... Welcome Ken Kinnett to the stage!*"

In the thunderous applause waves of people take to their feet...

Ted Ciuba's Famous...

How To Get Rich On The Internet™ BootCamp!

Wow, I thought, what a *great* celebration!!

But my fanny was on the line. Could we really pull it off?

At that point, confident as I was we *could* pull it off – the future was yet to tell.

We were in my own hickabilly Tennessee, not slick Las Vegas or Broadway, New York... We hadn't done the first rehearsal.

A lot had to happen, real quick. Smoothly.

The Challenge

In the weeks preceding the event I publicly promoted my challenge...

Give Me A Willing Person From The Crowd,

Loan Me A Laptop Computer With An Internet Connection,

Let Me Use A Few Internet Insider Secrets (which I'll fully reveal),
And I'll Make Them A Product, A Web Site,
and Money In The Bank Inside Of 72 Hours!
...that could go on making them money for years!

It was the stuff dreams are made of....

But if dreams go wrong, they turn into nightmares...

Was it as brash a boast as some whispered? Had I really been crazy? In public view, I was flying without a net.

How did we do it? How did 3 guys on public stage, starting with nothing but desire, a dream, and a dash of daring pull it off?!

5:12 p.m. Thursday

Here we are... Seconds whirring, less than four hours to brainstorm a product, create a web site, supercharge it with *AutoPilotRiches.com* and set a marketing campaign in motion... Sixty-eight hours after that to count the money...

I borrow a computer with a wireless Internet connection. Phil Huff sits down at the keyboard of a blank monitor...

Ken Kinnett, Phil Huff, and myself, and even the entire audience helping us – we begin...

How did we do it? How did three guys on public stage, starting with nothing but desire, a dream, and a dash of daring pull it off?!

How did we spend absolutely no more than $64.95 to build a web site, launch it live on the Internet within four hours, build a product, market it, and bring in $4,737.56 in less than 72 hours under the public scrutiny of the world?

How did we spend absolutely no more than $64.95 to build a website, launch it live on the Internet within 4 hours, build a product, market it, and bring in $4,737.56 in less than 72 hours under the public scrutiny of the world?

It Was All Sport For Me And Phil

Quite frankly, as Top-Gun Internet Marketers, men at the heights of their careers, it was all sport for me and Phil... We strapped in the fortunate Ken Kinnett with us for the show.

It was a skyborne demo done for you.

We took off! We began to ask ourselves what kind of product we *could* create and market within the upcoming 72 hour deadline we'd set ourselves...

The *full* event was captured and is available in Ted Ciuba's Famous *How To Get Rich On The Internet*™ *HomeStudy System*... If you don't have this amazing set yet, scoop it up at... *HowToGetRichOnTheInternet.com*

But I can share a few items with you now.

In direct defiance of all conventional Internet marketing wisdom, which dictates that we do our marketing mailing between Tuesday (after Monday's gone) and Thursday (before Friday and the weekend, when people have other things on their minds) we mailed out on a Thursday night!

Right in time for the Friday rush to ignore e-mail... With a 72 hour deadline – before Monday's dawn - on the mailing...

We woke in the morning with $693.95 worth of sales! Amazing!

But what was the product?

Next thing we knew it was Saturday afternoon, and I announced, "*We've made $2,248.81!*"

Orders came in from as far away as Madinat, Hamad!

A few hours later, at 5 p.m. we staged a *live* tele-conference – with 196 people in attendance. *That* was our first product. The teleconference itself.

Each of the Top-Gun Internet Marketers made their way to the telephone... And shared their greatest Internet marketing secrets... Ted Ciuba, Randy Charach, Kirt Christensen, Marlon Sanders, Armand Morin, Bill Levine, Rob Bell, Jeff Gardner, Michael Penland, Phil Huff, Carl Galletti, Lori Prokop, Mike Litman, Bob Silber... And others...

I announced we'd earned $3,129.76!

Then a very happy Ken Kinnett, winner of the web site we built, with *full* ownership rights – to the site, to the domain name, to the copy and the web page, to the product, and TO THE PROFIT$ – bounced up on stage with us again...

"*With what I've learned, I feel like I can now make three million dollars!*"

Indeed. A couple hours before the conference ended, I was handed a piece of paper...

5:00 p.m. Sunday

In the gala closing ceremonies of Ted Ciuba's Famous *How To Get Rich On The Internet*™ BootCamp I announced we'd made $4,371.70. Thus we finished our second product - tapes of the BootCamp itself - the product we strategically engineered in our offer as an upgrade.

I didn't know it, but at that moment we'd actually clocked in at **$4,737.56!**

Make $65.79 Per Hour In Your "Down" Time

Put the pencil to that and you'll see that - even counting the time of deciding on the product, building the web site, and 24 hours of sleeping time (eight hours every 24 hour period) – **hours around the clock**, including 67 hours of hands off time, from nothing but a concept to $4,737.56 cash in the bank – we made **$65.79 per hour!**

Twenty-four hours rockin' round the clock – eating, drinking, teaching, learning, praying, playing, talking on the telephone and *sleeping* – counting every second "on or off the clock" we made **$65.79 per hour!**...

Top-Gun Internet Marketing Team Clocks In At $947.51 Per Hour!

But if you only count the actual five hours of working time we put in on the project (like you would on a "real" job) we earned **$947.51 per hour!**

Not only that, but next day when I turned official ownership and control of the web site over to Ken after the conference was over, we'd pulled in an amazing **$5,965.52!**

The Internet Really Is A Field Of Dreams

Here's the short story of it all...

We PROVED *anyone* can start a worldwide business without any previous product or experience, education isn't important. And, if you follow the lead we gave you, you can do it in a single evening!

> ## The Internet Really Is A Field of Dreams
>
> *We PROVED anyone can start a worldwide business without any previous product or experience, education isn't important. And, if you follow the lead we give you, you can do it in a single evening! The Internet really is a field of dreams... The little ordinary guy really can get rich on the Internet almost overnight, at costs approaching the disappearing point.*
> *- Ted Ciuba*

The Internet really is a field of dreams... The little ordinary guy really can get rich on the Internet almost overnight at costs approaching the disappearing point.

Oh! Did I forget to mention that we didn't spend *one single cent* to market that site?! *Talk about LEVERAGE!*

How To Get An Infinite Return On Your Marketing Dollar

For those of you who have a little bit of business math experience, try calculating your R.O.I. (Return On Investment) on that one!!!

Want a higher math problemo?... Take our three days' winnings... Calculate it so that we make the same amount every three days, and that's a walloping $576,403 annually!

If you could keep one project like this going, and add only *one more* that only produced 73% of the results this one did, you'd roar past the money meters at $1,000,000 per year!

"YES! YOU CAN Get RICH On The Internet!"

Okay, so we did it... But can you?

Well, here's the question I posed to the entire line-up of top-gun Internet marketers on the stage at Ted Ciuba's Famous *How To Get Rich On The Internet*™ BootCamp...

"Is it possible for someone, who this is their first Internet BootCamp.... Is it possible for them to make more money than we – as the 'experts' - are currently making?"

They roared back in one tremendous voice...

"ABSOLUTELY!"

Reader, you've seen it all... It's all in your court, now...

Compare Information Marketing on the Internet with any other business opportunity on the planet!

Act on the sound Internet marketing advice you receive from Ted Ciuba and the Top-Gun Internet Marketers he's assembled for you and you almost can't help but get *RICH on the Internet* in record time at costs approaching the disappearing point!

Special thanks to the contributors to this show...

*Phil Huff * www.PhilHuff.com*
*Ken Kinnett * www.InternetMarketingMasterMind.com*
*Ted Ciuba * www.InstantInternetMarketing.com*

If you enjoyed this interview, there's more just like this!
Tune into *www.InternetMarketingInterviews.com*

Other resources to supercharge your progress!
  www.GetRichOnTheInternet.com
  www.GetRichOnTheInternet.com/seminars
  www.AutoPilotRiches.com
  www.KillerWebCopy.com
  www.ProtegeProgram.com
  www.MailOrderInTheInternetAge.com
  www.LowCostInternetAdvertising.com
  www.PrePaidLegal.com/go/parthenon

EXTRA!
FREE
BONUS
Advanced Training
Special Report

Who Else Would Like To?...

"Make $4,737 Your First Weekend In Your Own Internet Business Starting From Scratch, With No Previous Experience, Without Taking Any Risks, With No Product, At Home, On A Part-Time Basis!"

Ted Ciuba *America's Foremost Internet Marketing Consultant*

"Amazing Secrets To Internet Success Laid Bare With 1-2-3 Connect-The-Dots Simplicity!"

6:32 a.m. Tuesday – Villa de Leiva, Boyacá, Colombia, High Andes

Dear Friend,

You were in one of my recent *How To Get Rich On The Internet*™ BootCamps in the last chapter as Ken Kinnett was selected in a random drawing and brought on stage. With my coaching, he created a product, a website, and money in the bank - $4,737 to be exact - within 72 hours. With zero marketing costs! His first Internet venture ever.

If you know exactly how we did it, you could do it for yourself.

In fact, you could do better than we did. We actually didn't set any records of any kind. Ordinary people who are willing to reveal the ace Internet marketing secrets they've uncovered.

You've got great goals for your own Internet enterprise or you'd never have read to this point in this book. That's very good.

What a combo your goals and the opportunity of the times can be! The Internet is so happening any moderately executed Internet business can give you an independent living. Starting with peanuts! And it can happen fast, and it can happen to *you*!

Picture Yourself Successfully Living Your Internet Dream!

Go ahead and feel the feelings when you manifest your own Internet riches.

The liberty to do what you want when you want to...

The big house... The new cars – something you *want*... Not something you have strictly because you can afford it.

What does your house look like? Where is it? Are there any smells? Relish the experience!

The ease of living you enjoy.

Investments making you money – a secure, dignified retirement.

A life in which you appreciate every day!

Days when you don't make decisions based on how much something costs, but on whether you'd like to have it or not.

You travel as you wish, when you wish...

You help everyone you wish to help.

> *The Internet is so happening any moderately executed Internet business can give you an independent living. Starting with peanuts! And it can happen fast.*
> - *Ted Ciuba*

How you wish.

Your age doesn't matter, you make a generous full-time income working part time. You *like* your work.

You have the respect of everyone around you. Self-respect above all.

MasterMind Yourself To Internet Riches

How are you going to get from where you are now to where you want to be?

Nobody gets to the top by themselves. The easiest way to accelerate your progress is to hang out with those who are doing *successfully* exactly what it is you want to do.

That *is* a BIG qualifier. *People who are doing it...* Not just talking about it. You can't troop off to free evening seminars with hourly, salaried, or commissioned presenters and expect them to reveal the secrets of entrepreneurial home-based wealth on the Internet.

If they really knew what they profess to be teaching, they'd be *doing* it, not just talking about it.

That was the whole premise behind this book, *How To Get Rich On The Internet.* **Participating in a MasterMind session with top Internet marketers to get their greatest secrets.**

You've experienced the real gold in this book. Nothing false. Nothing foolish. Everyone of these experts are themselves knocking down solid six to seven-figure incomes, repeatedly. At will. Easier than they've ever done anything in their lives!

All their secrets are yours now. Each of the Internet marketing experts shared freely, giving you their own duplicable secrets – secrets that *you – Yes, YOU!* – can take, model, apply, and get equally as rich or richer, in less time!

You've broken bread here with the greatest Internet marketers on the planet, people who can turn your life around. Just to mention a few...

Terry Dean, who earned $33,245 in a three-day demo, and wasn't satisfied so went back and did it again, even better! $72,930 in 24 hours on the stage of *TheInternetBootCamp.com*

Jay Conrad Levinson, Internet Guerrilla Marketer extraordinaire, who showed you how to earn $625,000 on the Internet in four months time without spending one single penny on advertising!

T.J. Rohleder, who started with $300 from selling one of his junk vans to earning over $50,000,000. He just celebrated his first million dollar **month!!**

Kirt Christensen, while still a young man still in college, figured out a little bit about Internet marketing and made an $11.4 *million* windfall profit!

Joel Christopher pieced together the Internet puzzle after attending a quick series of Internet Marketing BootCamps and set himself a goal to double his list in 90 days. Turns out he *tripled* his list – and his income – in 99 days!

Phil Huff bought a computer, discovered he liked making web pages, and is now billed as "The Marketing Webmaster," with over 50 streams of Internet income that come in whether he works another day in his life or not!

Mike Litman, a struggling unknown, began to work the Internet and put his new book at #1 on *Amazon.com* – making him an international celebrity and tycoon.

Robert Allen set out with a goal to earn $24,000 in 24 hours. Heart trembling, he gave it his best shot. He wowed the cameras with an amazing $94,952 in 24 hours.

Ted Ciuba went from hiding out from bill collectors in a rebel trailer to billing as **America's Foremost Internet Marketing Consultant.** He can help you earn $1,000 per day in your own Internet business, from startup, and if you have that strength of ambition, how to turn that into million$. All at very low costs!

An incredible lineup! You learn massive Internet profit strategies from each of these MasterMind partners. An incredible opportunity for you!

It's Not Illegal, Unethical, Or Immoral
To Earn This Much Money

Occasionally someone who's family income has never rallied above $30,000 per year presents some questions about the morality of earning the kind of money we make on the Internet.

You saw some spectacular examples, but the truth is it's entirely possible for a rocking Internet entrepreneur to earn as much in a single day as others (including themselves, formerly) earn in an entire year of slavery.

No, it's not illegal, unethical, or immoral to earn this much money, this easily!

A lot of people hold some erroneous beliefs on this one... Much of it drilled into them by well-meaning but misguided, broke, authority figures. Misconceptions, pure and simple.

The truth is a lot different. Riches are genuinely healthful.

Given that you know what you're doing, the Internet is a setup for you finally getting rich.

First, there's definite advantages you enjoy on the Internet that make it likely that you'll earn a huge income.

What you do on the Internet costs practically nothing, goes out to an infinitely large global audience, makes money in seconds or minutes, not in weeks, months, or years, and stays put and keeps making you money forever!

Let me repeat that:

What you do on the Internet...

- **Costs practically nothing**
- **Goes out to an infinitely large global audience**
- **Makes money in seconds or minutes, not in weeks, months, or years**
- **Stays put and keeps making you money forever!**

It's nothing short of incredible!

Second of all, and this should be really important, given that you're *not* scamming anyone, that you're delivering a genuinely valuable product or service, the only way you can earn huge amounts of money is by delivering value to large amounts of people.

Money is a *value* exchange... Like George Tran says in Chapter 5, "Maximum Automation To Make Maximum Money With Minimum Effort," *give* a lot of **value**, and you'll *receive* a lot of **money**.

Of course, there's a GIGANTIC world market you can access when you put your wares up on the Internet. Ordinary people are doing it, and you can too.

Third, with money, you can contribute to the worthy causes in your heart and really make a genuine difference. Then, instead of being a single, broke individual with a big heart, you're able to fund entire efforts, putting dozens of able, dedicated, committed workers with big hearts laboring in the field. Talk about leveraging your success for good!

Just for your information, that's exactly what we are doing with this very project, our *How To Get Rich On The Internet*™ product line. We dedicate a portion of all profits to child development in Latin America. The contributions, while modest beside the contributions of a Ford or Vanderbilt Foundation, nevertheless fund entire projects – building schools, installing sanitation, educating young mothers...

If you want to get a current list of the charities we're supporting, send a blank e-mail to *sangre@realprofit.com*

When you have money it feels super good to contribute in a meaningful way to the worthy projects and causes of your own heart!

Doesn't seem to me there's anything illegal, unethical, or immoral about earning this much money on the Internet, nor in using it this way.

Announcing!...

Your Golden Opportunity To Continue
Your Internet Marketing Education!

Yes, you can start an Internet business in a few hours, work it as a lucrative global business one to two days a week, and earn more money in 24 hours on the Internet than most working stiffs get all month long! Hey, truth is, it's not the impossible dream to earn more in a single day than most people slave away for an *entire year!*

You don't need me to tell you this... If the people in this book are earning hundreds of thousands or millions on the Internet, so can you.

> *You've learned an incredible amount... Your education isn't over.*
> *- Ted Ciuba*

If others are doing it everywhere you turn, where do you think you should go to get rich quick and easy?

This baby is sizzling hot!

There's no better time you could ever jump on the Internet than right now.

You've learned an incredible amount in this extremely valuable book. This will probably be the most significant Internet book of your entire lifetime. Please let me know how much it's meant to you – I'd love to hear it.

In fact, if you send me an e-mail with a testimonial, if I use it, I'll also cite your web site, so it could be extremely profitable for you, too. Send your comments with "testimonial" in the subject line to *tedc@realprofit.com*

> *The more you learn, the more you earn.*
> *- Rich wise man*

You are to be congratulated for your drive. In a land where less than 10% of the books that are bought are ever read past the first chapter, you've made it all the way here!

On the other hand, your education isn't over.

It's just begun. You should reread this book one more time completely before the weekend ends, and twice again next week... With a highlighter to mark the book and a notebook for the action steps you'll take.

Then you'll begin to recognize the treasure of the Internet strategies, techniques, and applications you hold in your hands.

You should make it a practice to seek out the quality crowd on the Internet. You've just been introduced to 21 top-gun Internet marketers in this book. You couldn't have a better start.

> *Seminars and BootCamps are the best way I know to jolt you into effective action on your dreams and ambitions.*
> *- Ted Ciuba*

You'll quickly begin to piece it together.

There's several good courses you should have, including one which I'll tell you about shortly. Stuff so potent it could blow your hands off with all the money it'll unleash in the blast!

"The Greatest Internet Marketing Show On Earth!"
Ted Ciuba's Famous...
How To Get Rich On The Internet™ BootCamp

Catch the greatest secrets, live, straight from the Gurus' mouths! Charge up with a success energy you'll never find elsewhere!

You can't snooze on this one... We hold these gala super-conferences only one-time per year.

I can't give you too many details here, in a book, because every single conference is different.

But you can always get the skinny on the upcoming BootCamp – as soon as it's available – at *HowToGetRichOnTheInternet.com*

You should feel tingling in your toes telling you that you need to be at the next one.

You Can Find Out Which Are The Quality Internet BootCamps

You should attend as many of the quality live Internet marketing BootCamps as you can, as quickly as you can.

We keep an updated schedule of the few quality Internet BootCamps posted at *www.GetRichOnTheInternet.com/seminars* Check it out anytime. You get recommendations to the best BootCamps I know.

Seminars and BootCamps are the best way I know to jolt you into effective *action* on your dreams and ambitions.

Consulting Sessions Put You On The Fast Track

If you're really serious about taking your income to the next level, we offer coaching and consulting programs. These are for the very elite. Those who want instant, solid success. To check out one of our coaching programs visit *ProtegeProgram.com*

Consulting generally is NOT a "one-size-fits-all" phenomenon. If you have something different in mind, call our office at (615) 662-3169.

Let me tell you about several other things you can do to make your own story as big and as good as any you've heard about in this book...

These Are The Tapes You've Heard About!...
Ted Ciuba's Famous...

How To Get Rich On The Internet Radio Tapes

Yes, these are the amazing radio tapes you've heard so much about!

If you have any interest at all in seeing and figuring out the process of maximum leverage when creating an information product, you've got to grab the radio tapes of this epic *How To Get Rich On The Internet* show.

You see, the product, the book, How To Get Rich On The Internet... I, little ole Ted Ciuba, *I* didn't write it.

It was all done on the radio, live.

Then we decided to *multi-purpose* it. Without one lick more work we had it transcribed, ran it through five different editors... And, *presto*! We had a book...

We then created another product out of

> *"Ted Ciuba can show you how you can make money on the Internet... Not just a little bit of money, but your own Million Dollar success!"*
> - KFNX, Phoenix, Arizona

the work we did one time... We had a radio show, we spun off a book, we spun off *The Radio Tapes*. That's a splendid inside look at what's available to you easily and effortlessly.

Further, as good as this book is... And even though it's been cleaned up to get rid of the "uh's and ah's" of a live broadcast... What I'm saying is that the energy in the tapes of the live, on-the-air audios is out of this world!

You get to *hear* the speakers' enthusiasm, their inflections, where they pause, what they emphasize... You understand in a way you could never otherwise experience it!

Besides which... Those editors? Who knows what else they cleaned out? Perhaps it wasn't just the bad grammar.

Every single chapter in the book – you can listen to it *live*. Unedited. Exactly as it took place. Live broadcasting on the air.

The program comes with a 30-day money back guarantee, you only have to return the program in resalable condition for a no-questions asked, cheerful, and prompt refund.

Your investment in this priceless knowledge, captured during the live radio broadcasts is only $199 plus $20 shipping and handling.

These tapes are a valued collector's item, only those who act quickly can even get in on this.

We've got people waiting on your call 24 hours a day, toll-free, *1-877-4RICHES*. (International please call +615-662-3169, if you get voicemail, we will return your call as soon as possible.)

You Can Get The Radio Tapes FREE

But you want one better than that? I'll give you these amazing tapes absolutely **FREE**! Stay tuned for the details, I'll reveal them shortly.

Here's The BIG One For You!
Ted Ciuba's Famous...
How To Get Rich On The Internet™
HomeStudy System

This system puts it all together for you. Talk about amazing, usable Internet information!

Like the "challenge" event... Selecting a person from the crowd, brainstorming a product, building and automating a site, marketing it, and banking $4,737 during the next 72 hours.

You read all about that in the free bonus report, "How To Become A Millionaire On The Internet In Record Time At Costs Approaching The Disappearing Point."

I've selected the best who have appeared at my *How To Get Rich On The Internet*™ BootCamps, and put them on tape for you. You won't find any outdated stuff in this program. It is so cutting edge it's red hot sizzling!

> *The fastest, easiest, and simplest way to make a fortune is to find out how others are doing it - and then use their best secrets.*
> *- Ted Ciuba*

America's 21 Top-Gun Internet Marketers give you the real lowdown on Internet marketing.

The *great* news is that you can get this system for yourself for a tremendous discount, which I'll share with you shortly.

You get to take in this high-powered Internet info from the convenience of your own home, car, or office, at a fraction of what live attendees pay.

Undercover Confessions

The fastest, easiest, and simplest way to make a fortune is to find out how others are doing it - and then use *their* best secrets. Now you can cash in on the golden expertise of America's top Internet Marketers!

Discover The Secrets To Internet Success, Money, And Freedom That Will Transform Every Aspect Of Your Life!

21 Of America's Top-Gun Internet Marketers & Business Experts Reveal Their Quick-Start Internet Income Secrets!

Ted Ciuba's Famous...

How To Get Rich On The Internet™ HomeStudy System

These guys and gals are top-gun marketers.

The current instability in the economy and political situation won't bury those who have the persuasion and marketing secrets you get at this incredible BootCamp!

> *"If we could be alive at any one time to get rich, it would be here and now, because of the Internet."*
> *- Forbes*

Quite literally, these guys can teach you more in one day than you're likely to discover otherwise in your entire life!

These are the guys...

Look around you. How many people do you suspect are actually earning cushy six- and seven-figure incomes on the Internet?

> *You told me anybody could earn $100,000 on the Internet. You were right, I've done it that easy!*
> *- Chuck Smith*

Everybody has their right to an opinion... But do you want to act on blind opinions?

Quit relying on the Internet false prophets. The profits they promise you – doing it their way - are indeed false!

Quit buying the charlatan programs of the latest TV pied piper who pockets your money and sends you merrily off the cliff into opportunity oblivion.

Quit relying on your broke friends, your bearded philosopher uncle (also broke) and your beautiful mother. They can't help you. (Not when it comes to earning giant sums of money easily on the Internet.)

Your experts are not University instructors who have never made a genuine entrepreneurial dollar in their lives...

These guys are the proven commodity. True gold. Top-Gun.

With the home study audios, videos, and other materials, you can tune into them time and time and time again, so that you really *get it*! That's how you get *rich* on the Internet. Going to those who know how to do it, because they're *doing it*, and learning directly from them.

Here's The Celebrity Lineup Of Top Internet Marketing Experts Who Reveal Their High-Flying Secrets...

How To Get Rich On The Internet With Little Or No Cash Outlay In Record Time

Take a look at this list of top-gun Internet marketers who can help you get *rich* on the Internet!

They all have done it, they can help you get rich on the Internet!

- **Terry Dean** - A Simple System For Web Success
- **Ted Ciuba** - *AutoPilotRiches.com* - Hands-Off, Automatic Selling Strategies For Breakaway Internet Profits
- **Kirt Christensen** - Riskless Profits On The Internet - Guarantee Your Income *Before* You Do The Deal
- **Armand Morin** - How To Create Your Own High Profit Products With No Experience

Bonus! 2 Killer FREE Gifts at www.Get-Rich-On-The-Internet.com

- **Randy Charach** - Niche Magic – The Actionable Secrets Of Getting Rich in Your Niche
- **Carl Galletti** - The Greatest Internet Marketing Secret Of All Time
- **Marlon Sanders** - Make HUGE *Daily* Profit$ Applying Low-Cost Internet Marketing Secrets
- **Phil Huff** - Secrets Of The Techno Geeks To Super Charge Your Internet Marketing
- **Bill Levine** - The Best Way To Shop, Earn Money, Fundraise, And Do Business In The 21st Century
- **Jeff Gardner** - How You Can Make $500,000 Or More Every Year With A Tiny List Of Customers
- **Fred Gleeck** – Insider Secrets To Triple Your On-Line Sales With A Line Of Back-End Products And Services
- **Lori Prokop** - How To Become An Internet Celebrity In Less Than 30 Days
- **Bob Silber** - CyberLaw: Doing Business On The Internet and Staying "Clean"
- **Steve Duce** – Unveiling The Formula That Made Me $1.2 Million My First Year On The Internet
- **Michael Penland** - Instant Cash Internet Marketing Secrets
- **Raleigh Pinskey** - How To Get Millions In Free Advertising And Make Your Web Site *RICH* and Famous Overnight!
- **Mike Litman** - The Magical Internet Formula For Wealth
- **David Cooper** - A Secret New Technique To Accelerate Your Online $ales
- **Robert Shemin** - Get Rich Selling A Little Something Everyone Needs From Your Web Site
- **JoHan Mok** – Secrets Of Killer Web Copy
- **Frank Garon** – How To Tap Into The Amazing Secret That Underlies All Internet Success

Also Featuring Guest Appearances by... Bret Ridgway, George Callens, Debbie Bunnell, Rob Bell, Rod Beckwith, and Dick Desich.

Imagine the financial returns you'll get from having this group of Top-Gun Internet Marketers in your pocket!

The secrets and formulas these experts share have the potential to make you huge amounts of cash on the Internet. They have the power to take you from zero to wealthy in as little as 30 days!

Panel Sessions Get The Real Secrets Out

You'll *love* these sessions! During these live events a whole lot of new ideas come up. Sparks fly. This is a live environment! Participants ask their most important questions - and they apply to YOU!

That's right! We've picked and culled to get the most hard-hitting, direct, universally applicable questions from the audience on tape for you!

It's funny... Sometimes the most valuable *single* thing you get from an entire home study system comes from the remarks during panel sessions.

That's because they're spur of the moment. The speakers don't control what's asked... *You* do! Anything could come up, and *does* on these tapes!

These questions, brought up from audience members, seem to uncannily match what you're wondering about in your own head!

You don't want to miss out on these tapes! One little technique or trick you learn – out of dozens presented – could easily earn you back 10, 20, 100 times your investment in the entire system within days of applying it!

A Specific Plan To Follow

Loads of people want Internet success, but it eludes most people. Why?

One of the biggest problems I see is that people don't have a definite step-by-step, connect-the-dots, day-after-day plan to success.

Not surprisingly, many think that this is the most valuable component of the entire home study course.

A specific, day-by-day plan you follow to your Internet marketing success.

Will it make any difference in your life? Well one couple changed their Internet ambitions from "Someday Isle..." To a definite date. That's exciting!

> *"We already have a game plan that we have anticipated by March 31 that we will have earned $100,000 on the Internet from what we've learned today."* – Michele and Larry Schulman

Surprise!... That's what this system is all about – putting *action* behind your own Internet marketing success story!

You could do as well – or better!

Incredible Gains!

How To Get Rich On The Internet Gives You All The Hot Action, Insider, Time-Saving, No-Cost / Low-Cost Internet Secrets You Need To Launch A Million Dollar Empire!

Learn from those who have done it.

You can learn how to get *one million dollars* of free publicity, from someone who's made millions, and rock the rector scale of your personal wealth.

A real copywriter shaker and mover can tell you what makes copy electric. Put the right combo together and...

You Are Only One Web Page Away From A Million Dollars!

You discover exactly what works, what gets results, complete with figures and illustrations, all in the celebrity's own voice, and you can see his or her facial expressions, body language, and all the other things that make a live appearance so incredibly meaningful!.

Hard-hitting, actionable, Internet insider secrets – no matter what you're marketing, whether the Internet's a portion of your business or 100% of it, whether you're a budding entrepreneur or a seasoned Top 50 executive!

Others are raving over the hot, action-able, money-making secrets, tools, and resources Ted Ciuba and his group of America's Top-Gun Internet Marketing MasterMind partners bring you!

> *"You are only one web page away from a Million Dollars!"*
> *Ted Ciuba*

Here is what just a few of thousands say about their Ted Ciuba experience...

"Over the years, I've purchased materials from just about every so called "marketing guru" around. But none of the materials comes close to the timeliness, clarity, integrity, and stupendous value of your products. And thanks a million for your superb service and genuine concern after the sale."

RODNEY MORTILLARO, TRENTON, NEW JERSEY

"I made my first sale for $535.90 the second day I owned Ted's course."

SCOTT SOSSAMON, DUNCAN, OKLAHOMA

"Ted, what you are doing is helping Linda and me convert our own big-heartedness into something that really succeeds and pays us

back... I'd gotten bits and pieces before, but you're the one who is giving me the paint-by-numbers canvas, putting the brush in my hand, opening the paint cans, and saying, 'Ready, Fire! ...Aim.'"
SANIEL BONDER, SAN RAFAEL, CALIFORNIA

"The only course that has ever made me any money is yours! And I've spent bloody thousands on other courses! $17,000 in one day."
CHRISTIAN NAEF, LONDON, ENGLAND

"I was captivated by two of your ideas, so I tested them... And lo and behold, I've brought in an extra $749,543 from rolling out these ideas!"
T.J. ROHLEDER, GOESSEL, KANSAS

"I made an astonishing $18,895 within 5 weeks... Since that time I have done $1.985 million dollars worth of business. I now consider Ted Ciuba a valuable resource to my business and a close friend."
GREG CHAFFIN, DALLAS, TEXAS

"From a trailer park to Internet wealth! Ted Ciuba really is a 'Rags To Internet Riches' story. He reveals all his top secrets for making big money on the Internet. Just one of his secrets could make you thousands of dollars a month, and they could begin making you money the very same day you use them!"
INTERNET MARKETING ASSOCIATION

"Author Ted Ciuba cuts right to the chase... Ted Ciuba will give you an unbeatable marketing edge, regardless of your business."
MILLIONAIRE MAGAZINE

"Your course changed the direction of our life. For this Donna and I will forever remember and thank you."
GARY & DONNA STANTON, LAMPE, MISSOURI

"I'm overwhelmed with the amount of information that I've got. I've got a web site going. It is amazing. I've learned all the new stuff that I need to do in order to get my stuff going. I've had 12 years of education after high school, and with the information that I've got, to me it's worth more than that."
JON JON PIERRE, SAN ANTONIO, TEXAS

"I've never seen so many unbelievable experts in one place that were willing to share their secrets and actually work with people."
LEN THURMOND, MARRIETTA, GEORGIA

"What was amazing for me is I came not knowing anything about Internet Marketing, and what I discovered, very simply, is that even without any experience it's possible to make money quickly."
MICHELE SHULMAN, BELLEVUE, TENNESSEE

That's the whole story of Internet marketing. Anyone who gets the insider secrets to high-profit marketing on the Internet can do it.

"It doesn't matter whether you're young or old, black or white, man or woman, these opportunities are available to everyone." Los Angeles Times

The problem, of course, is *finding* that info... Where in the world are you going to find people in the know willing to spill their guts?... And you gotta have a camera running when the magic pours!...

The solution is Ted Ciuba's Famous... *How To Get Rich On The Internet*™ HomeStudy System! It's like receiving outrageous Internet success on a silver platter!

Nowhere else in the world can you find this summit of victorious top-gun Internet marketers showing their colors!

I'm waiting to hear the good news from you!

Earning A Six-Figure Income On The Internet Is Surprisingly Easy!

In a nutshell, the secret to earning a 6-figure income on the Internet is to run an *information* publishing business on the Internet, set it up so that it does its own lead generating, follow up, and order taking, as well as delivery of the product along with upsells for your backend products.

Of course, once you "get" it - why stop with *one* automated web business?

It's as close as you can get to a truly autopilot business.

Imagine it for yourself!...

Now you can make it yours.

Get it straight, summarized, broken down into pieces you can immediately apply and profit from!

Bonus! 2 Killer FREE Gifts at www.Get-Rich-On-The-Internet.com

Each speaker has something unique and valuable to contribute to your Internet marketing success.

There are literally thousands of different and distinct things you could discover, see in a new way, or get motivated to act on – any one of which could pay back your investment thousands of times over!

For starters...

- How to find out with an hour's research in strategic Internet databases if the kinds of products, services, and information you're thinking about offering are hot on the Internet or not. This inside info - used properly - practically guarantees your success.

- Discover the seven elements to create the perfect product – one that a hungry well-heeled audience wants, that's simple to create, that has HUGE margins in it, that can be delivered digitally, and that requires no customer service.

- How to get money for all your Internet ventures so that you never have to put up a dime of your own. These precious secrets have never been revealed in any Internet marketing materials before.

- How to publish a book and keep 100% of the product sales price. This was unheard of before the Internet came along! Today it's a snap!

- Inside secrets to getting your site listed in the top 30 of the powerful search engines that drive the world! Apply what you learn here and these secrets alone could be all you need to get rich on the Internet.

- **Stampeding profit$!** Insider tricks you can set off that stampede visitors to your site!

> *Sell a product once and get paid forever! It's easier than you ever imagined!*
> *- Ted Ciuba*

Automate Your Web Site To Pull In The Leads, Customers, and Profit$

We're not even winding up yet! You'll be learning our deepest secrets about how to build and automate a web site that pulls in the leads, customers, and profit$!

Here's just a small sample of the immediately profitable information you'll discover in Ted Ciuba's Famous *How To Get Rich On The Internet*™ HomeStudy System...

- How to **sell a product once** and **get paid forever!** It's easier than you ever imagined, and you get tips on how to select from various options.

- Want to guarantee your success? In any market? Remove the mystery behind getting the perfect product! It's as simple as a four-word question!

- How to "upsell" a $337 purchaser into a **$99,639 bonanza!** You'll get every single step of the simple four-step process! It's a secret you haven't even imagined and you can duplicate it in your business.

- Say you don't have a product? Discover the secrets marketing superstars use to create valuable products in as little as 60 minutes! These products are perfect for autopilot hands-off delivery!

- Seven simple steps to advertising your web site on thousands of other web sites – for FREE!

- Traffic, traffic, traffic! Every single speaker delivers! Dozens of different ways to drive traffic to your site. Hordes of hungry buyers with $100 bills in their paws, eager to spend them with you!

- How to make money – even if you don't have a product to sell on the Internet! Find out the deceptively simple secrets you can put to work on your site within 47 minutes!

- How your Internet "competition" can actually help you make MORE money! Little-known secret that turns "competition" on its head.

- How to grab all your competitors' best customers! You won't believe it – it's almost too simple... Like the "obvious mystery" in Edgar Allen Poe's *The Purloined Letter.*

- Are you stuck trying to produce a new product, sales letter, or web page right now?... Here's a simple "trick" that will demolish writer's block and get the words and graphics flowing like water for you! You'll see a demo that will make it click for you!

- Heard about all the money to be made in rehabbing real estate? Why not apply the same principles to cyber real estate? Kirt Christensen shows you simple steps that could make you a fortune!

- What ONE thing every web site owner desperately needs and will pay you for. This cuts across all boundaries with all web sites! Tap into this baby and you could make the million dollars you're dreaming about in ONE year!

- Frank Garon reveals how you can trash 99% of all the wisdom the Internet gurus are dispensing... If you get this one giant secret right... It's so simple a truck driver knows it – but so overlooked on the web!

- Your most valuable asset. If you have this, guard it, because you've got your own Internet money-making machine that can crank out MONEY ON DEMAND!

- How to rocket your way to millions through the bright lights of Media Exposure! The Internet has made publicity easier and faster than ever before!

- Nothing has the leverage of media. It can make you a millionaire overnight. Yet less than 2.5% of businesses use it in any form! That makes the media easy pickins for you!... If you play the game right.

- The Media runs 24 hours a day in thousands of different outlets! Their demand for material and personalities to make famous is insatiable! Internet resources make high-stakes publicity a snap!

- All you have to do is hop on the moving train and they'll take you, your product, philosophy, or company to fame, stardom, and Internet riches.

Cut Years Off Your Internet Learning Curve

This HomeStudy System lets you shortcut years off your learning curve!

> *"It's allowing me the opportunity to begin at a level where if I had to go back and go through all the trial and tribulation that the experts went through to get where they're at now, I don't have to do all that. I can start at their level, where they're at right now, and be able to go on from there. They've got the cookie cutter all made. All I've got to be able to do is have enough sense to follow these directions and do exactly the way they say to do it."* – Dan Harvey

Snag the inside scoop of what it took these top-gun marketers years of trial and travail to learn and you make it yours! Instantly you can "start at their level"!

- Unmask the latest, most powerful marketing stealth tactics so that you can steal up on your competitors and bury them in ash!

- Undercover spell-binding no-cost marketing strategies that allow you to simply *ask for money and receive* mountains of it!

- Plant time bombs… One enterprising Internet marketing student applied this secret and pulled in $625,000 in less than 4 months! 100% online. With ZERO advertising costs!

- A subtle way of hypnotizing your prospect… Only the best copy-writers on the planet know how to use this secret and JoHan

Mok unveils the secret in this system.

- Discover six specific no-fail psychological ploys you can seed in the pages of your web site so that you have people wagging their tails like a happy hound dog begging to give you their money!

As you get more successful you'll be hiring people to write copy, create products, create web pages and graphics, and do some programming for you.

- Armand Morin reveals one simple sentence you can put into your bids to slash the price you pay - yet maintain top quality!

"Writing" A Book Will Make You Rich And Famous

Writing a book will make you rich and famous. Everyone knows that. But what's holding you back? It won't be know-how after you dig into your *How To Get Rich On The Internet* HomeStudy System!

You discover!

- The simple "25 x 4" formula that you can use to create a book in a single weekend, and a whole line of products in 2 weeks.
- Fred Gleeck has 12 books right now on *Amazon.com* and reveals why you don't need to be an expert to create a best-selling info product – this is a little-known tactic nearly every hugely successful Guru adopts early on!
- Confidential contacts that can ghostwrite your book for you for pennies!
- How to springboard your book to celebrity status and BIG paydays! From a marketer's point of view, this advice could mean millions.
- An *Amazon.com* strategy that gets you thousands of free leads for your Internet business.
- Mike Litman reveals how to put your book at #1 on *Amazon.com* – he can teach it, because he's done it. And the best thing is that anybody can do it. It's just like the old saying… "Knowledge is power." This will open millions in opportunities for you.

Literally, you could become a millionaire from implementing this one strategy! Is that powerful, or what?!!

It makes your investment in the magic *How To Get Rich On The Internet* HomeStudy System puny, indeed.

Shoot Lawsuits Dead At The Doorstep

Once you make your millions, others may come back at you saying they were responsible for your success... But with the three word phrase revealed in this System in all your agreements you'll shoot 'em dead at the doorstep!

- Bob Silber, the "Net's" #1 attorney, reveals everything you need to foil the bad guys with the legal system.

Amplify The Power Of Your Internet Promotion

And there's tons of other clever, profit taking, making, boosting, and protecting tricks you discover!...

- Add an arsenal of **diabolically clever tricks** you can spring to **confound your competitors** and enrapture your "fans", so that they and *you* come out a winner every time!

- Craft a clever upgrade offer – based on your original offer – that can entice 80% of your customers to give you more money! All you do is follow the formula! You get every piece of the formula.

- A crazy piece of offer psychology that works every time... It's like you call "Rover!" and Rover can't resist coming – and buying. You'll laugh when you see how simple this is, you'll celebrate the first time you use it!

- Exactly because most people NEVER do it you can get all the free advertising you want! Ted Ciuba reveals how you could earn $109,967 in 10 weeks developing this deadly secret.

- Terry Dean reveals his simple 4-part marketing system that's made him a millionaire online. The hardest part about his simple system is you'll try and goof it up by overcomplicating it!

- Jeff Gardner reveals a product you can sell "with a lit fuse"... It explodes, has it's impact, and they have to come back to you again... And again!

- Discover a little used copywriting technique that never fails to make you more money. Using this one technique in your offers can multiply your income overnight!

- Randy Charach reveals how, with no previous Internet experience, you can earn $100,000 your first five months online. These tricks work in any market, every time!

- Armand Morin introduces his "Holy Crap!" factor... If your product elicits the "holy crap" response – you know you've got a winner... Discover the three key leverage points to harness it!

- Ted Ciuba reveals how "time travel" makes you a better copywriter and a more profitable marketer. You've never heard this one before, but you'd getter get in on it now – or suffocate behind your competitors who do! Includes instructions.

♦ The three things you must learn to be successful at Internet marketing... They're all tied together... And together they constitute the single biggest reason for failure on the Internet! The good news is it's easy to solve this puzzle... Like with all "tricks" there's a simple sleight of hand that you must know to make it work – it doesn't take "work"!

♦ How to use "risk-reversal" to make the most money! The conclusions defy logic... The more generous you are the more you make! But it works every time!

♦ How to master the scariest word in this industry... A word so powerful that every expert you hear from in this industry does it! It's the difference between a life spent wishing and outrageous online success.

> *You get exact references to sites where you can go and see - and analyze and model! - exactly what the Marketing expert is referring to.*

♦ Download a million-dollar resource for finding and choosing the perfect URL (name) for your web site.

♦ The secret, unannounced way the savviest, richest marketers are using the Internet! If you want to multiply your sales overnight, this is the big secret you're looking for!

It's incredible what you find inside Ted Ciuba's Famous *How To Get Rich On The Internet™ HomeStudy System*!

♦ Resource sites where you can pick up every tool you need to market successfully on the Internet.

♦ Deceptively **simple secrets** revealed... A **secret software** that lets you license your way to riches with just a single e-mail!

♦ How to duplicate one give-away e-book strategy that made its author over $1,000,000!

♦ The six **throat-grabbing, eyeball-popping thrillers** that the top web copywriters slip into their killer copy. These psychological principles could be worth *hundreds of thousands of dollars*! Also, if you don't understand them, they're using them **against you**!

♦ **The amazing connection between creating a product and writing the copy that no one reveals!** This one secret can make you 22.7% times more money on the very next product you create!

- The right way to use graphics to multiply your sales 474% – and how to track it to the penny!

- *Customers leave clues*! Discover the secrets that reveal buyers' behaviors! *Why* people buy isn't important, but the *triggers* that make them buy will make you *rich*!

Let's Sum It Up

In short, you get EVERYTHING these **Internet Marketing Top-Guns** normally keep hidden only **for themselves** and their **most coveted clients**!! – Everything you need for...

- More Effective Marketing
- More Effective Ads
- More Effective Web Sites
- More Effective Products
- More Effective Automation
- More Effective Deployment
- More Buying Traffic
- More money in your account!

> Why *people buy isn't important, but the triggers that make them buy will make you rich!*
> - Ted Ciuba

On Every Internet Marketing Topic...
You Get It Straight From The Horse's Mouth!

You discover...

- How to select winning products from the market that you can use to get rich with by understanding "Net Value." And this ain't the "net value" on a balance sheet, though it affects it hugely!

- What kind of business you should enter. The answer may surprise you! You'll know it before you leave. This alone can be worth multiples of your investment in this amazing HomeStudy System.

- Why, if you think it's wise to "follow the leader," you'll develop your own Internet Membership Site right away!

Instant Wealth

Online you really can make money overnight...

- How to make money overnight online! And really *BIG* money within 7 days. This secret shatters all myths and crusty pre-conceptions you may have had!

- A little-known secret adapted from the practices of the greatest mail order marketers of history that works even better to give you massive, reliable, consistent sums of spendable cash every single month! The riches from applying this one secret can absolutely transform your life.

- ◆ A secret way to get rich giving stuff away! This lethal tactic pierces right to the heart of your prospects. Your job is half done when they request your free gift!!! Get skillful at this and you'll always have more business than you could ever handle!

- ◆ How to turn nothing but a $100 nestegg into a thriving Internet business!

That's a lot of hard hitting, immediately actionable Internet profit info you get! But it's only the beginning of what you discover in these coveted tapes. In the interest of time I must cut it short... But I'll tell you that I personally know three different people who took over 50 pages of notes! Hot, actionable, take-it-to-the-bank notes!

Buckle In!...

Here's Exactly What You Get In Ted Ciuba's Famous... How To Get Rich On The Internet™ HomeStudy System

This whole shooting match is so big you'd better make sure you eat your Wheaties the day it arrives! This will become your Internet Success Library. You'll refer to it again and again.

The complete home study system contains 27 cassette tapes in two beautiful albums, 12 VHS videos packed in three albums, a 193 page manual, and presents you an entire BootCamp, beginning to end!

And then you get the bonuses...

Some special super bonuses such as a hot copy of the famous "challenge" event.

How about the tape of the incredible live *tele-conference* call we did from the event? It's **yours**! Every marketer shared their one, single, greatest, most powerful secret to spectacular Internet marketing success!!!

And then there's an incredible, comprehensive set of notes taken by one of the most intelligent attendees there, that will give you an immediate and decided advantage when you go to digest this huge volume of incredible Internet marketing cutting-edge information!

Which includes **special one-on-one time with America's Foremost Internet Marketing Consultant, Ted Ciuba!** He'll give you the penetrating advantage and keep you from making any costly mistakes.

Let me explain...

The Complete System Consists Of 12 Amazing Parts

The complete *How to Get Rich On The Internet*™ HomeStudy System consists of an amazing 12 parts!

The meat of the system is in the audios, the videos, the manual, the notes, the "challenge" tapes, and the special teleconference. But it even gets better than that!

I don't have a lot of space, but I'll try and do you justice in describing that you get *everything*!

#1 Audios: Ted Ciuba's Famous... How To Get Rich On The Internet™ BootCamp Official Audios

You get 27 riveting cassette tapes – Every speaker, every word, every nuance... Every secret that came off the speakers' lips – you have *it*!

Plug into these tapes at your convenience! Jogging, walking, working, driving down the road. Yes, shut off that radio and plug in your "University on Wheels"!

Considering the value of the secrets they reveal and the earning ability they give you, they could be priced at $4,995 and still be a steal.

You could earn millions of dollars off what you receive here - others are.

Even if these tapes were to cost that, which they decidedly do not, they'd be worth every penny of it. They're high-quality productions. But more important than that, the *information* they contain reveals exactly *how to get rich on the Internet*!

What is that worth?!!

#2 Videos: Ted Ciuba's Famous... How To Get Rich On The Internet™ BootCamp Official Videos

You get 12 smashing VHS video tapes – Don't you think it's about time you got some super videos! From beginning to end, the camera caught the very best of everything! And these aren't those cheap schlocky one-camera shoots that just has the camera running all the time...

These are high-quality productions. Hard-hitting, direct, meat and potatoes – but delivered Hollywood style. These tapes can make you **rich** on the Internet.

Most people try and pawn off on you "unedited tapes," claiming they're somehow special. In reality, that's just a synonym for lazy and cheap.

These are TV quality shoots! Of the highest quality. You'll think you're in the auditorium with the speakers! Then you zoom in so close you can see into the speaker's eyes!

You learn without effort!

I know you'll enjoy them. I paid *mucho más* than the average American worker earns in an entire year just to get these high-quality tapes produced for you!

Jammed full of immediately actionable Internet marketing secrets you can take to the bank! Outside of the incredible offer you receive in this special report, these hard-to-get videos have a price tag of $2,799.

#3 Manual: How to Get Rich On The Internet™ Official BootCamp Manual

This is a comprehensive 193 page manual – you follow along, page by page. Nothing is left out, you're not cheated out of anything. Far from it!...

You get special note-taking pages that make it a breeze to take notes that you'll refer to again and again to develop your business! Our motto when it comes to taking notes?...

Actually, we like two of them!...

"Take it easy."

"A place for everything, everything in its place."

Having the manual is a great way to integrate the learning you're getting from the tapes and videos... For instance, you might listen to the audios while you're in the car... And catch up with the manual later. Then apply it and get rich.

Or, if you're watching the videos – keep the open manual at your side and take relevant notes!

It's *yours* FREE!

With much effort, we put this manual together in our office to give you the very best of the presenters featured in your amazing HomeStudy System. It will multiply your learning experience.

Were we to sell the manual alone, but we won't, it could command an easy $495.90.

#4 The Challenge Tapes: The Entire Event On Tape – Bonus

The Challenge Tapes could be the most valuable part of this whole show… Getting the instructions – point-by-point – as master Internet marketers *do* it. But it's not a classroom experiment…

You are *THERE* as we go to work and…

1. Brainstorm a product
2. Create it
3. Build a web site
4. Automate it with *AutoPilotRiches.com*
5. Launch it live on the Internet
6. Make deals
7. Market it
8. Celebrate the MONEY!

> *Yes, you really can get a website up in a few hours and start making money overnight… Hundreds of dollars overnight!*
> *- Ted Ciuba*

This has never been captured on film or audio before – and no telling if it ever will be again.

We picked a willing person from the crowd… Seconds whirring, less than 4 hours to brainstorm a product, create a web site, super-charge it with *AutoPilotRiches.com,* and set a marketing campaign in motion… Sixty-eight hours after that to count the money…

We took the 72-hour challenge, and we pulled it off…

> *Give me a willing person from the crowd,*
> *Loan me a laptop with an Internet conection,*
> *Let me use a few insider secrets (which I will fully reveal),*
> *And I'll make them a product, a web site,*
> *And money in the bank inside of 72 hours.*

We *PROVED* you can do it, overnight.

Nothing was done that wasn't done from the stage –

Nothing is hidden, everything is revealed!

What do you think you can learn from this?!!

Yes, you can put up a web site, automate it, and start making money within 4 hours!

The Challenge

These are two cassette tapes plus pages of notes. The cost of the materials is less than $10. If you've already put up dozens of success-ful, e-automated sites, and make $4,737 in your first 72 hours, there may not be much value in these tapes to you. But if you haven't yet celebrated your first $1,000 day... Let alone $1,000 month, this step-by-step system could be worth *million$* to you!

Right Before Your Very Eyes!

Nothing was hidden! Everything we did we did on stage!

You are there as it unfolds... Feel the magic. Discover the secrets. $673 overnight... $4,737 in 72 hours!! All on public stage!

Almost ridiculously too easy it could be *you*!

You get this bonus for *free*. Conservative Value $4,737. After all, that's what you could earn in the first three days you activate the secrets for yourself.

#5 Recording Of Historic How To Get Rich On The Internet™ Teleconference Call

When we started brainstorming what kind of product we could cre-ate and sell within 72 hours, the idea of a teleconference came up quickly.

After all, it only takes a few quick e-mails and you've got a rowdy crowd of spenders on site! And... **It can be promoted, produced, and delivered inside of 72 hours!**

So we invited America's 21 Top-Gun Internet Marketers to share their biggest single secret to outrageous Internet marketing success!

There's an incredible, live energy! This was done from the stage of Ted Ciuba's Famous *How To Get Rich On The Internet™* BootCamp.

Imagine it! This exclusive tape alone, with each speaker sharing their *one, single, biggest Internet marketing success secret* can blast you to immediate success on the Internet!

You'll never get another chance like this!

What am I talking about?... We made history that evening. You can only do that one time. We were the first people in all the world to take the tele-seminar to a new level... We had a single telephone on stage... 183 people in the audience, 21 Top-

> *We made history that evening. You can only do that one time.*
> *- Ted Ciuba*

Gun Internet Marketers on the dais... People all over the globe with their earballs glued to their telephones...

Ted Ciuba, host of the gala event... Speaker after speaker... Audience... Experts... Callers together.

You just have to experience it!

Participants paid $39.77 to be on the call, but received multi-million dollar advice. You couldn't duplicate this spontaneous event for less than $77,000. Real world Vvlue $495.

#6 Notes of Ted Ciuba's Famous... How To Get Rich On The Internet™ BootCamp

Bite into 55 pages of solid gold! – These comprehensive notes were taken by a motivated front-row attendee who attends our BootCamps. He took a heap of notes... Then he spent the next seven weeks processing, cleaning up, and refining his notes. Him and his partner. In my opinion, these will make your learning experience 10 times easier, 1,000 times faster, and 22 times as profitable.

A ready reference with everything in order, complete with principles, details, examples, and web site references.

I happen to know that this guy, who's identity you will discover when you receive his notes, made his first $5,229 online within four days of leaving one of our BootCamps!

What are the insider notes of a $9,997 Internet Summit Conference worth? $1,000? $20,000? More!

That kind of money, that fast, isn't that bad! You know what I'm saying?... Conservative value $1,299.

$14,820.90 Worth So Far!

According to my calculator, that's $14,820.90 worth of valuable, incisive Internet marketing knowledge in your shopping cart so far...

And There's MORE!

You would think with all the insider quick start, high profit tools, tips, tricks, and strategies that you're getting so far, that would be more than enough...

But it's not. I'm piling on the bonuses, so that you'll get 25-30 times your money's worth!

Ted Ciuba's Get You RICH Quick On The Internet "Super-Pak" FREE Gifts!

If you really want to take what you learn from all 21 Top-Gun

Internet marketers Ted's put together for you, there's just a few more things that you must have!

And you get them all in the Ted Ciuba **Super-Pak** To Get You *RICH Quickly* On The Internet!

I throw this in for *FREE* – at no cost to you whatsoever!

#7 Video: 21 High Leverage Secrets You Absolutely Must Know To Get Rich On The Internet Today

Make no mistake about it! The uninformed do lose money. In fact, they get slaughtered. In this rare video capture of a live performance Ted Ciuba reveals *21 High Leverage Secrets You Absolutely Must Know To Get Rich On The Internet Today.*

These secrets break down into two distinct sections, which I've titled...

- "The 13 Deadly Internet Marketing Mistakes Almost Every Business Is Making... And How You Can Avoid Them"
- "Thrive In Your Internet Business When You Focus On The 8 Basic Missions Of A Business" Value $797.

> *Make no mistake about it! The uninformed do lose money. In fact, they get slaughtered.*

#8 Consulting: One-On-One Consulting With America's Foremost Internet Marketing Consultant, Ted Ciuba

I'll be frank with you... I'm offering this because I've been exactly where you are before. (In fact, I still go to advisors who have made more money than I have, for the same reason.) I'm talking about you would like someone looking over your shoulder, checking out your product, your sales copy, your marketing plans, your web site...

Making sure that you're on the right track. Making sure you can reach the goals you've set for yourself. Making a few suggestions to an already excellent campaign that can boost it from mediocre to spectacular!

Equally as important, making sure you don't make any fatal mistakes. A single setback can wipe out years of wealth accumulation!

"Ted Ciuba can show you how you can make money on the Internet... Not just a little bit of money, but your own Million

Dollar success!" – KFNX, Phoenix, AZ

My biggest concern is that you really get it – and that you don't let some little meaningless trivia hang you up. I'll be there for you for the broad strokes and the little details that matter...

The only way I know to make sure you get it is to work with you one-on-one. So that's what I'm doing!

I'll take your calls and me, my coaches, and my network of winning Internet marketers will work on your case to make you succeed. (You must agree to keep this number for your own private use only.)

Normally that's prohibitive for most startup Internet entrepreneurs, because I bill my time out at $1,000 per hour with a minimum $9,997 twelve-month commitment. If you want to check me out on this one, surf up to *www.ProtegeProgram.com*

I also reveal in this incredible system how you can put yourself into the enviable position of billing yourself out at $1,000 per hour - and have more eager clients than you could ever handle! That's 4.4x the billing rate of a high-falutin medical doctor.

This bonus alone has a bona fide value of $2,000, even though it can earn you a lot more!

However, this *How To Get Rich On The Internet*™ HomeStudy System is a pet project of mine. I want it to succeed, and I want it to succeed big time!

So I'm committed to doing whatever it takes to make it the best it can be. Here's what that means for you...

I'm making Internet millionaires all over the world.

I'll give you the best I have to offer!

Two hours worth of my time – time that can make you millions.

Two hours that can cut ten *years* off your learning curve.

You'll get the full details of how to contact Ted Ciuba with your complete *How To Get Rich On The Internet*™ HomeStudy System.

This *free* gift can save you *thousands* in futile efforts and dead ends. Certain failure staring you in the face... We can head it off at the pass.

It could mean the difference between a project or a career that gets mired in the muds of mediocrity and "me-to-ism" or one that jumps off the runway and soars into million$!

Truly incredible! Don't miss out on your chance to have America's Foremost Internet Marketer keep you from making any costly mistakes!

Note: Because this requires so much of my personal attention, this is one of the bonuses that I just can't give you if you don't accept the *complete* system, I hope you understand.

#9 Internet Marketers Resource Toolbox

I've put together a complete Internet Marketer's Resource Toolbox, jam-packed with everything you need to build an Internet marketing empire. I should know – because I use it regularly as a marketing tool!

But it's more than just my own tools... Just like I do with all my top-quality systems, tools, and resources, I've gathered the best used by the best!

This insider's guide reveals resources used by the top marketers to make tons of money online! Legends such as Corey Rudl, Ted Ciuba, Jonathan Mizel, Terry Dean, Yanik Silver, Alex Mandossian, Armand Morin, and about 15 other Internet marketing greats.

It will become your indispensable guide to building your business on the Internet. It's worth far more than the measly $399 I sell it for. It's your *free*.

That's An Additional $3,196 Worth Of Internet Success Power!

Add up those special "Super-Pak" FREE Gifts I throw in, $3,196 that buys million dollar specific-to-you advice, and the meter shows me that you've busted past the $18,000 mark. $18,016.90 to be exact!

How About A Few More Valuable FREE "No-Strings-Attached" Bonuses?

You would think $18,016.90 would be more than enough, but there's more! I'm throwing some bonuses in for you! These are *"no-strings-attached" bonuses* – you get to keep these puppies even if you send the system back for a refund!

#10 Book: How To Get Rich On The Internet by America's Foremost Internet Marketing Consultant, Ted Ciuba

This is *the* Internet marketing book. So many people are buying and gifting this breakthrough Internet marketing book that you may already own it! If you do, give this one to someone you know can appreciate it!

Ted Ciuba corners America's Top Internet Marketers and squeezes their most closely-guarded secrets out of them! You get it all so that you can follow in their footsteps and build your own Internet marketing empire!

It's the best bargain on the planet for a mere $19.95!!!

#11 Resale License To The How To Get Rich On The Internet™ HomeStudy System

I'll also throw in the resale license to the homestudy system for free, a $495 value. This will let you make tons of good money with this very same high-quality product. Think of it! You didn't do any of the work to create or organize it. You didn't have to labor to write the sales materials, e-zine ads, or web pages. We do it all!

You'll get sales letters, web files, and URLs to promote. Yes!

There's a global market for this product – people are *hungry* for information on how to get rich on the Internet.

If you play your cards right, you could get rich on the Internet from just this one product!

Get your share, the easy way!

I'll give you a full 50%.

It don't get no better than this! Income with no work!

This is what I'm talking about when I say... *Only on the Internet*!

What if you really get behind this as an extra source of income?...

You could potentially gross $100,000, almost without lifting a finger. That's just sales of 63 units.

Do the math! If you were to only average ten sales per week, that's over $830,000!

I'm not suggesting you get dizzy like they do at multi-level meetings... And any time we get into income calculations I am compelled to remind you that we make no representations nor guarantees of income and that *your results will vary*. But I do suggest you check out what the dispassionate mathematics can do for you.

> *A little serious marketing on the Internet can make you wealthy!*

If you amp up your marketing machine you can earn $2 Million Dollars!

It's a mind-blower! A little serious marketing on the Internet can make you wealthy!

#12 *Mail Order In The Internet Age* By Ted Ciuba

This is the blockbuster book that woke the world up to the fact that to be successful on the Internet you've got to treat it like a "mail order" business. Such things as split testing a web page design, headline, or offer. Such things as tracking your ads, to know where you're horsepower is really coming from. Sequential mailings to suck the most money possible out of a list of customers. A strong backend...

Some have called it the greatest Internet marketing book in history. I don't know about that, but I know it gives you the real lowdown on success with an Internet site.

Sells for $19.95, worth $2-Million, yours *free*.

These super free bonuses are special! You see, I know you're taking this homestudy system on a trial basis. Well, I want you to keep these super bonuses – even if you send your homestudy system back! That's right, these super bonuses are yours to keep forever, just for giving my system a try! That's an additional $534.90, guaranteed yours, even if you send the amazing wealth-busting system back.

You'll Need A Dedicated UPS Truck To Deliver All Your Goodies!

Whew! That's a *LOT of STUFF*!

My calculations show you're getting $18,551.80 worth of materials and bonuses! And $534.90 worth of that is yours to keep even if you send this amazing Internet money-making system back!

With this much value it's only natural you're wondering...

"Alright, Ted, What's My Investment In This Life-Changing How To Get Rich On The Internet™ HomeStudy System Gonna Be?"

I'm glad you asked... That's a very good question.

First, let me ask you... Forget the fact that you're getting $18,551.80 worth of goods and services. Ask a more important question. What's a home study system that teaches you how to get rich on the Internet really worth?

That magical ability to market on the Internet and make money on demand, to make money 24 hours a day - on a permanent vacation... What's that worth to you?

Maybe $200,000 worth of income in your first 12 months?...

"I believe within the next 12 months I can easily make $200,000 to $300,000 with the knowledge that I've learned. I

know I can get rich on the Internet with Ted Ciuba's incredible plan and the plans from all the experts that he's brought together."   – Linda Adams, New York, New York

Maybe **half a million dollars!**...

"The information that I've received, over the next 12 months, will probably give me a gross dollar amount of close to a half-million dollars.   The price of the information that you receive is easily worth $10,000 to $25,000. And that's a low esti mate."   - Luann Allen, St. Augustine, FL.

Bottom line: this special system could cost a fortune and still be an incredible value.

That being said, it was still an adventure deciding what to price it at. Many of my marketing friends suggested that the information was worth way more than the $9,997 people pay at the door for my events. After all, you have a lot more opportunities to learn when you can repeat parts of the course as many times as you like!

And I agree. It's incredibly powerful stuff!

And that doesn't take into account the other expenses associated with travel and lodging. So you're sitting on top of $11,000 - $12,000, not to mention that you've got to take off work 4-5 days of inconvenience...

Of course, what is the magical ability to market on the Internet and make money on demand, to make money 24 hours a day on a permanent vacation worth?

Most people would say it's certainly worth more than $10,000.

Compare it for a moment with an automobile. Sure, a car is a necessity in today's American society - but that being the case, you could drive any car you wanted.

Yet most Americans go into debt for 4-6 years for a car that costs $28,000.

And, sure, that car may enable you to get back and forth from work... And keep your lousy job...

Whereas, if they'd invest a fraction of that amount into an opportunity, they could make enough to pay cash for hundreds of cars!

There's a value mis-adjustment in here somewhere, don't you feel?

This *How To Get Rich On The Internet* HomeStudy System is the stuff of Top-Gun Marketers... The secret knowledge in this home study system will give you an arsenal of secret weapons you can use and deploy to immediately make yourself independent and to make huge sums of money for decades to come!

Truth is, you should be willing to invest whatever within reason is required... And when it's plum dumb an outright steal, you should jump on it within seconds, because it may not last!

Nevertheless, I'm not about to charge as much as it costs to attend a live event. It's worth it, and it can open up a million dollar career for you, but if I priced it at $9,997, or even at $2,997, a lot of people on the verge of turning it all around simply couldn't afford it at this point in their lives.

Home study courses are supposed to be less expensive than the big seminar productions.

So I'm slashing the price and saving you all the travel, lodging, and incidental expenses to boot! Put it together and you save up to $10,000 by taking the home study system. A non inconsequential sum.

> *Compare it for a moment with an automobile. Sure, a car is a necessity in today's American society - but that being the case, you could drive any car you wanted. Yet most Americans go into debt for 4-6 years for a car that costs $28,000. And, sure, that car may enable you to get back and forth from work... And keep your lousy job... Whereas, if they'd invest a fraction of that amount into an opportunity, they could make enough to pay cash for hundreds of cars!*
> *- Ted Ciuba*

Your one-time investment in the entire package is **only $1,497**.

The Price Is Trivial

That price is trivial side by side with what you stand to gain...

In fact, just with the resale license you get as a *free* bonus – it would only take 2 sales for you to earn back 100% of your money. With numbers like that you just can't go wrong, can you?

In fact, with the info, tools, resources, and personal help you get in Ted Ciuba's Famous... *How To Get Rich On The Internet*™ HomeStudy System, you could launch a new career! It could be bold, or it could be humble... The choice is yours...

> *"It's hard to believe, because so many claims are made by so many people, but I truly believe that you could make your income go 10 times what it is now, at least, by learning what you learn here."*
> – Ken Kinnett

That's right, you get the complete *How To Get Rich On The*

Internet™ HomeStudy System, including personal Internet consulting with Ted Ciuba, America's Foremost Internet Marketing Consultant, for only $1,497!

Introductory Option Available

And if you can't see your way to separate with that small investment in yourself, I've even put together an *Introductory Option*.

Your investment in that package is only $797.

However, you should be aware...

> *"Buying the complete set will give someone the next best thing to being here live, in person, because these speakers pour out their souls, their hearts, and their knowledge, in detail. Having this set will go a long way in helping someone get started. And all their information will be accessible, so that people could still access these speakers on their own as well."*
>
> – Linda Adams

Of course, to get the reduced pricing you have to give up certain crucial things. You'll give up items 7 – 9 of the complete system... Unfortunately, these are the specific items that could help you accelerate your way to wealth most rapidly!

You won't get the incredible video, *21 High Leverage Secrets You Absolutely Must Know To Get Rich On The Internet Today*. You won't get the real foundational secret leverage points that you can apply to make a fortune in your business in this video.

You won't get the *Internet Marketers Resource Toolbox*. This has hundreds of the hottest, cheapest, sources of everything you need to market on the Internet. From beginning to end. From A to Z. Alpha to Omega. These are the very tools this top-gun rank of Internet marketers use to make million$.

If you can imagine it, it's like an airplane pilot trying to fly in a foreign land without any maps. If you wouldn't mind that, you won't mind trying to make money on the Internet without the instruction, guidance, direction, contacts, and resources the *Complete* System gives you.

But by far the worst thing you'll give up is the personal consulting help Ted Ciuba offers you. As America's Foremost Internet Marketing Consultant, if it's related to the Internet, he can help you.

From sales copy to automation. From a viral marketing campaign to selling ebooks for a fortune... It doesn't matter *who* you are, what your product, service, or cause is, or how big or small you currently are. Ted Ciuba can help you make a fortune online!

That's a lot to give up, but if that's what it takes to make it inside your current budget, it's far better to invest in the strip-down model now than put off your success!

Your Better-Than-Risk-Free Guarantee

Of course you are protected by my iron-clad guarantee. It's as strong and as risk-free as I know how to make it!

You have a full 60 days after you purchase this product to send it back for a prompt and courteous refund for 100% of the purchase price. That honestly ought to be more than enough time for you to get it in your house, look it over, and decide if it can benefit you. Should you not see its immediate overwhelming value to you, pack it up and send it back. Only one condition - that it be in resellable condition. You'll get a no questions asked, cheerful, prompt refund.

You get to convince yourself it's everything I say it is, and can get you rich on the Internet. You get to *prove it to yourself!*

And even if you should decide to return this product for a full refund, you get to keep the *FREE* Super Bonuses you receive as our special gift to you. It's our way of thanking you for giving us a try.

This way, even if you decide it's not right for you, the worst that could happen is you'll get a $534.90 value absolutely FREE.

How's that for a *better-than-risk-free guarantee?*!

How can you go wrong? You can't. How could I be fairer? I couldn't, and you know it.

Get Started Now

To order immediately call *right now* toll-free *1-877-4 RICHES*. Ask for the *How To Get Rich On The Internet* HomeStudy System. Ask for either the *Complete* System or for the *Introductory* System. If you'd like to chat a moment about the system and your opportunities before investing, business hours you can call +615-662-3169.

You can also fill in the form at the end of this chapter and mail or fax it in.

Finally, if you'd like to order online, and why not?! Just scoot up to *www.GetRichOnTheInternet.com/now*

Don't Let Negativity In The Land Of Opportunity Hold You Back

You know, it's sad, here in the "land of opportunity" how many doubting Thomas's there are. Sure, a measure of skepticism is a good quality... But at the same time you're moving forward with *due* caution *move forward adventurously*!

Negative, fearful thoughts ask the question:

What if it doesn't work?

Let's address that. The down side is simple. If it doesn't work, you can get a full refund on the materials and still come out $534.90 ahead, because you can keep the bonuses.

Since you have no downside risk, the real question becomes...

What if it DOES work?!

If it does work, you could become an Internet millionaire almost overnight, working at home, starting from scratch.

If it does work, and you didn't step up to the plate, you've traded a glorious Internet future for a few dollars of misplaced skepticism. That's the BIGGEST risk of all.

Imagine Your Feelings When You Get Rich On The Internet!

It's not an exaggeration to say that with just one idea, one application, one resource, one product, or one new motivation you receive from this program you could easily earn $100,000. In fact, that's ridiculously conservative....

Some of the people who enter this system will earn millions from what they learn here, I'm convinced of it.

The Internet revolution that is sweeping across the US and the whole world is creating more millionaires than anything else in history, and at a faster pace than anyone could have possibly imagined even three or four years ago...

Make it *yours*! Get the wealth you would like and...

Everything being wealthy means. Independence... Vacations... Private schools... A better house... Secure retirement... Respect – of your neighbors, your family, and, above all, self-respect.

It continues to happen on the Internet...

Why can't it happen to you?

It CAN happen to YOU!

Just follow the connect-the-dots plan to Internet success revealed in Ted Ciuba's Famous... *How To Get Rich On The Internet*™ HomeStudy System.

Like Ken Kinnett was awestruck when it happened to him...

"Quite frankly, I was awestruck! I grossed over $4,000 in the first 2 1/2 days, and $6,000 by day five... And this was my first Internet marketing venture ever!"

It happened to Ken, it can happen to you. I'll make sure of that.

Just like the chapter title says, you too can make $4,737 your first weekend in your own Internet business starting from scratch, with no previous experience, without taking any risks, with no product, at home, on a part-time basis!

I don't just "believe" you can do it, too. I *know* you can.

But you must *start* now. Don't lose the advantage of timing, you'll find it more difficult if you don't get started *now*.

You have absolutely *nothing* at risk! With your generous 60-day inspection guarantee, if you don't like what you get, send it back! And even if you do, you get to keep the "No-Strings Attached" Bonuses! So the worst that could happen is you come out $534.90 ahead!

Order Now While You Still Can

Don't let anything stand in the way of your Internet success!

Order the *How To Get Rich On The Internet* HomeStudy System now, while you're thinking about it! There's five easy ways...

1. **Call** right away *toll-free 1-877-4 RICHES (1-877-474-2437)* and ask for Ted Ciuba's Famous *How To Get Rich On The Internet* HomeStudy System. Ask for either the *Complete* System or for the *Introductory* System.
   Business hours you can call our offices 615-662-3169.

2. **Online** at *www.HowToGetRichOnTheInternet.com/now*

3. **Fax** your enrollment information to 615-662-3108 –
   there's a convenient Rush Enrollment Request at the end of this special report.

4. **E-mail** everything in to *tedc@realprofit.com* – just include all the information that's requested on the Rush Enrollment Request at the end of this special report.

5. **Mail** the Rush Enrollment Request (at the end of this chapter) to:
   Parthenon Marketing Inc.
   2400 Crestmoor Rd #36
   Nashville, TN 37215

Don't hate yourself later for missing out on this incredible Internet opportunity. Start now or you'll lose the advantage of timing. Don't let it happen to you. Supplies are limited and we could have to return your check or credit card authorization if it arrives too late. So rush your order in now.

Get the further education you must have. Follow the lead of the Internet celebrities in this book. Act on your dreams!

And, yes! YOU *CAN* get *RICH* on the Internet!!!

Sincerely,

Ted Ciuba, President Parthenon Marketing Inc.
Author, America's Foremost Internet Marketing Consultant

P.S. Hurry. I may be raising the price soon, because it's so trivial side-by-side with what you stand to gain... In fact, just with the resale license you get as a *free* bonus – it only takes two sales for you to earn back 100% of your money! With numbers like that you just can't go wrong, can you?

P.P.S. Remember, I said I'd give you the *How To Get Rich On The Internet* Radio Tapes with your enrollment in the complete *How To Get Rich On The Internet* HomeStudy System. These are the original interviews you enjoyed so much in this book, and they're yours *free*! **Value $199**

That brings the total value of everything you receive to a whopping $18,750.80. Jump into this baby act *today*!

In any moment a decision you

make can change the course of

your life forever...

The very next person you stand

behind in line or sit next to on

an airplane,

the very next phone call you

make or receive,

the very next movie you see

or book you read

or page you turn

could be the one single thing

that causes the floodgates to open,

and all of the things that you've

been waiting for to fall into place.

- Tony Robbins

For Rush Service
Call, Fax Or Go Online

Order NOW Toll Free:
1-877- 4 RICHES *(1-877-474-2437)*

615-662-3169 / fax: 615-662-3108
www.HowToGetRichOnTheInternet.com/now
tedc@realprofit.com

Or Mail This Form To

Parthenon Marketing, Inc.
2400 Crestmoor Rd #36
Nashville TN 37215
USA

☑ "Yes, Ted, I Want To Make $4,737 My First Weekend In My Own Internet Business Starting From Scratch, With No Previous Experience, Without Taking Any Risks, With No Product, At Home, On A Part-Time Basis!"

☑ **Yes,** I am stoked! I've marked my choice below, let me have your amazing *How To Get Rich On The Internet* HomeStudy System right NOW!

☑ Send me everything just the way you outlined it, including my no-questions-asked, cheerful, prompt 60-day guarantee!

☑ FREE EXTRA BONUS! With my purchase I get 2 FREE months membership to InternetMarketingInterviews.com Thereafter $19.95 is conveniently billed to my credit card until I cancel, which I may do at any time.

☐ The COMPLETE *How To Get Rich On The Internet*™ **HomeStudy System – Total Value $18,551.80** **$1,497**

☑ Just like you described in this bonus special report, I get the audios, videos, manual, Challenge Tapes, historic tele-conference call, and comprehensive notes of the whole event! *Value $14,820.90*

☑ FREE GIFTS! Plus you give me your "Super-Pak" FREE Gifts! That's the Ted Ciuba personal component, which includes a special video with 21 secrets, personal consulting, and a copy of Ted's very own Internet Marketer's Resource Rolodex. *Value $3,196.00*

☑ As if that wasn't enough, I also get your FREE "No Strings Attached" Bonuses. Two of Ted Ciuba's breakaway Internet books plus a Resale License! That's a value of $534.90, mine to keep even if I send your amazing system back!

☐ The Introductory *How To Get Rich On The Internet*™ **HomeStudy System – Total Value $15,355.90** **$797**

For a 50% savings I get the Introductory version! Yep, I know that when I order the 'strip-down' version of The How To Get Rich On The Internet™ HomeStudy System for only $797 I lose all the Super-Pak FREE Gifts– including 2 hours of consulting time with Ted Ciuba that could save my tail and make me a fortune! But that's okay, give me your killer materials now!

☐ CD Option - Instead of audio cassettes send me CD's (at no extra charge)

☐ I'm ordering the Complete version of the How To Get Rich On The Internet™ HomeStudy System, so be sure and include my hot How To Get Rich On The Internet™ Radio Tapes for FREE! This is an additional $199 value on top of everything else I get!

9.75% Tax for Tennessee residents (Complete: $138.47, Introductory: $ 77.71) TAX _____

Shipping for Giant package, add $34 priority, $59 overnight, $67 International SHIPPING _____

Order Now Toll-Free: GRAND TOTAL$ _____
1-877-4Riches (1-877-474-2437)

It's Easy to Enroll: Call, mail, fax, or e-mail this form or this information to us!
To register right now rush to www.HowToGetRichOnTheInternet.com/now

Name_____

Address_____

City_____ State/Province_____

Postal Code_____ Country_____

Phone/fax_____ E-mail_____

☐ Cash, check, money order ☐ Please charge my Visa, MasterCard, AMEX, or Novus/Discover

Card #_____ Exp date_____ Amount_____

Signature_____ Date_____

Parthenon Marketing, Inc * 2400 Crestmoor Rd #36 * Nashville, TN 37215 * tedc@realprofit.com

For Rush Service
Call, Fax Or Go Online

Order NOW Toll Free:
1-877- 4 RICHES *(1-877-474-2437)*

615-662-3169 / fax: 615-662-3108
www.HowToGetRichOnTheInternet.com/now
tedc@realprofit.com

Or Mail This Form To

Parthenon Marketing, Inc.
2400 Crestmoor Rd #36
Nashville TN 37215
USA

Index

How To Make
Money
24 Hours A Day –
While On
Permanent
Vacation

Ted Ciuba Fans $1,000,000

**America's Foremost Internet Marketing Consultant
Reveals How To Get Rich On The Internet!**

Ted Ciuba is America's Foremost Internet Marketing Consultant. He takes clients and students at any level to wherever they want to go on the Internet. His methods have been hailed by thousands, in all different types of businesses and stages of Internet marketing.

How does he do it? *Millionaire* magazine says it superbly:

> *Ted deftly incorporates traditional mail order techniques with clear-thinking online marketing tips, to create a winning combination anyone can use.*

His goal for you?... The "Internet Lifestyle"...

That magical ability to market on the Internet and make money on demand, to make money 24 hours a day - while on permanent vacation.

Ciuba is the author of a number of business programs, including *How To Get Rich On The Internet, Mail Order in the Internet Age, Internet Membership Sites, Internet Joint Ventures, Money On Demand, Paper Profit$, The 13 Deadly Internet Marketing Mistakes Almost Every Business Is Making ...And How You Can Avoid Them,* and many more books, courses, and programs.

Ted is the host of the popular *"How To Get Rich On The Internet"* show broadcast from *InternetMarketingInterviews.com,* widely hailed as one of the Net's model membership sites.

What gets the most press is his famous *How To Get Rich On The Internet*™ BootCamps. Like when he selects someone from the audience and starts the profit-taking brainstorm... And accelerates from concept to money-in-the-bank within 72 hours! He plays to international audiences.

Ted has shared the stage with such marketing celebrities as Jay Conrad Levinson, Dan Kennedy, Ron LeGrand, Terry Dean, Corey Rudl, Wade Cook, Randy Charach, Declan Dunn, Frank Kern, Marlon Sanders, Ken McCarthy, Jonathan Mizel, Robert Allen, Mike Enlow, Bob Gatchel, Carl Galletti, Kirt Christensen, T.J. Rohleder, David Cooper, Russ von Hoelscher, Yanik Silver, Jim Straw, Michael Penland, & dozens more top performers!

Ted Ciuba – independent entrepreneur, successful investor, noted author, publisher, speaker, promoter, and famed Internet Marketing Consultant...

But it wasn't always so good. The Internet Marketing Association tells it...

> Ted Ciuba really is a "Rags To Internet Riches" story.
> He once lived on the county line at the end of a long dirt road in rural Tennessee... Hiding out from bill collectors.

Today his money-making methods have been featured in scores of major radio shows, newspapers, magazines, web sites, and live seminars throughout the world.

There's magic in his methods! Tune in, you'll discover how to make your own fortune on the Internet!

Book Ted Ciuba at your event! Speeches, workshops, copywriting, consulting. Contact publisher.